Cover image: Soldiers from the 4th Infantry Division's 2nd Battalion, 77th Field Artillery Regiment, fire a test round downrange from a newly arrived M777A2 howitzer at Kandahar Airfield, Afghanistan. US Army photo by Specialist Ariel Solomon.

Original tear graphic: Designed by Layerace/Freepik, freepik.com
Original paper texture: Created by Freepik, freepik.com
Composite cover design: Arin L. Burgess and Michael P. Serravo, Army University Press

This book is part of *The US Army Large-Scale Combat Operations Series*, which includes:

Weaving the Tangled Web: Military Deception in Large-Scale Combat Operations

Bringing Order to Chaos: Historical Case Studies of Combined Arms Maneuver in Large-Scale Combat Operations

Lethal and Non-Lethal Fires: Historical Case Studies of Converging Cross-Domain Fires in Large-Scale Combat Operations

The Long Haul: Historical Case Studies of Sustainment in Large-Scale Combat Operations

Deep Maneuver: Historical Case Studies of Maneuver in Large-Scale Combat Operations

Into the Breach: Historical Case Studies of Mobility Operations in Large-Scale Combat Operations

Perceptions Are Reality: Historical Case Studies of Information Operations in Large-Scale Combat Operations

Lethal and Non-Lethal Fires

Historical Case Studies of Converging Cross-Domain Fires in Large-Scale Combat Operations

Edited by
Thomas G. Bradbeer

Army University Press
Fort Leavenworth, Kansas

Library of Congress Cataloging-in-Publication Data

Names: Bradbeer, Thomas G., 1957- editor. | Army University Press (U.S.), issuing body.

Title: Lethal and Non-Lethal Fires: Historical Case Studies of Converging Cross-Domain Fires in Large-Scale Combat Operations / edited by Thomas G. Bradbeer.

Other titles: Historical Case Studies of Converging Cross-Domain Fires in Large-Scale Combat Operations.

Description: First edition. | Fort Leavenworth, Kansas : Army University Press, 2018. | Series: US Army Large-Scale Combat Operations Series Subjects: LCSH: United States. Army--Artillery--Drill and tactics--Case studies. | Tactics--Case studies. | Military planning--United States--Decision making--Case studies. | Military doctrine--United States--Case studies. | Unified operations (Military science).

2018

Army University Press publications cover a variety of military history topics. The views expressed in this Army University Press publication are those of the author(s) and not necessarily those of the Department of the Army or the Department of Defense.

Editors
Diane R. Walker and Lynne M. Chandler Garcia

Foreword

Since the Soviet Union's fall in 1989, the specter of large-scale ground combat against a peer adversary was remote. During the years following, the US Army found itself increasingly called upon to lead multinational operations in the lower to middle tiers of the range of military operations and conflict continuum. The events of 11 September 2001 led to more than 15 years of intense focus on counterterrorism, counterinsurgency, and stability operations in Iraq and Afghanistan. An entire generation of Army leaders and Soldiers were culturally imprinted by this experience. We emerged as an Army more capable in limited contingency operations than at any time in our nation's history, but the geopolitical landscape continues to shift and the risk of great power conflict is no longer a remote possibility.

While our Army focused on limited contingency operations in the Middle East and Southwest Asia, other regional and peer adversaries scrutinized US military processes and methods and adapted their own accordingly. As technology has proliferated and become accessible in even the most remote corners of the world, the US military's competitive advantage is being challenged across all of the warfighting domains. In the last decade, we have witnessed an emergent China, a revanchist and aggressive Russia, a menacing North Korea, and a cavalier Iranian regime. Each of these adversaries seeks to change the world order in their favor and contest US strategic interests abroad. The chance for war against a peer or regional near-peer adversary has increased exponentially, and we must rapidly shift our focus to successfully compete in all domains and across the full range of military operations.

Over the last two years, the US Army has rapidly shifted the focus of its doctrine, training, education, and leader development to increase readiness and capabilities to prevail in large-scale ground combat operations against peer and near-peer threats. Our new doctrine, Field Manual (FM) 3-0, *Operations*, dictates that the Army provide the joint force four unique strategic roles: shaping the security environment, preventing conflict, prevailing in large-scale combat operations, and consolidating gains to make temporary success permanent.

To enable this shift of focus, the Army is now attempting to change its culture shaped by over 15 years of persistent limited-contingency operations. Leaders must recognize that the hard-won wisdom of the Iraq and Afghanistan wars is important to retain but does not fully square with the exponential lethality, hyperactive chaos, and accelerated tempo of the multi-domain battlefield when facing a peer or near-peer adversary.

To emphasize the importance of the Army's continued preparation for large-scale combat operations, the US Army Combined Arms Center has published these volumes of *The US Army Large-Scale Combat Operations Series book set*. The intent is to expand the knowledge and understanding of the contemporary issues the US Army faces by tapping our organizational memory to illuminate the future. The reader should reflect on these case studies to analyze each situation, identify the doctrines at play, evaluate leaders' actions, and determine what differentiated success from failure. Use them as a mechanism for discussion, debate, and intellectual examination of lessons of the past and their application to today's doctrine, organization, and training to best prepare the Army for large-scale combat. Relevant answers and tangible reminders of what makes us the world's greatest land power await in the stories of these volumes.

Prepared for War!

Michael D. Lundy
Lieutenant General, US Army
Commanding General
US Army Combined Arms Center

Contents

Illustrations

Introduction
Thomas G. Bradbeer

The Russian rocket attack on Ukrainian forces at Zelenopillya on 11 July 2014 was the first example of Russia's contemporary reconnaissance-strike model on display. The strike targeted a large Ukrainian assembly area where Ukrainian forces were preparing to uncoil and conduct an offensive. At approximately 0400 on 11 July, drones were heard overhead; at around the same time, Ukrainian forces lost the ability to communicate over their tactical radio network. A few minutes later a bevy of rockets and artillery fell on the assembly area. The result was carnage—upwards of 30 Ukrainian soldiers were killed and dozens were severely wounded, while more than two battalions' worth of combat power was destroyed.[1]

—Majors Amos C. Fox and Andrew J. Rossow

According to Army doctrine, the word *Fires* describes the use of weapon systems to create a specific lethal or nonlethal effect on a target.[2] Similarly, the Fires Warfighting function, which evolved from the Fire Support Battlefield Operating System less than a decade ago, specifically deals with the related tasks and systems that collectively provide coordinated use of Army indirect fires, air and missile defense (AMD), and joint fires through the targeting process. Army fires systems are tasked to deliver fires in support of offensive and defensive operations to create specific lethal and non-lethal effects. To accomplish this, the fires warfighting function must accomplish three critical tasks: 1) deliver fires; 2) integrate all forms of Army, joint, and multinational fires; and 3) conduct targeting.[3] Furthermore, fires assists operational forces in "seizing, retaining, and exploiting the initiative . . . and enhanc[ing] freedom of action and the movement and maneuver of ground forces."[4]

From the evolution of artillery systems such as the catapult and ballista used by the Roman Legions to present-day cannons, missiles, and rockets, the purpose of fires has remained constant: to be the maneuver commander's most responsive combat arm and by doing so assist the other arms in accomplishing their battlefield missions. As the Army prepares for the possibility of conducting large-scale ground combat operations (LSCO) against a peer or near-peer threat, it must confront the likelihood that US Army and joint fires—especially cannon, rocket, and missile artillery—will be vastly outnumbered and outranged. Additionally, for the first time in nearly 70 years, US and Allied air and naval forces may not have air superiority—let alone air supremacy—during the opening engagements and battles of the war. To ensure US and Allied forces do not suffer the same fate experienced by the Ukrainian army in July 2014, we must take advantage of our intellectual capital throughout the Army and our military to make up for our potential technological disadvantages in weapons systems if we are to be successful on tomorrow's battlefields.

Precision and near-precision munitions with stand-off capability are at risk of losing effectiveness against adversaries that contest our hegemony in the space domain, across the electromagnetic spectrum (EMS), and through anti-access/area denial (A2/AD) capability.[5] Our ability to provide flexible response and deterrent options to combatant commanders rests in the aggregated efforts of the greater fires community across the land, air, and maritime components—with varying levels of buy-in from host nation, regional, and Allied partners.

This volume is a collection of historical case studies involving lethal and non-lethal fires from the period 1917 through 1991 with lessons for military professionals who will be engaged in future large-scale combat operations. Though the chapters range from the First World War through Desert Shield/Desert Storm, they are not organized chronologically. This will allow the reader with time constraints to read and analyze those specific battles and operations that strike a specific interest or need. The concluding chapter written by the Commanding General, Fires Center of Excellence, reviews the future of fires and the requirements and expectations for lethal and non-lethal fires to accomplish the numerous and complex missions the warfighting function will be expected to successfully execute during the conduct of multi-domain operations.

The authors were asked to provide a concise overview of an engagement, battle, or campaign that would be the centerpiece of their case study. They were to present the doctrine the organizations were using or attempting to use, the challenges the leaders encountered with the doctrine and the operational environment, as well as their actions and decisions during the conduct of the operation. Most importantly, they were to address the lessons learned by the leaders in these large-scale combat operations and how they were applied or ignored. Lastly, they were to identify how these lessons learned are applicable to US Army leaders today and in the future.

Chapter 1 by Joe R. Bailey, the Assistant Command Historian for the US Army Combined Arms Center and Fort Leavenworth, examines the use of airpower during the planning and execution of Operation Overlord. The focus is on how General Eisenhower overcame parochial and competing interests between the different services and nations to ensure that airpower effectively supported the seaborne and ground assault. In Chapter 2, Lieutenant Colonel (Retired) Thomas G. Bradbeer, the Major General Fox Conner Chair of Leadership Studies for the US Army Command and General Staff College at Fort Leavenworth, provides a chapter on the November 1917 British offensive operation against Cambrai. He will argue that by using the latest scientific and technological advancements in gunnery, the British Royal Artillery was able to overwhelm the German defenders along the Hindenburg Line, enabling the successful armored assault which followed.

General David M. Rodriguez' 1989 School of Advanced Military Studies (SAMS) monograph in Chapter 3 analyzes two mid-east wars—the Sinai Campaign in 1973 and the Bekaa Valley Campaign in 1982—to illustrate the impact of electronic warfare on operational maneuver. In Chapter 4, Lieutenant Colonel (Retired-USAF) Mark E. Grotelueschen, a professor in the US Air Force Academy's Department of Military and Strategic Studies, discusses the US Army's major offensive in 1918 into the Meuse-Argonne and examines how significant changes made at the army, corps, and division levels affected the way firepower was planned and employed during the battle, resulting in the most successful attack for the American Expeditionary Forces (AEF) during the war. Major Lincoln R. Ward, Joint Plans Officer, Combined Joint Task Force-Horn of Africa, describes how the division artillery can achieve the Army Chiefs of Staff objective of readiness using Operations Desert Shield and Storm as a case study to analyze preparations for deployment and the use of artillery during offensive operations against a near-peer threat in Chapter 5.

In Chapter 6, Major Jeffrey S. Wright, an instructor in the Department of Military Instruction, US Military Academy at West Point, analyzes the February 1943 Battle of Kasserine Pass, the first major engagement between American and Axis forces in Africa during the Second World War. He examines how both the maneuver and field artillery commanders learned from their initial mistakes and were able to set the conditions to mass, demonstrate flexibility, and effectively synchronize fires to defeat follow-on Axis attacks. Lieutenant Colonel G. Kirk Alexander is the battalion commander for 1st Battalion, 31st Field Artillery, Basic Combat Training at Fort Sill, Oklahoma. Using the Korean War as a case study in Chapter 7, he examines the principles of fire support in the defense: mass, unity of command, and security. He argues that operational success in the Korean War largely depended upon the US Army's ability to provide artillery support at the decisive place and time to defeat the North Korean and Chinese offensive operations. He also discusses whether our current doctrine and organizations can execute these principles against a near-peer threat in large-scale combat operations.

In Chapter 8, Boyd L. Dastrup, the US Army Field Artillery School Branch Historian, analyzes the performance of the US Army Field Artillery during the Vietnam War. First and foremost, he argues that the field artillery demonstrated adaptability and flexibility, most especially with its shift to incorporate airmobile operations in support of maneuver forces. He also identifies that the Army became too reliant on firepower to accomplish its missions and that this was not always the most effective way to conduct operations. In Chapter 9, Lieutenant Colonel (Retired) Mark T. Calhoun, an Associate Professor at the US Army School of Advanced Military Studies, examines the use of strategic bombers in close support of US ground troops using the Normandy campaign, and specifically Operation Cobra, as a case study. His chapter contrasts well with Bailey's Chapter 1, ensuring that multiple perspectives are provided on the role and use of US and British airpower during the invasion of France in 1944.

David Thuell, a graduate student at the Norwich University, and Lieutenant Colonel (Retired) Thomas G. Bradbeer analyze how the Canadian Corps applied new doctrine in the employment of fires and maneuver to successfully capture the German-held Vimy Ridge during the Battle of Arras in April 1917 in Chapter 10. Five of the six tenets of today's Unified Land Operations—flexibility, integration, lethality, adaptability, and synchronization—were displayed by the leaders and Soldiers of the Canadian Corps during the assault on Vimy Ridge. The concluding chapter by Major General Wilson A. Shoffner, Commanding General, Fires Center of Excellence and Fort Sill, Oklahoma, presents his vision of the future of lethal and non-lethal fires and the critical role they will serve in ensuring that the combined arms team will win the first battle of the next conflict against a near-peer opponent.

The volume provides three chapters focusing on battles from the First World War; three on battles and campaigns from the Second World War; and one each on the Korean War, Arab-Israeli Wars, and First Gulf War. The work analyzes the use of lethal and non-lethal fires conducted by US, British, Canadian, and Israeli forces from 1917 to 1991. The coverage is comprehensive and focuses heavily on the successful use of fires in large-scale combat operations against near-peer threats.

This work would not have been possible without the voluntary time and work of the authors; they are the experts. The authors are a mix of active (four) as well as retired officers and civilian scholars (seven). Several authors are current or past Army historians with a significant depth of expertise. Some are scholars who have devoted a lifetime of study to master the sources, understand the context, analyze the breadth and depth of the subject, and develop a skill for presenting each case study in a comprehensible format.

I owe special thanks to the staff of Army University Press for putting this volume into physical and electronic form as part of *The US Army Large-Scale Combat Operations Series*. Special thanks to Colonel Paul E. Berg, book series general editor; Donald P. Wright for production; Robin D. Kern for graphics; and Diane R. Walker and Lynne M. Chandler Garcia for copy editing and layout. Russell P. "Rusty" Rafferty, Chief, Classified Services, Ike Skelton Combined Arms Research Library, as well as Ken A. Turner and Lieutenant Colonel David M. Ward, Field Artillery—two instructors from the Department of Command and Leadership, US Army Command and General Staff School—deserve special praise for their willingness to locate photographs to support each of the chapters, as well as their cogent advice and recommendations. They have made this volume better for their contributions. As the general editor of this volume, I am responsible for any errors, omissions, or limitations of this work.

Notes

1. Amos C. Fox and Andrew J. Rossow, "Making Sense of Russian Hybrid Warfare: A Brief Assessment of the Russo-Ukrainian War," Association of the United States Army Institute of Land Warfare, Land Warfare Paper No. 112, March 2017, 10.

2. Department of the Army, Army Doctrine Reference Publication (ADRP) 3-09, *Fires* (Washington DC: 31 August 2012), 1-1.

3. Department of the Army, ADRP 3-09, 1-1 and 1-2.

4. Department of the Army, Army Techniques Publication (ATP) 3-09.90, *Division Artillery Operations and Fire Support for the Division* (Washington DC: 12 October 2017), vii.

5. Headquarters, Combined Arms Center, CALL Handbook No. 18-28, *Operating in a Denied, Degraded, and Disrupted Space Operational Environment,* (Fort Leavenworth, KS: Headquarters, Combined Arms Center, June 2018), 6.

Chapter 1

"In This Thing With Both Feet": Eisenhower and Operation Overlord's Airpower

Joe R. Bailey

Multi-Domain Battle requires the ability to maneuver and deliver effects across all domains in order to develop and exploit battlefield opportunities across a much larger operational framework. It must include whole-of-government approaches and solutions to military problems and address the use of multinational partner capabilities and capacities.[1]

—General David Perkins, Commanding General
US Army Training and Doctrine Command

In January 1944, General Dwight Eisenhower assumed his new post as Supreme Commander of the Allied Expeditionary Force in Europe, the headquarters responsible for the cross-channel invasion of continental Europe, also known as Operation Overlord. Among the many problems Eisenhower encountered was the necessity of making airpower an asset for the coming invasion. This consumed enormous amounts of his time, particularly his effort to gain operational control of American and British strategic bombers.

As the Army implements multi-domain operations into its doctrine, leaders should look to the ways in which Eisenhower skillfully maneuvered these choppy winds and made airpower a viable cross-domain fire that directly supported the cross-channel invasion. To achieve this, the new Supreme Commander fought to establish effective command arrangements and organization for the use of airpower. He not only overcame parochial and competing interests between different services but did so while establishing a complex, multi-national command. Eisenhower also negotiated a complex web of organizational, political, and ethical problems as the air support plan unfolded.

Eisenhower knew that airpower would be a decisive component in the coming invasion. The first step in making it effective meant ensuring unity of command and bringing all air forces under his strategic and operational direction. In keeping with his background as an infantry officer, Eisenhower had concluded that Germany would ultimately have to be defeated on the ground. Thus, he argued that strategic bombers should directly support Overlord's ground forces for a limited period before and after the invasion. He disagreed with strategic bombing advocates who argued the primary mission of airpower was to destroy Germany's economic centers and defeat the military capacity of Germany to fight. He also disagreed that their use of strategic bombing would render an invasion of Europe unnecessary.[2]

Eisenhower clearly saw the joint nature of airpower. Although he believed that the first mission of airpower was support of ground troops, he never opposed the strategic bombing of Germany. To his thinking, strategic airpower could weaken Germany and achieve air superiority for his Allied ground forces. Time and again, however, Eisenhower called on strategic bombers for operational missions that diverted them from bombing Germany. In giving strategic bombers operational missions directly supporting the invasion, Eisenhower established that support of ground forces took precedence over the strategic bombing of Germany.

After the war, Eisenhower explained his belief in the dual role of airpower. He noted,

> Many ground soldiers belittled the potentialities of the airplane against ground formations. Curiously enough, quite a number of Air Force officers were also antagonistic to the idea, thinking they saw an attempt to shackle the air to the ground and therefore a failure to realize the full capabilities of air attack. It was patiently explained over and over again that, on the contrary, the results of coordination would constantly advance the air bases and would articulate strategic bombing effects with ground strategy, so that as the air constantly assisted the advance of the ground forces its long-range work would not only be facilitated but destruction of its selected targets would contribute more effectively and directly to Nazi defeat.[3]

Eisenhower and the Challenges of Unity of Command

Eisenhower's problems with airpower organization and command structures that threatened unity of command began even before he assumed his position as Supreme Commander of the Allied Expeditionary Force. In 1943, British planners for Overlord urged the Combined Chiefs of Staff to decide the organization of tactical airpower for the invasion. In a message to Army Chief of Staff George C. Marshall on 31 December 1943, Eisenhower bitterly complained about those arrangements. He pleaded with Marshall, "I most earnestly request that you throw your full weight into opposing the tendency to organize in advance the sub-echelons of the Overlord operation in such a way as to tie the hands of the command and Allied staff." Eisenhower also noted that he and many of his staff had learned the dangers of such arrangements during his tenure as Allied commander during Operation Torch in North Africa, and he urged the Army Chief of Staff to let him apply that experience to Overlord's organization.[4]

As he became familiar with the organization of the command he was about to assume, Eisenhower also found that Air Chief Marshal Arthur Tedder, a Royal Air Force officer with vast experience in the Mediterranean, had been assigned as his Deputy Supreme Commander, although this officer came "without portfolio [without definite responsibilities]." On the other hand, Air Chief Marshal Trafford Leigh-Mallory was given command of the tactical air forces although he styled himself as commander of all air forces for Overlord. These arrangements and divided authority troubled the Supreme Commander deeply. Eisenhower's Chief of Staff, General Walter B. Smith, told him, "I personally believe that Tedder should be the real air commander and your advisor on air matters, which Mallory now considers himself. I don't think there is a place for both of them." Before assuming command in England, Eisenhower took a short leave back to the United States. After a few days of travel with his wife, Eisenhower arrived in Washington to meet with Marshall and Chief of Staff for the Army Air Forces, General Henry "Hap" Arnold. Eisenhower continued his protest of the air arrangements proposed by the Combined Chiefs of Staff and also voiced his displeasure at the controversy over Leigh-Mallory and Tedder.[5]

At the same meeting the new Supreme Commander argued that both American and British strategic bombing commands should come under his operational control for the invasion. Commanders of both strategic bombing forces, Air Chief Marshal Arthur Harris and General Carl Spaatz, however, wanted to continue their strategic bombing of Germany, insisting that this more effectively employed the bombers. Eisenhower referred to their opinions as "dangerous nonsense" and insisted that the most effective use of strategic air forces was to directly support Overlord.[6] Eisenhower left Washington for his new command without a satisfactory solution to his airpower problems. The topic received much attention and debate over the next several months.

One of the many insights that Eisenhower gleaned from his time as the Allied commander in the Mediterranean regarding airpower came from the landing at Salerno. This bloody affair, where Allied forces landed on the Italian Peninsula and established a beachhead, cemented within the Supreme Commander's mind that Soldiers on the ground needed responsive airpower at critical times. This experience shaped his future view of airpower organization for Overlord. Eisenhower later stated, "My insistence upon commanding these air forces at the time was further influenced by the lesson so conclusively demonstrated at Salerno: when a battle needs the last ounce of available force, the commander must not be in the position of depending upon request and negotiation to get it." He added, "It was vital that the entire sum of our assault power, including the two Strategic Air Forces, be available for use during the critical stages of the attack." [7]

Very early, Eisenhower attempted to achieve some consensus on the consolidation of airpower for Overlord. In fact, the Supreme Commander began this implementation before he left Washington to take his new command. Trying to bring the American and British strategic bomber commands under his operational control consumed much of his time. On 5 January 1944, he sent a message to Smith anticipating difficulty in making the necessary arrangements to integrate the tactical and strategic air forces according to his plan. He told Smith that Tedder should be sent to consult with Spaatz, head of US Strategic Air Forces, to begin planning for this integration. Eisenhower was already directing Tedder, his deputy commander without portfolio, in matters concerning airpower.[8]

On the same day, Lieutenant General Thomas Handy, the Army's Chief of Staff for Operations, sent a message to Spaatz telling him that the Supreme Commander saw his strategic bombers and those of Air Chief Marshal Harris, his British counterpart, as the "big guns" for Overlord. Through Handy, Eisenhower asked Spaatz to operate in conjunction with Harris and his British Bomber Command. Eisenhower had also noted, "While the above conception has not been officially approved by all concerned, it offers the only chance of success, and therefore I am confident will be accepted by everyone shortly."[9] Nothing, however, could have been further from the truth. Argument through diplomatic and military channels over airpower concerns continued for several months. This proved to be only the first in a long series of debates that emerged about the use and control of airpower in support of Overlord.

The Supreme Commander, while uncompromising in his requirements for Overlord's airpower needs, was willing to negotiate in order to achieve acceptance of his plan by the Americans and the British. In a message to Arnold, Eisenhower stated, "To get what I want, I am perfectly willing to avoid terms and language that may startle anyone. But there can be no evasion of the certainty that when the time comes, the Overlord Commander must have the full power to determine missions and priorities for all forces." Eisenhower anticipated little trouble from British Prime Minister Winston Churchill but was prepared to present his case to the Combined Chiefs of Staff, if necessary.[10]

The Air Plan to Support Overlord

Eisenhower directed his staff, under the leadership of Tedder, to begin a plan that could be presented to the Combined Chiefs of Staff. On 9 February 1944, Eisenhower told Marshall that the air plan would be completed in the next few days. He stated, "This plan will not only lay out exactly what we have to do, with our priorities, but will also fix our recommended dates for the passage of command over Strategical Air Forces to this Headquarters. Before I present it to the Combined Chiefs of Staff, I am going to have a Commanders-in-Chief meeting on it so that thereafter it becomes 'doctrine' so far as this Headquarters is concerned."[11]

Eisenhower's desire to bring American and British strategic bomber forces under his operational control during Overlord brought many objections from, not only the British government, but also from the strategic commanders Spaatz and Harris. One objection that British and American air commanders had was the appointment of Leigh-Mallory as the Commander in Chief for Air of the Allied Expeditionary Force. Both Spaatz and Harris remained reluctant to take orders from Leigh-Mallory, a commander whose experience was with tactical air forces and not strategic bombers. Eisenhower also experienced objections from Prime Minister Churchill.[12] During this debate, Eisenhower told Marshall, "The Prime Minister was quite violent in his objections to considering Leigh-Mallory as the overall Air Commander-in Chief, although this was his definite assignment."[13]

In order to gain Churchill's approval and that of the Combined Chiefs of Staff, Eisenhower was willing to negotiate on parts of the air plan, but stood fast and refused to consent to losing operational control of the Allied strategic bomber commands. On 29 February 1944, Eisenhower told Tedder about Churchill's objections to Leigh-Mallory's command of the strategic bombers and urged Tedder to find solutions with Spaatz and Harris. If a solution could not be found, he warned, "the P.M. [Prime Minister] will be in this thing with both feet." He explained his conceptual basis for operational control and told Tedder, "I'm quite prepared, if necessary, to issue an order saying I will exert direct supervision of all air forces—through you—and authorizing you to use headquarters facilities now existing to make your control effective. L.M.'s [Leigh-Mallory's] position would not be changed so far as assigned forces are concerned but those attached for definite periods or definite jobs would not come under his command."[14]

On 9 March 1944, Eisenhower solved some of these problems with airpower organization. A new directive gave Tedder overall command of the air forces for the invasion. Eisenhower would exercise control of these air forces through Tedder; Leigh-Mallory would command the tactical air forces that consisted of the US Ninth Air Force and the British Second Tactical Air Force. General Spaatz and Air Chief Marshal Harris directed their respective strategic bombing units under Tedder's supervision. The turnover of Spaatz's and Harris's bombers to Eisenhower's operational control would take place after the Supreme Commander and British Air Chief of Staff, Air Chief Marshal Charles Portal, agreed on an overall air plan for their use in Overlord. Eisenhower sent a message to Marshall telling him, "This morning it appears to me the air problems are at last in good order and will be presented officially to the Combined Chiefs of Staff quickly. All air forces here will be under Tedder's supervision as my agent, and this prospect is particularly pleasing to Spaatz." The Supreme Commander also messaged Arnold, "I think we have our Air Forces pretty well straightened out. As you can well imagine it has not been simple because of the independent status that so many of these Air Forces have heretofore enjoyed."[15]

Feeling confident that his plans were moving forward, Eisenhower was surprised a week later when the British raised objections to the wording in the agreement with the Combined Chiefs of Staff regarding his control of the strategic bombing forces. Eisenhower's frustration was evident when he observed that, "the air problem has been one requiring a great deal of patience and negotiation." He recorded in his diary:

> In the messages coming back and forth from Washington, a sudden argument developed over the use of the word "command." The whole matter I had considered settled a week ago, after many weeks of argument. This did not seem important at the time the drafts were first drawn up, but as long as the question was raised I have recommended to General Marshall that a word be adopted that leaves no doubt in anybody's mind of my authority and responsibility for controlling air operations of all three of these forces during the critical period of Overlord.[16]

The Supreme Commander made it clear that he would have the ability to give strategic bombers tactical missions in support of Overlord, or he would quit. Eisenhower was insuring that all military assets under his command would work to further the objectives of the all-important invasion.

Eisenhower Threatens to Resign

Growing increasingly frustrated by the constant bickering of those objecting to his airpower plan, Eisenhower determined to wrestle control of the strategic bombers or to go home. He noted that he would have one more meeting with his air commanders to attempt implementation of his plan and wrote, "If a satisfactory answer is not reached, I am going to take drastic action and inform the Combined Chiefs of Staff that unless the matter is settled at once I will request relief from this command." On 6 March 1944, General George Patton walked into Eisenhower's office in the middle of a telephone conversation between Tedder and the Supreme Commander. Patton arrived in time to hear Eisenhower say, "Now, listen, Arthur, I am tired of dealing with a lot of prima donnas. By God, you tell that bunch that if they can't get together and stop quarreling like children, I will tell the Prime Minister to get someone else to run this damn war. I'll quit." Eisenhower also told Churchill that if he did not receive a total commitment of the bombers that he would "simply have to go home."[17]

Evidently Eisenhower's threats to resign did not fall on deaf ears. Churchill, eventually, agreed to the Supreme Commander's arrangement to exercise operational control of the strategic bombers. After being informed of wording problems associated with his "command" of the strategic bombers and noting that he would resign short of a satisfactory solution, later that

Figure 1.1. General Dwight D. Eisenhower and his key leaders meet to discuss planning for Operation Overlord. Front row (left to right): Air Chief Marshal Sir Arthur Tedder, Eisenhower, General Sir Bernard Montgomery; back row: Lieutenant General Omar N. Bradley, Admiral Sir Bertram Ramsay, Air Chief Marshal Sir Trafford Leigh-Mallory, Lieutenant General Walter Bedell Smith. Photo courtesy of Imperial War Museum, CH12110.

day Eisenhower added a postscript to his diary stating that the chiefs-of-staff found the word "direction" acceptable, and he expressed relief.[18]

Although Eisenhower won operational control of the strategic bombing commands under Spaatz and Harris, the Supreme Commander still experienced trouble attempting to perfect the new organization. Many British and American authorities remained confused about who would actually give the strategic bombers their instructions. They also remained confused about when Eisenhower's direction of the bombers would begin. On 12 April 1944, he wrote Marshall telling him, "For the past two weeks all air operations have been under my general direction and although it takes a little time to get new operational lines completely sorted out where there have been so many independent voices and authorities, everything in that particular field is working satisfactorily."[19]

The problems associated with organizing his air plan remained on Eisenhower's mind for several months. On 22 May 1944, he mentioned these problems in his diary. He complained, "One of our most difficult problems here has been the setting up of a completely satisfactory air organization. This comes about because of the widely scattered interest of the air forces and the great strength of units that have been acting in almost an independent way. However, somewhere about 10 April, a special arrangement was worked out that gives the supreme commander all the authority necessary to secure full support from all the air forces in England."[20]

While fighting to gain operational control of the strategic bombers, the Supreme Commander faced a concurrent argument about how to best employ strategic airpower to support the invasion once the bombers were under his direction. Initially, Eisenhower believed that the invasion's success hinged on Allied air superiority. In his postwar report as Supreme Commander of the Allied Expeditionary Force, Eisenhower declared, "The Strategic Air Forces also would be given definite tactical responsibilities during critical periods [in preparing for the invasion], although their principal mission would be to continue their attacks on the industrial potential of Germany, with emphasis now placed on the facilities for aircraft production. They had also definite tactical responsibilities at critical periods of the battles."[21] Eisenhower told Marshall that the Strategic Air Forces of Spaatz were taking every opportunity to "force the *Luftwaffe* to fight, and noted that Spaatz's operations were "taking a big toll of the enemy."[22]

To Eisenhower, Allied air superiority was vital to Overlord's success. Air superiority allowed freedom of action that enabled the stockpiling of men and equipment in England essential to the invasion. Secondly, establishing a firm beachhead in France necessitated the *Luftwaffe* be weakened to the point that they could not oppose the Allied landings. The Supreme Commander recalled, "Quite apart from the direct assistance these attacks lent to the success of our landings, they were essential also as a preliminary to the intensive bombing of German industry." Eisenhower once again exhibited that he supported strategic missions so far as they assisted in the conduct of Overlord, but one could not mistake that the invasion was his priority for the use of strategic airpower.[23]

The Transportation Plan

Having largely achieved air superiority during Big Week, when the strategic air forces forced the *Luftwaffe* to fight and incur damaging losses in planes and pilots, Eisenhower focused on ways to more effectively employ airpower as part of the invasion. In his postwar report on operations of the Allied Expeditionary Force, the Supreme Commander conveyed his intent. He recalled, "Until January 1944, the view had been held that the heavy bombers of the Strategic Air Forces could make sufficient direct contribution to the assault in a period of about a fortnight before D-day. Further consideration, however, indicated the need to employ them for a much longer period—about three months—and a plan was finally adopted which aimed at the crippling of the French and Belgian railway systems and the consequent restriction of the enemy's mobility." This plan became known as the Transportation Plan, and it called for a large role to be played by both the tactical and strategic air forces.[24]

The Transportation Plan intended to deprive the Germans of the ability to concentrate troops rapidly in the invasion area. To do this, the Transportation Plan called for attacks by the tactical air forces against railroads, bridges, and communications centers beginning two months before the invasion. The Supreme Commander ultimately hoped that the plan would "hinder his [German] efforts to maintain an adequate flow of reinforcements and supplies, forcing him to move by road with resultant delay, increased wastage in road transport and fuel, and increased vulnerability to air attack." In order to conceal the actual place of the invasion, however, Eisenhower's planners had to avoid concentrating all of their attacks on the invasion area. Instead, they attacked targets in a wide area and, shortly before D-Day, they began concentrating their attacks on areas vital to Overlord.[25]

The Transportation Plan enjoyed support from Tedder, Leigh-Mallory, and most of the ground commanders. Like much of his entire air plan, however, Eisenhower's Transportation Plan encountered resistance. Among those objecting to the plan were the commanders of the American and British strategic bombing forces, Prime Minister Winston Churchill, and the British War Cabinet. Allied predictions of the Transportation Plan noted that it would kill 10,000 to 15,000 French citizens if implemented. Churchill and the War Cabinet, considering the possible political ramification for postwar France, balked at this idea and urged Eisenhower to develop another plan. Churchill recommended that the air forces should engage "bases, troop concentrations, and dumps." On 29 April 1944, Eisenhower told Marshall that Churchill's recommendations were simply not practical. He noted, "The fact is that any large dumps are obviously located near marshalling yards while troop concentrations are by battalion in little villages. Any immediate attempt to bomb the German troop units throughout France would probably kill four Frenchmen for every German." The Supreme Commander also noted that there was simply no other way the Allied Air Forces could help him in the period before Overlord commenced. Eisenhower argued for the necessity of the Transportation Plan.[26]

Eisenhower had previously told Churchill something very similar on 5 April. He remarked, "After long study by our transportation experts as well as by our senor airmen, it was decided that the only preparatory field in which our air force could be profitably employed, other than its normal task of destroying the hostile air force, was against the enemy's transportation system." The Supreme Commander also told Churchill that he simply did not see any other way of effectively using airpower to aid Overlord, and noted that he thought the estimates of French casualties were "grossly exaggerated."[27]

Eisenhower continued this discussion with Churchill on 2 May 1944. He told the Prime Minister that he had taken steps to reduce French civilian casualties during the conduct of the Transportation Plan. These steps included issuing warnings to the population before attacks occurred and waiting to attack large rail centers in close proximity to large civilian populations at the latest possible date. Eisenhower did, however, indicate that civilian casualties were inevitable in any operation using airpower and once again noted that the estimates of French lives that would be lost were likely overstated. On the other hand, Eisenhower argued that the bombing of rail centers would inflict very heavy casualties upon French railroad personnel. Finally, Eisenhower told Churchill that he had consulted with his staff and found no alternative to implementing the Transportation Plan, writing that he appreciated "the gravity of the issues raised," but stated, "The 'Overlord' concept was based on the assumption that our overwhelming air power would be able to prepare the way for the assault. If its hands are to be tied, the perils of an already hazardous undertaking will be greatly enhanced."[28] He explained to the Prime Minister in no uncertain terms that he understood the political ramifications in a postwar world between France and the Allies if bombing killed large numbers of French civilians. Eisenhower argued, however, that the Transportation Plan was a vital component to the success of Overlord and must proceed regardless of the casualties it inflicted on French civilians.

While the British War Cabinet and Prime Minister opposed the Transportation Plan because of the projected casualties to French civilians and

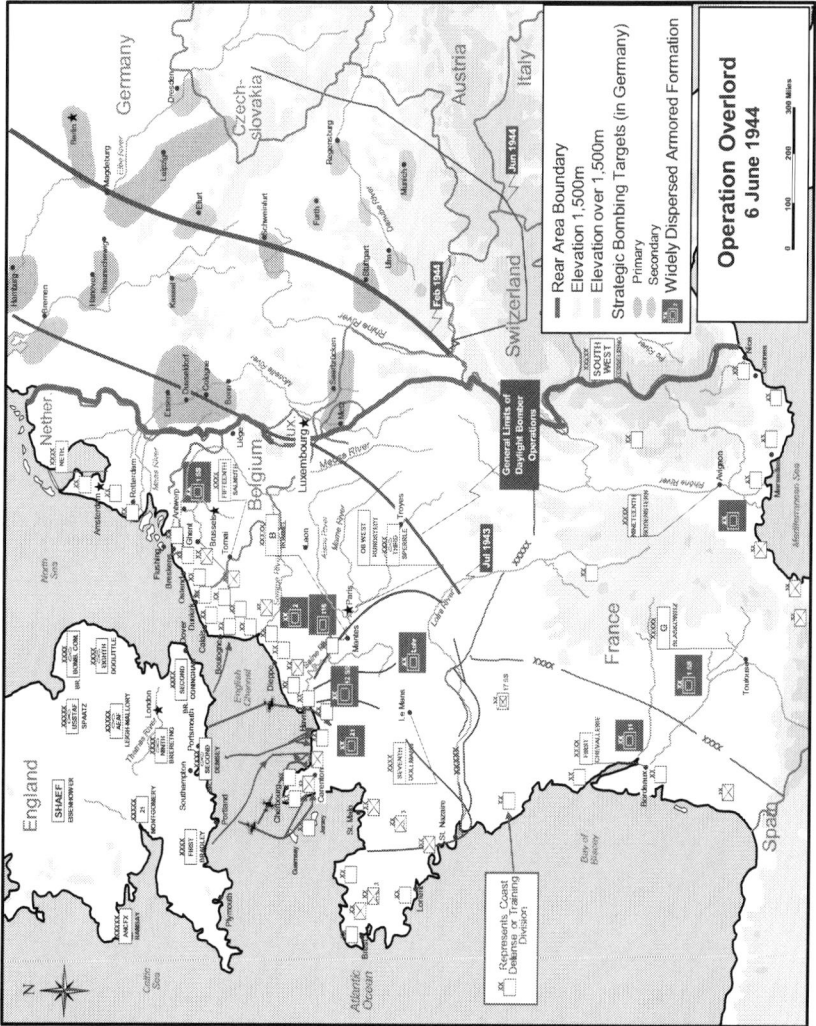

Figure 1.2. Map of Operation Overlord. Map courtesy of US Military Academy, West Point.

the fear of resulting political ramifications, the Allied strategic air force commanders opposed the plan for other reasons. They thought that the strategic bombing campaign against Germany was of vital importance, and that it should not be discontinued for the more tactical role of preparing the French coastal areas for the invasion. Most strategic bombing advocates argued that the continuation of Operation Pointblank, the strategic air assault against Germany, would render the invasion of Normandy unnecessary.

In early February 1944, General Carl Spaatz, commanding American strategic forces in Europe, and Air Chief Marshal Arthur Harris of Royal Air Force (RAF) Bomber Command objected to the Transportation Plan. Spaatz believed that targets under the Transportation Plan were of little value and jeopardized achieving air superiority before the invasion. Harris wanted to continue the area bombing of German cities. General James Doolittle, commanding the Eighth Air Force later noted that he thought "the Strategic Air Forces could render more effective aid to the war effort by denying the enemy the facilities he required than by giving direct support to our ground forces." In other words, Doolittle thought that the continued strategic bombing of Germany was more effective than using strategic bombers as part of Eisenhower's Transportation Plan.[29]

Eisenhower consistently attempted to convince strategic bombing advocates that he did not want to discontinue Operation Pointblank. The Supreme Commander had viewed the continued strategic bombing operations as a way of gaining air superiority by forcing the *Luftwaffe* to fight. Now that Eisenhower had gained the desired control of the air, he argued that strategic bombers would be most useful in helping achieve the goals of the Transportation Plan although he never wished to completely abandon Pointblank. During his fight to secure control of the strategic bombers, he told Tedder, "It is equally important that the plan recognize the tremendous advantages accruing to Overlord through current Pointblank operations and therefore be so developed that from the very beginning the air operations of Pointblank and Overlord are completely integrated."[30]

Nevertheless, the objections by Spaatz and Harris continued. Before D-Day, Harris warned Eisenhower that a temporary stop of the strategic bombing to assist the invasion would allow Germany, within five months, to fully restore its war production.[31] Although Eisenhower made the decision to use strategic bombers as part of the Transportation Plan, he demonstrated again that he recognized the significance of Pointblank. In May 1944, he wrote Harris noting, "I have of course been familiar with the over-all strategic effort against Germany from the air, but since you showed me last night the photographs and charts portraying the extensive damage inflicted upon the enemy within the boundaries of his own country, I am more impressed than ever."[32] After the invasion gained a foothold, Harris reminded the Supreme Commander of his warning and urged that the Allies return to the strategic bombing of Germany as soon as possible. Eisenhower told the British air commander, "I hope I have never left any doubt as to my desire to return all the Strategic Air Forces to the bombing of Germany to the greatest extent at the earliest possible moment. I have been quite pleased, lately, to note the extent which Bomber Command and the Eighth and Fifteenth Air Forces have been hitting the centers of German production. Of course we always have the emergencies of the battle front, and, most of all, the necessity for beating down Crossbow."[33]

Counter to the Transportation Plan: The Oil Plan

In March 1944, General Spaatz briefed a plan he thought was more effective than the Transportation Plan. Spaatz's alternative became known as the Oil Plan because it called for the destruction of Germany's oil production facilities and redefined Pointblank operational priorities. Spaatz argued that the Transportation Plan was not viable. In short, he believed that the plan included too many targets, and it would take too long to see any noticeable effects. The Oil Plan, however, would only require 15 days of visual bombing for the 8th Air Force and 10 by the 15th Air Force to reduce the German oil production to 80 percent. Advocates of the Transportation Plan, however, argued that the effects of the Oil Plan would not be timely enough to support the invasion. Tedder wrote after the war, "It was considered that, since the enemy would almost certainly be holding ample stocks of oil in France to meet the immediate emergency, attack on the oil industry was not likely to give the immediate assistance which the assault required. It was therefore decided that the primary target system for the Allied strategic bomber forces should be the transportation system upon which the movements of enemy reinforcements would depend."[34] After protracted debate, Eisenhower settled on the Transportation Plan. Now, with his airpower plan complete, the strategic bombers came under his operational control and Ike settled his command arrangements with his air commanders.

Airpower over Normandy

On 6 June 1944, Operation Overlord commenced, and both strategic and tactical air forces saw large-scale use. On that day alone, 8th Air Force and RAF Bomber Command flew 5,309 sorties and dropped 10,395 tons of bombs. The tactical air forces flew 5,276 sorties. Targets on D-Day remained largely confined to enemy troop concentrations, defensive works, gun positions, and communications centers.[35]

Eisenhower and his staff continued contemplating the role of airpower after a lodgment was established. On 3 June 1944, Eisenhower wrote that he envisioned offensive operations moving forward in two distinct zones of advance, one British and the other American. At that time, he planned the establishment of a second army group commanded by General Omar Bradley, which would pursue this strategy. The Supreme Commander wanted each one of the groups to be supported by its own contingent of fighters and fighter-bombers. Eisenhower stated, "At that time a certain portion of the so-called 'tactical' air force, that is, medium bombers and possibly some of the long-range fighters, will remain under the commander in chief, AEF (Allied Expeditionary Force). This portion of the tactical air force will be available to assist either army group."[36]

Eisenhower's vision for a second army group came to fruition after the invasion gained a stable beachhead. In addition to the tactical air forces that supported each army group, Eisenhower continued using strategic bombers to support the ground campaign. Eisenhower wrote, "In addition to the strategic bombing of oil, aircraft, and communications targets, we were, during the campaign, to call upon the Strategic Air Forces for tactical support. At the time of the breakthrough in Normandy . . . strategic bombers were employed in strength to attack enemy positions, supply bases immediately supporting the enemy front, and strongpoints and communication centers within the battle area. In these instances of tactical assistance, the Strategic Air Forces aided immeasurably in turning the decision of battle in our favor."[37]

One of Eisenhower's more effective uses of airpower after the landings was its use in breaking up enemy troop concentrations. Before the invasion, he noted in a memorandum, "Because the enemy in great strength is occupying a country that is interlaced with a fine communication system, our attack can be looked upon as reasonable only if our tremendous air force is able to impede his concentrations against us and to help destroy the effectiveness of any of his counterattacks." Five days later, after Allied troops had landed on the Normandy beaches, Eisenhower noted that the situation was fluid and that added to the difficulty of assigning targets to air assets. He was, however "confident that if weather permits our air will intervene effectively in any attempted counter attacks by the enemy."[38]

Although tactical aircraft engaged enemy troops, equipment, and transportation, the Allied strategic bombers did not receive another substantial

Figure 1.3 US Air Force B-17s attack marshalling yards in support of Operation Overlord, 29 May 1944. Photo courtesy of Imperial War Museum, FRE11844.

mission until the commencement of Operation Goodwood, an offensive operation planned in the British sector of Normandy. On 18 July 1944, approximately 1,700 bombers from RAF Bomber Command and the 8th Air Force, in addition to other bombers belonging to the 9th Air Force, dropped 8,000 tons of bombs in advance of ground operations. In this operation, commanders learned from previous experience and avoided cratering the ground that ground forces would need to cross by only using fighter bombers in attack lanes established for armored divisions. They also ordered ground units to "attack immediately after the air strike in order to capitalize on the paralyzing effect of the bombardment on the Germans."[39]

Operation Cobra, a breakout attempt in the American sector, included plans for massive air support preceding the offensive. The planners arranged target areas and bombing durations for the various types of participating bombers, timetables for the withdrawal of American Soldiers to a zone of safety, and made arrangements to mark the target areas for the aircraft. Tragically, despite the elaborate planning, the situation went awry almost immediately. On 24 July, the day the attack was to commence, Air

Chief Marshal Leigh-Mallory was on the ground to observe it. Realizing that the sky was too overcast for the planned air support, Leigh-Mallory attempted to call the bombardment off but could not reach all of his aircraft. Some bombers reached their targets and subsequent accidents and miscalculations resulted in dropping bombs on positions occupied by American infantrymen. [40]

Commanders halted the operation until the next day. Another bombardment commenced on 25 July 1944. Formations of heavy, medium, and fighter bombers dropped more than 4,150 tons of bombs in support of Operation Cobra. Despite further planning to prevent such occurrences, again, poor weather conditions and human error resulted in short drops that killed 111 American Soldiers and wounded another 490. Among the dead was Lieutenant General Lesley McNair, commander of Army Ground Forces. Eisenhower subsequently told Bradley that he would never again use heavy bombers in support of ground forces, but later changed his mind.[41]

Referring later to Goodwood, Eisenhower remarked, "Although only temporary in effect, the results of the bombing were decisive so far as the initial ground attack was concerned. Actual casualties to the enemy, in his foxholes, were comparatively few, but he was stunned by the weight of the bombing and a degree of confusion was caused which rendered the opposition to our advance negligible for some hours." He also noted, "At the same time, the spectacle of our mighty air fleets roaring in over their heads to attack had a most heartening effect upon our own men." The Supreme Commander said similar things about airpower in support of Cobra. While the bombardments did not inflict large numbers of German casualties, "the bewilderment of the enemy was such that some men unwittingly ran toward our lines and four uninjured tanks put up white flags before any ground attack was launched." The Supreme Commander also lauded the success of airpower in other ways. He stated, "The closeness of the air support given in this operation, thanks to our recent experiences, was such as we should never have dared to attempt a year before. We had indeed made enormous strides forward in this respect." He added that "from the two Caen operations we had learned the need for a quicker ground follow-up on the conclusion of the bombing, for the avoidance of cratering, and for attacks upon a wider range of targets to the rear and on the flanks of the main bombardment area." Despite the setbacks, airpower proved valuable in these operations.[42]

Conclusion

Eisenhower faced similar challenges in organizing and coordinating airpower on the eve of the Normandy invasion in 1944. As today's commanders work to implement cross-domain fires, they would do well to study Eisenhower's airpower accomplishments in support of Overlord.

Airpower served as a valuable, albeit imperfect, cross-domain fire in the period before, during, and after Overlord. Although critical to the invasion, the effectiveness and success of airpower in Normandy was not inevitable. On the contrary, Eisenhower, in his role as Supreme Commander, engineered the attainment of effective airpower. Through the force of his personality and experience, Eisenhower achieved unity of command for airpower operations supporting Overlord and created an organization ensuring that all components worked toward the same goal. Additionally, Eisenhower overcame inner- and inter-service rivalries, differing international priorities, and political challenges while deftly and diplomatically orchestrating his own version of multi-domain battle. Today's commanders face similar challenges while establishing cross-domain fires, in addition to establishing multi-domain organizational frameworks. For example, Field Manual (FM) 3-0, *Operations,* refers to the responsibilities of a theater army commander, noting, "These forces are either allocated or assigned to the combatant commander, who establishes command and support relationships with the theater army as required." FM 3-0 also addresses the role of coordinating cross-domain fires. According to the manual, "Commanders ensure the coordinated use of indirect fires, AMD, and joint fires to create window of opportunity for maneuver and put the enemy in a position of disadvantage. This is accomplished through the operations process, fire support planning, and targeting. . . . Commanders use long-rang fires (rocket, naval, surface fire support, and rotary and fixed-wing air support) to engage the enemy throughout the depth of their AO [Area of Operations]."[43]

Notes

1. US Army Capabilities Integration Center, "Multi-Domain Battle: Evolution of Combined Arms for the 21st Century, 2025–2040," December 2017.

2. Stephen Ambrose, *Eisenhower: Soldier and President* (New York, NY: Simon and Schuster, 1990), 121. Lieutenant Colonel Michael J. Finnegan has also addressed Eisenhower's effort to achieve unity of command in "General Eisenhower's Battle for Control of the Strategic Bombers in Support of Operation Overlord: A Case Study in Unity of Command," (US Army War College, 1999).

3. Dwight Eisenhower, *Crusade in Europe* (New York: Doubleday and Company, 1955), 47.

4. Eisenhower to General George Marshall, December 31, 1943, ed. Alfred D. Chandler, *The Papers of Dwight David Eisenhower, The War Years* 3 (Baltimore: Johns Hopkins University Press, 1970), 1648–49.

5. Walter Bedell Smith to Eisenhower. 30 December 1943. *The Eisenhower Papers*, 1648, n. 1.

6. Ambrose, *Eisenhower: Soldier and President,* 121.

7. Eisenhower, *Crusade in Europe*, 221–22.

8. Eisenhower to Smith, 5 January 1944. *The Eisenhower Papers*, 1651.

9. General Thomas T. Handy to General Carl Spaatz, 5 January 1944, *The Eisenhower Papers*, 1654.

10. Eisenhower to Henry Arnold.23 January 1944, *The Eisenhower Papers*, 1677.

11. Eisenhower to Marshall, 9 February 1944, *The Eisenhower Papers*, 1715.

12. Eisenhower to Tedder, 29 February 1944, *The Eisenhower Papers,* 1755–56; Arthur Tedder, *With Prejudice* (Boston: Little, Brown and Company, 1966), 508–12; *The Eisenhower Papers*, 1756, n. 1.

13. Eisenhower to Marshall, 3 March 1944, *The Eisenhower Papers*, 1758.

14. Eisenhower to Tedder, 29 February 1944, *The Eisenhower Papers*, 1755–56.

15. Dwight Eisenhower, *Report of the Supreme Commander To The Combined Chiefs of Staff On the Operations In Europe of the Allied Expeditionary Force 6 June 1944–8 May 1945* (Washington, DC: Center of Military History, 1994), 9–10; Eisenhower Memorandum, 22 March 1944, *The Eisenhower Papers*, 1784; Eisenhower to Marshall, 10 March 1944, *The Eisenhower Papers*, 1766–67; Eisenhower to Arnold, 15 March 1944, *The Eisenhower Papers*, 1768.

16. Eisenhower Memorandum, 22 March 1944, *The Eisenhower Papers*, 1784–85.

17. Eisenhower Memorandum, 1785; Ambrose, *Eisenhower: Soldier and President*, 126

18. Eisenhower Memorandum, 22 March 1944, *The Eisenhower Papers*, 1784, 1786, n. 9.

19. Eisenhower to Marshall, 12 April 1944, The Eisenhower Papers, 1817.

20. Memorandum for Diary, 22 May 1944, *The Eisenhower Papers*, 1880–81.

21. Eisenhower, *Report of the Supreme Commander*, 9–10.

22. Eisenhower to Marshall, 12 April 1944, *The Eisenhower Papers*, 1817.

23. Eisenhower, *Report of the Supreme Commander*, 9–10.

24. Eisenhower, 10.

25. Eisenhower, 9–10.

26. Eisenhower to Marshall, 29 April 1944, *The Eisenhower Papers*, 1838; Eisenhower to Churchill, 2 May 1944, *The Eisenhower Papers*, 1842–43, 1844, n. 1.

27. Eisenhower to Churchill, 5 April 1944, *The Eisenhower Papers*, 1808.

28. Eisenhower to Churchill, 2 May 1944, *The Eisenhower Papers*, 1842–43.

29. Wesley F. Craven and James L. Cates, eds. "Europe: Argument to V-E. Day," *The Army Air Forces in World War II*, (Washington, DC: Office of Air Force History, 1983), 74–75; James. H. Doolittle, *I Could Never Be So Lucky Again*, (New York: Bantam Books, 1991), 387–88.

30. *The Eisenhower Papers*, 22 March 1944, 1784; Eisenhower to Tedder, 9 March 1944, *The Eisenhower Papers*, 1765–66.

31. *The Eisenhower Papers*, 2033, n. 1.

32. Eisenhower to Harris, 25 May 1944, *The Eisenhower Papers*, 1888.

33. Eisenhower to Harris, 27 July 1944, *The Eisenhower Papers*, 2033; Operation Crossbow was the Allied attacks against German long-range weapons facilities.

34. Craven, "Europe: Argument to V-E. Day," 76–77; Richard Davis, *Carl A. Spaatz and the Air War in Europe*, (Washington, DC: Center for Air Force History, 1993), 345–46; Arthur Tedder, *Air Power in War*, (London: Hodder and Stoughton, 1947), 108. See also Richard Davis, *Bombing the European Axis Powers: A Historical Digest of the Combined Bomber Offensive, 1939–1945*, (Maxwell Air Force Base, AL: Air University Press, 2006).

35. Eisenhower, *Report of the Supreme Commander*, 19–20.

36. Eisenhower Memorandum, 3 June 1944, *The Eisenhower Papers*, 1905–06.

37. Eisenhower, *Report of the Supreme Commander*, 16.

38. Eisenhower Memorandum, 3 June 1944, *The Eisenhower Papers*, 1905; Eisenhower to the Combined Chiefs of Staff, 8 June 1944, *The Eisenhower Papers*, 1916.

39. Martin Blumenson, *Breakout and Pursuit, The United States Army in World War II: The European Theater of Operations,* (Washington, DC: Center of Military History, 1984), 188–91.

40. Blumenson, 221–22, 228–29.

41. Blumenson, 233–36; Omar N. Bradley, *A Soldier's Story*, 349.

42. Eisenhower, *Report of the Supreme Commander*, 35–37

43. Department of the Army, Field Manual (FM) 3-0, *Operations* (Washington, DC: October 2017), 2-3, 2-45.

Chapter 2

Gunners at Cambrai, 1917: How the Royal Artillery Set the Conditions for the Successful Armored Assault

Lieutenant Colonel (Retired) Thomas G. Bradbeer

At 0620 hours on 20 November 1917, 1,003 medium and heavy guns of the Royal Artillery opened fire on the German trenches southwest of the French town of Cambrai. This was the signal for 476 Mark IV tanks to begin the crossing of no-man's land.[1] Six infantry divisions supported by nearly 300 aircraft of the Royal Flying Corps (RFC) were directly behind the tanks. Their objective: penetrate the Hindenburg Line (identified as the *SiegfriedStellung* or Siegfried Line by the Germans) and secure the high ground that was the Bourlon Ridge to the north and crossing over the St Quentin Canal in the south.[2] If the British could achieve their objective, they would capture Cambrai, a critical logistics and communications base, secure "the passages over the Sensee River, and cut off the troops holding the German front line."[3]

Foregoing the days or weeks long artillery barrage that had signaled the start of all previous offensive operations, the British artillery barrage was synchronized to begin when the tanks and infantry began to cross no-man's land. The Germans, dug-in behind the Hindenburg Line, were taken by surprise and stunned by the overwhelming intensity of the barrage fire. The combined arms assault of artillery, tanks, infantry, and aircraft achieved greater results in one day than any previous British Army offensive operation on the Western Front in over three years of warfare.

The artillery fire pinned the German defenders in their dugouts, allowing the tanks to crush the immense barbed-wire obstacles that had earned the Hindenburg Line its impregnable reputation, and to overrun the enemy trenches and strongpoints. The British captured numerous fortified villages and made an initial crossing over the St Quentin canal. In less than four hours of the first day, the British had "smashed" through the outpost line and two heavily fortified German trench systems, breeching the Hindenburg Line on a front of six miles to a depth of four miles. The British Third Army captured more than 4,200 prisoners and 100 artillery pieces at the cost of 4,000 casualties.[4] The German Supreme Command was so shocked by the British advance that they seriously considered ordering a withdrawal from the entire Hindenburg Line. If the British could exploit their gains achieved on the first day of the battle, it might signal the beginning of the end of the war.[5]

When the news of the successful attack reached London on 21 November, church bells rang out all over the country to signal a major victory on the Western Front. It was the first time the bells had rung since the start of the war in August 1914.[6]

Significance of Battle of Cambrai to Unified Land Operations

Today, military professionals remember the Battle of Cambrai as the first battle in which tanks were used *en masse* in an attempt to break the deadlock of trench warfare. More importantly, by synchronizing advances in military technology as well as organizations and doctrine to achieve combined arms maneuver in offensive operations, Cambrai initiated a revolution in military affairs (RMA) in 20th Century warfare.[7] More importantly, is the critical influence that artillery had on shaping the initial success of the armored breakthrough. Using new techniques and tactics, in concert with detailed planning, coordination and synchronization, as well as the fire support provided by the Royal Artillery can be found in the fire support doctrine of today's US Army contained in Field Manual 3-0, *Operations* as well as Field Manual 3-09, *Artillery Operations*.

The use of indirect fires, such as that displayed at Cambrai, was the beginning of what would later be identified as a major component of the "modern style of warfare" or as noted artillery expert and historian Jonathan Bailey has stated, "the advent of three-dimensional conflict."[8] The doctrine employed by the Royal Artillery at Cambrai would be used for the remainder of the war and during offensive operations of the British Army during the Second World War. Many of the tactics, techniques, and procedures first used at Cambrai remain an integral part of most artillery formations in the 21st Century.[9]

The Tank's Baptism of Fire

The British first used tanks in September 1916 during the attack on Flers-Corcelette during the Battle of the Somme. Field Marshall Sir Douglas Haig, commander of the British Expeditionary Force (BEF), had requested 150 tanks be shipped to France in time for the start of the Battle of the Somme in July with the hopes that the new weapon would assist his force in achieving a breakthrough of the German positions. Only 60 Mark 1 tanks arrived by early September under very tight security. When the attack commenced on 15 September, only 30 tanks were operational, and owing to insufficient doctrine, were used in small groups to support the infantry assault.[10] The debut of the tank had mixed results. Several tanks did very well leading the infantry over the German trenches and capturing strongpoints

Figure 2.1. British Mark IV tank moving through Arras, 1917. Photo courtesy of Imperial War Museum Q6418.

to include the village of Flers. They also managed to induce panic amongst several German units, which resulted in surrender or pell-mell retreat.[11]

In the after-action review detailing the tanks performance in combat, Haig admitted that the tanks had not achieved his expectations but "had saved many lives and justified their existence."[12] He then requested delivery of an additional 100 Mark 1 tanks and placed an order for 1,000 more tanks that were to be modified based on the lessons learned at Flers-Courcelette.[13]

Tanks were used throughout the remainder of the Battle of the Somme and again during the Battle of Arras (April 1917) and the Battle of Messines (June 1917). In each battle, the tanks provided valuable support to the infantry. Also in June 1917, Haig approved the creation of the Tank Corps with its own commander and staff. Lieutenant Colonel Hugh Elles, an engineer, was selected to be the commander and Major John Frederick Charles Fuller, an infantryman, was to be his chief of staff.

It was during the Third Battle of Ypres (July–November 1917), fought on the flooded plains of Flanders, where the Tank Corps suffered its highest casualty rate and a major blow to its reputation. More than 200 tanks served in the five-month campaign and at the end of the fighting with the

British capture of Passchendaele ridge, the majority of the tanks had been destroyed by German artillery in the direct fire mode when they became bogged down in the mud forming a "tank graveyard" along the Menin Road.[14] The Tank Corps received criticism and blame for the lack of its success in supporting the infantry and the subsequent heavy casualties the British infantry suffered. There were even rumors amongst the British senior leadership of dissolving the Tank Corps.

Salvation and a chance at redemption came from the BEF commander. Haig, more than most, knew the difficulties that the Tank Corps had faced in the trying conditions around the Ypres salient. In his official dispatch after the battle he provided both a rationale for their performance as well as a tribute to their efforts:

> Although throughout the major part of the Ypres battle, and especially in its later stages, the condition of the ground made the use of tanks difficult or impossible, yet whenever circumstances were in any way favourable, and even when they were not, very gallant and valuable work has been accomplished by tank commanders and crews on a great number of occasions. Long before the conclusion of the Flanders offensive these new instruments had proved their worth, and amply justified the labour, material and personnel diverted to their construction and development.[15]

A Tank "Raid" or Surprise Attack?

A month into the Battle of Third Ypres, Elles and Fuller began to analyze the terrain along the Western Front in an attempt to find a location that could best support the capabilities of the new Mark IV tanks. They identified two critical factors required to support the cross-country capability of the tank. The first was an area that had seen little to no serious fighting and thus was not heavily cratered by near-constant artillery fire. This would allow better trafficability for the tanks, as well as the infantry and artillery. Second, the area must not have a low water table and must be absent of swampy or muddy ground.

Both Haig and his staff had considered the possibilities for offensive action against the German positions west of Cambrai. For more than a year, both the British and the Germans had used the Cambrai sector as a location to allow their corps and divisions to rest and rebuild their strength after the intense fighting on the Somme, Arras, and Ypres during 1916 and 1917. Cambrai was considered a quiet sector experiencing little fighting in the first three years of the war.

After a detailed analysis, Elles and Fuller identified the ground just west of Cambrai as ideal for the use of tanks. The British Third Army, commanded by General Sir Julian Byng, was responsible for the Cambrai sector. Byng had commanded the Canadian Corps when it had captured the key terrain that was Vimy Ridge during the Battle of Arras in April 1917, and he was considered a rising star for future high command.

In early August 1917, Elles and Fuller submitted a plan to Third Army headquarters outlining a "tank raid" using 200 tanks whose objective was to destroy the German artillery behind the Hindenburg Line near Cambrai. The plan called for a "hit and run" attack that would last no more than 48 hours. Nearly simultaneously, another plan for an attack on Cambrai arrived at Third Army headquarters that called for a "surprise attack" in the IV Corps sector, a subordinate unit of Third Army.

Though much of the historiography of the Battle of Cambrai gives Elles and Fuller credit for identifying the Cambrai sector as the location to conduct an offensive operation with tanks *en masse*, as well as devising the operational plan for the attack, it was in fact an artillery officer, Brigadier General Henry Hugh Tudor, the commander of the 9th (Scottish) Division's artillery and a leading artillery tactician, who provided the critical elements of for what would become the operational plan for the attack against Cambrai in November 1917.[16]

Tudor's divisional artillery supported the Third Army's IV Corps. He proposed a surprise attack in which the artillery would not open fire until the tanks and infantry left their positions and began to cross no-man's land. This was a new concept for the use of artillery in supporting a ground attack. In all previous offensive operations, British, French, and German artillery had conducted days or weeks long preparatory artillery barrages to destroy the enemy's trenches and artillery while preventing reinforcing units from moving into the battle zone. These lengthy barrages prevented all efforts at surprising the enemy, and in fact did just the opposite, alerting the defenders to the impending assault.

Tudor's plan called for the tanks to be in the lead to cut lanes through the massive wire obstacles of the Hindenburg Line, some of which were hundreds of yards deep, while the artillery neutralized enemy artillery and forced the infantry to remain underground until the tanks were on top of their positions. The most critical factor of Tudor's plan however, called for the artillery to forgo registration on enemy artillery batteries and other important targets and thus eliminate the requirement for a days or weeks long artillery bombardment. Instead they would use "silent registration" and "predicted fire" to achieve surprise.

It was only because of the many technological and scientific advancements within the Royal Artillery between 1915–1917 that allowed Tudor to be so confident that a surprise attack against Cambrai was both feasible and realistic. He firmly believed that by applying the latest gunnery techniques and procedures, of which silent registration was but one new technique, the artillery would fire fewer shells but with greater precision and thus be far more effective than in previous offensive operations. Achieving precision and surprise would be the two most critical components of the Cambrai offensive.

General Byng approved "The Tudor Plan" as it was known, on 13 October. Byng and his staff briefed the plan to Field Marshall Haig three days later. Recommendations from Elles and Fuller's plan were also included. Realizing that the fighting in Flanders was turning into another battle of attrition, Haig approved the plan for an attack on Cambrai and directed that the Cavalry Corps with its five divisions be included into the order of battle with the intent of exploiting any breakthrough of the Hindenburg Line. When Byng briefed the plan to his corps and division commanders on 26 October, he stressed the importance of secrecy for the operation to achieve complete surprise.

The preparation for the battle was immense. Six infantry and five cavalry divisions, along with three tank brigades consisting of three tank battalions each, had to be assembled and organized for what was to become one of the war's first combined arms battles. Additionally, 14 squadrons from the Royal Flying Corps would observe and direct artillery fire as well as provide close support to the attacking armor and infantry units. A detailed training plan was developed that ensured every infantry battalion had at least two days to train with the tanks that would support them. One thousand and three artillery pieces were allocated to support the attack with many having to be transferred from the Ypres sector. More than 150 new battery positions had to be prepared and massive amounts of ammunition, of a variety of calibers, had to be moved by train, truck, and mule to these new battery positions.[17] In short, the logistics for the battle were herculean and all of it had to be done without providing any telltale signs to the Germans that an attack in the Cambrai sector was imminent.

As training between the infantry and tanks took place from late October through mid-November, the artillery units began to occupy their positions during the hours of darkness. Haig provided additional guidance to Byng and the final plan code-named "Operation GY" was issued on 13 November. In his briefing to his corps and division commanders, Byng identified three phases with multiple objectives within each phase:

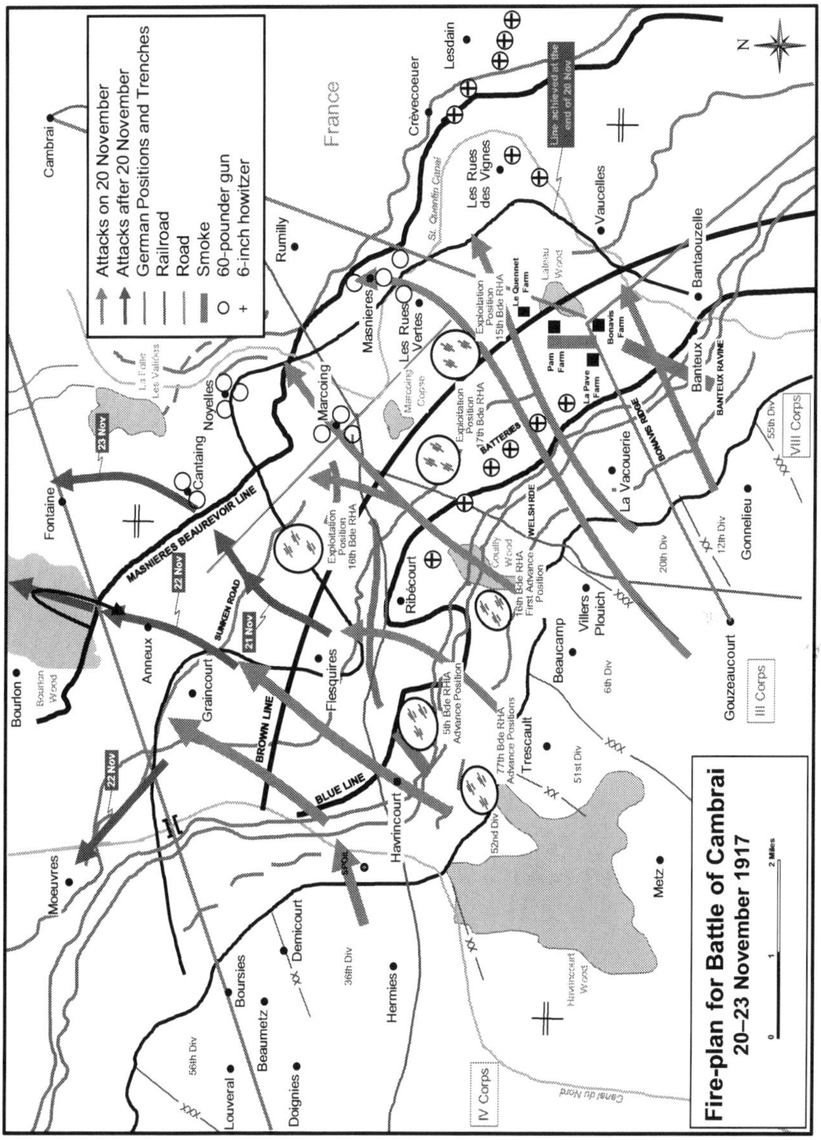

Figure 2.2. The Royal Artillery fire-plan for the Battle of Cambrai, 20 November 1917. Map recreated by Army University Press; reproduced by kind permission of the Royal Artillery Institution.

1). The breakthrough of the Hindenburg Position; the seizing of the canal crossings at Masnieres and Marcoing; and the capture of the Masnieres-Beaurevoir line (the German Second Position) beyond.

2). The advance of the cavalry, through the gap made, to isolate Cambrai and seize the crossings of the Sensee river; and the capture of Bourlon Wood.

3) The capture of Cambrai and the quadrilateral defined by Haig and the defeat of the German forces cut off.[18]

Haig realized that the attack required detailed synchronization among the tanks, infantry, cavalry, and the squadrons of the Royal Flying Corps. He also informed his subordinate commanders that he would call off the attack after 48 hours if the attack failed to attain the seven objectives identified in the plan. Haig believed that if a breakthrough did not occur in the first 48 hours, the Germans would have the necessary reinforcements in place to blunt any further advance in the Cambrai sector.[19]

For the combined arms attack against Cambrai to succeed, much depended on the ability of the British artillery to destroy, neutralize, or suppress critical targets while providing supporting fires to the advancing tanks and infantry as they crossed no-man's land. It is therefore important to review the organization, capabilities, and doctrine of the Royal Artillery from the start of the war through November 1917.

The Royal Artillery: Organization, Capabilities, and Doctrine

When the war started the Royal Artillery consisted of three branches: the Royal Horse Artillery (RHA), the Royal Field Artillery (RFA) and the Royal Garrison Artillery (RGA). The RHA provided artillery support for cavalry units and was considered the *corps d'elite* within the Royal Artillery.[20] The RFA provided support to infantry divisions. The RHA and RFA were equipped with the horse-drawn 18-pounder Quick Firing gun Mark I, the 13-pounder Quick Firing gun Mark I, and the 4.5-inch (114mm) Quick Firing howitzer.[21] A well-trained crew could fire 20 rounds a minute to a maximum range of between 6,600 yards to 7,800 yards depending on which weapon they were equipped with. Divisional heavy batteries were equipped with the 60-pounder gun Mark I which had a maximum range of 10,300 yards. The RGA Heavy artillery consisted of the obsolete 6-inch 30-cwt howitzer with a maximum range of 5,200 yards. These would be replaced with the more improved 12-inch and 15-inch guns.[22] The RGA was organized for use in coastal forts against enemy ships but also provided the army with mountain batteries of light guns and howitzers. As the war progressed the RGA attached a heavy battery to each infantry division within the BEF. By the start of the Cambrai offensive, the most numerous artillery pieces in the Royal Artillery were the 6 and 8-inch howitzers, the 18-pounder gun, the 60-pounder gun, and the 9.2-inch siege howitzer.[23]

At its lowest level, the organization of the Royal Artillery was the battery. By 1917 each RHA and RFA battery was equipped with six 18-pounder field guns and all howitzer batteries had six 4.5-inch howitzers. A major commanded a battery with an additional four officers and about 200 men.[24] The next echelon within the Royal Artillery was the artillery brigade, which was the equivalent of an artillery battalion in the US Army today and was commanded by a lieutenant colonel. Two RHA Brigades were attached to a cavalry division with each brigade having two batteries. By 1917 the divisional artilleries were reduced to two brigades but contained four batteries, with three 18-pounder field gun batteries and one 4.5-inch howitzer battery. Army field brigades were formed and were used by the army commander to provide reinforcing fires to artillery brigades supporting major offensive operations.[25]

The Royal Artillery did not have a corps artillery organization in its force structure when the war started. Within the corps headquarters the senior gunner was the Brigadier-General, Royal Artillery (BGRA). He was an advisor to the corps commander and not a commander. By the time of Cambrai, however, the BGRA was recognized as the corps artillery commander (GOCRA) though the position continued to be filled by brigadier generals.

At the divisional level, a Commander, Royal Artillery (CRA), also a brigadier general, commanded the artillery. The CRA was assigned a Brigade-Major Royal Artillery (BMRA) to assist with the coordination and synchronization of all artillery matters. Each of these positions was created shortly before the start of the war and had evolved from lessons learned from the British Army's experiences in the Anglo-Boer War (1898–1902).

The major lesson learned from the Russo-Japanese War (1904–1905) by the Royal Artillery (as well as the artillery formations of the European nations and the United States) was the significant impact indirect fire had on the outcome of the land battle. At the Battle of Sha-ho (September 1904), the Japanese positioned their artillery on reverse slopes where the Russian artillery or their observers could not see them. From their concealed positions, they neutralized the Russian guns and devastated the Russian infantry. They also massed fires by controlling their artillery batteries using wireless telephones.[26]

Though the Royal Artillery revised its doctrine in 1906 to incorporate the lessons learned from the war in South Africa and the Russo-Japanese

War, stressing the importance of indirect fire as the primary form of artillery fire, the RHA and RFA spent most of its time in the inter-war period training to conduct direct fire. Both branches of the Royal Artillery learned painful lessons in the opening battles of the First World War. Using direct fire tactics against the advancing German Army during the fighting at Mons and Le Cateau in August 1914, both the RHA and RFA suffered severe losses to their battery leadership and gun crews.[27] The high casualty rate convinced senior British artillery commanders they had to incorporate indirect fire as the primary means of engaging the enemy.

With the evolution of artillery as a major weapon system on the battlefield in the late 19th Century, the increasing incorporation of scientific advancements and methodologies on artillery systems and procedures was not fully accepted within at least two of the three branches of the Royal Artillery. The RFA had earned a reputation of being resistant to change, most especially with the advancements that science was having on gunnery in the decade before the start of the First World War. The majority of leaders within the artillery branch thought that the use of artillery had more to do with art than science. It was believed that intuition and judgment were two critical attributes that were more important than scientific advancements in gunnery for artillery to be effective on the future battlefield.[28]

"The RFA did not practice temperature corrections, map shooting was unknown, and communications were by visual signal, sometimes by short telephone line, but more usually by megaphone."[29] The RGA, however, embraced the scientific advancements. When the war began it was using indirect fire as its primary method of engagement, using instruments to ensure all of its guns and howitzers were firing in a common direction and using calculated data to account for weather and maps to attain a more accurate firing solution. The RGA also incorporated techniques to include camouflage as a means to improve battery survivability.[30]

The Artillery-Aviation Team

After trench warfare set in along the Western Front in the Fall of 1914, the Royal Artillery as a whole recognized that it had to transition to use indirect fire as its primary *modus operandi* if it was to be of value in future offensive operations. As part of this learning curve, infantry and artillery commanders also began to recognize the valuable role aircraft could play to augment and enhance their own capabilities.

Within the first few days and weeks of the war in France and Belgium, the senior leadership of the British Army came to recognize that aircraft could be a force multiplier. On 22–23 August 1914, the RFC conducted almost continuous reconnaissance missions during daylight and identified that the advancing German Army was attempting to envelop the two British Corps near Mons Belgium. With these observation reports from the RFC, Sir John French, the BEF commander realized the danger to both of his flanks and ordered a retirement that would save the British Army.[31]

In September, reports provided by RFC aircrew, identified that the German commander, Field Marshal von Kluck, had left his right flank exposed. In what became known later as the "Miracle on the Marne," the French were able to conduct a counter-attack that forced the Germans to retreat 40 miles to the River Aisne and dig-in. During the Allied counter-attack on the Marne, the commander of the BEF, Field Marshal Sir John French, notified the Prime Minister and the War Cabinet:

> I wish particularly to bring to your Lordship's notice the admirable work done by the Royal Flying Corps under Sir David Henderson. Their skill, energy, and perseverance have been beyond all praise. They have furnished me with the most complete and accurate information, which has been of incalculable value in the conduct of operations. Fired at constantly both by friend and foe, and not hesitating to fly in every kind of weather, they have remained undaunted throughout.[32]

During the subsequent Battle of Aisne and the First Battle of Ypres, the evolution of aircraft continued as a weapon of war in support of the ground commander. The RFC began to experiment with aerial photography focusing on enemy dispositions and artillery emplacements. The end result was that by 1916, hundreds of thousands of photographs were taken along the entire Western Front, and in coordination with Field Survey Companies from the Royal Engineers, produced accurate and detailed maps that highlighted enemy trenches, unit locations and artillery emplacements. These maps enabled British artillery commanders to accurately fix the location of each of their batteries as well as the locations for enemy targets. Battery commanders were provided with a specially prepared map known as a "plotting table" or "Artillery Board." From these maps, gunners in the Fire Direction Center applied mathematical calculations to determine the angle and elevation for their batteries.[33]

The RFC in coordination with the Royal Artillery also began to experiment with directing artillery fire from the air using wireless. By the Battle of Cambrai, the techniques for the conduct of aerial reconnaissance, aerial photography, and directing artillery fire had become established doctrine within both the RFC and the RA.[34]

Advancements in weapon systems and gunnery techniques

As the war entered its third year, advancements by the Royal Artillery greatly increased both the range and lethality of its guns and howitzers. In tandem with better artillery systems, there was a corresponding increase in the complexity of the ammunition fired by the guns. Shrapnel was used almost exclusively from 1914 through 1916 with good effect against personnel and barbed wire obstacles but the use of high explosive (HE) shells was often less effective due to the fact that the fuse often delayed detonation until after the shell buried itself in the ground, and the force of the explosion was primarily upward.[35] By 1917 this problem was solved with the introduction of the No. 106 fuse, which enabled a HE shell to detonate before it hit the ground. The blast went horizontal rather than vertical and proved to be more effective than shrapnel at cutting barbed wire. Even better, by exploding above the ground the shell did not create deep craters that would impede the advance of infantry and tanks.[36] A smoke shell was also developed to be fired by the 18-pounder.

This combination of improved weapon systems and ammunition, the 18-pounder and 4.5-inch howitzer and smoke shell specifically, and the No. 106 fuse, with a plentiful supply of HE ammunition, made the artilleryman's contribution to offensive operations much more effective than in the first three years of the war.[37]

Other scientific techniques used by the Royal Artillery to improve its lethality and effectiveness included "flash-spotting" and "sound-ranging" of enemy artillery batteries. The German artillery used these same techniques, but the British were much more committed in their development and application. Commanders such as Brigadier General Hugh Tudor stressed the importance of using new and experimental methodologies to locate and neutralize German artillery batteries and to ensure that these efforts were coordinated from brigade through army headquarters. Much of these efforts would be codified in evolving doctrine directed by the War Office when it issued a pamphlet titled "Artillery Notes No. 4-Artillery in Offensive Operations."[38]

By November 1917, the Royal Artillery had proven itself to be superior to its German counterpart, both tactically and technically.[39] The use of sound-ranging and flash-spotting were so effective that the Germans feared them.[40] The data produced from these two processes could determine a German artillery piece's location to within 15 yards as well as accurately locate the fall of shot from British guns. By using these methods and by working with the RFC, the counter-battery units within each corps were able to win the artillery duels that took place during the battles of Arras (April 1917) and Messines (June 1917). The end result was that the RA now focused more heavily on neutralizing the German artillery and less on bombarding enemy tranches.[41]

Having started the war with a 19th Century mindset, the RA had made significant and lasting advancements in the development of its weapon systems and tactics. Under the visionary leadership of men like Major General Sir Herbert Uniacke, MGRA Fifth Army, Lieutenant General Sir Noel Birch, MGRA Fourth Army and Brigadier General Hugh Tudor, CGRA 9th Division Artillery, the RA had by the final planning stages for the Battle of Cambrai proved it was more than ready to assume a greater and more significant role in the coming combined arms battle.

Silent Registration

The final piece of the puzzle to convince the ground commanders (as well as some of the non-believing artillery commanders) that a surprise attack was feasible by not conducting the traditional days and or weeks long preparatory artillery barrage, was the introduction of a new method for calibrating artillery pieces. The proven technique had been to calibrate guns while conducting registration fire on enemy targets as part of the initial bombardment but this eliminated any chance of surprise.

Instead, Tudor proposed that every gun and howitzer involved in the Cambrai offensive be sent to ranges in the rear area before moving into the line prior to the start of the battle. At the range, crews would ascertain their piece's muzzle velocity by conducting calibration of the gun or howitzer tube; this eliminated the requirement to calibrate the gun or howitzer by conducting live-fire and was termed "silent registration." Once the guns occupied their positions behind the trenches, critical information for a target was taken from a map and then a gunnery solution was developed and recorded to be used when the barrage started. By doing this, Tudor argued, the element of surprise would be maintained up until the start of the attack.[42]

The Battle of Cambrai

With the mission of neutralizing enemy artillery batteries west of Cambrai in the opening attack, General Byng had 36 artillery brigades (battalions by modern standards) plus an additional 16 batteries of General Headquarters artillery units and 11 batteries from Third Army bringing the total to 1,003 guns and howitzers to support his six attacking divisions. Third Army Intelligence identified that the Germans had only nine batteries, totaling 34 guns supporting the 20th Landwehr Division, the 9th Reserve Division and the 54th Division deployed between Havrincourt and La Vacquerie. The 54th had spent July and August fighting at Ypres and was in the process of reconstitution due to its heavy losses.[43] The German artillery was thus the first priority on the high priority target list. The fire-plan directed all 60-pounders to fire gas on the German artillery units and then switch to known reserve assembly areas in the villages behind the front lines. The 6-inch guns were to continue the bombardment of the German artillery positions until directed otherwise.[44]

To prevent German observation of the attack, a smoke screen was to be fired and maintained by the British artillery on the Havrincourt-Flesquieres Ridge throughout the first two hours of the attack, weather permitting. The fire-plan also reminded all artillery commanders that there would be no pre-registration on targets and that all RA batteries would use a "lifting barrage," from one objective to the next at timed intervals, instead of a "creeping barrage" that had been introduced during the Battle of the Somme the previous year. The 13- and 18-pounders were to fire one-third shrapnel, one-third high explosive and one-third smoke. Of the 1,003 artillery pieces providing fire support to the attacking tanks and infantry, the most predominant system was the 18-pounder of which there were 498 at the start of the battle.[45] The operations order also provided detailed instructions on the routes and timings to be followed for those artillery units who were to move forward as the battle progressed.[46] Additionally, for the first time in the war, the British also developed a detailed air defense plan to support the attack. Twenty-eight anti-aircraft guns were deployed throughout the sector with most of them well forward to provide coverage up to 4,000 yards ahead of the British front-line trenches.[47]

The last batteries moved into their firing positions on the night of 17–18th November. Haig and Byng were confident that the detailed plan to use tanks, infantry, artillery, cavalry, and aircraft as a combined arms force would rupture the Hindenburg Line east of Cambrai. The two commanders agreed that with limited reinforcements available to sustain the attack they had 48 hours to achieve their objectives. After that time, they realized the German commander at Cambrai would receive reinforcements and these units would most likely determine the ultimate success or failure of Operation GY.

A thick mist appeared over the impending battlefield on the morning of 20 November, limiting visibility to less than 200 yards. At 0610 the tanks, the first echelon of the 476 that would take part in the battle, with infantry units behind them, moved forward along a front of 6 miles.[48] Ten minutes later, at zero hour the British artillery opened fire, their shells landing 200 yards in front of the advancing tanks and lifting forward to the German trenches per the fire-plan.[49]

"The synchronization was excellent and it was a most impressive sight to see the hillsides burst into a perfect sheet of flame." Major E.F. Norton, commanding D Battery, RHA stated.[50] The British tanks and infantry crossed no-man's land with their own artillery fire bursting all along the front with an accuracy that surprised both the infantry and the artillery commanders. The concept of "Predicted Fire" that Brigadier General Tudor had argued so hard for was vindicated in the first minutes of the assault.

Haig and Byng had feared for weeks that if the element of secrecy was lost and the Germans learned of the impending attack against Cambrai, the advancing infantry would suffer heavy losses. In fact, all along the Hindenburg Line, the Germans were taken by surprise as the British tanks, in platoon and company formations, crushed the massive wire obstacles and breeched the German first line trenches within the first hour of the attack.

Field Marshal Paul von Hindenburg, German Army Chief of the General Staff, confirmed that at all levels, the German leadership had been caught by surprise with the attack against Cambrai. More importantly, he recognized that the British had changed their strategy by using a combined arms approach in an attempt to break-through what had been considered an impregnable defensive position.

On November 20 we were suddenly surprised by the [British] near Cambrai. The attack at this point was against a portion of the Siegfried

Figure 2.3. Royal Artillery (RFA) 18-pounders in action. Photo courtesy of Imperial War Museum Q2017.

Line which was certainly very strong. . . . With the help of their tanks, the enemy broke through our series of obstacles and positions which had been [previously] entirely undamaged. . . . With the Battle of Cambrai the [British] High Command had departed from what I might call the routine methods which hitherto they had always followed.[51]

Though directed to neutralize the German artillery, the Royal Artillery destroyed many of the German batteries west of Cambrai. The accuracy of the massed British guns might have surprised the British commanders but shocked the German leadership who later would question how the Royal Artillery was able to achieve such effects without conducting their usual barrage to register their guns.[52] The answer lay primarily with the "Flash-Spotting" and "Sound Ranging" units of the Royal Engineers and the herculean work the sappers had done to survey every British gun and howitzer location prior to the start of the battle. The RA was able to achieve a 90 percent accuracy rate in locating the German artillery positions.[53] It was a combination of each of these three techniques that convinced Tudor that predicted fire based on "silent registration" was not only feasible but would ensure that a surprise attack against Cambrai would catch the Germans unawares and set the conditions for a success unlike anything the British had experienced on the Western Front up to that time.

A few of the German guns attempted to conduct counter-battery fire against the British batteries but the overall effort was negligible, and in turn, they were destroyed or neutralized by returning British artillery or by RFC aircraft searching for the German batteries to bomb or to call for fire on these high priority targets. A single example is noteworthy of the effort of the RFC that day. In poor weather with heavy fog, four DeHavilland five aircraft located and attacked German battery positions on the reverse slope of Flesquieres Ridge, which was at the extreme range of the British guns. Flying at less than 200 feet, the four pilots dropped their bombs and then strafed each gun position. An hour later a reconnaissance aircraft confirmed the German guns were neutralized with their crews dead around their guns.[54]

By mid-day it was evident that the British had achieved a major breech in the Hindenburg Line. Tanks and infantry were advancing on Graincourt and Bourlon Wood in the west, toward the villages of Marcoing and Masnieres in the center, and the St. Quentin Canal Crossing in the east while the massed batteries of the RFA and RHA continued to lay down fires on high priority targets west of Cambrai as part of the scheduled fire-plan. Assigned batteries began to move forward to better provide supporting fires as British units advanced closer to Cambrai.

The lone German success on the first day of the battle occurred in the center in the fortified village of Flesquieres, which sat atop the Flesquieres Ridge and so looked down upon the advancing British tanks and infantry. Two battalions of German infantry, along with several batteries of artillery, which were dug-in on the reverse slope of the ridge, managed to put up a resolute defense, withstanding several intense artillery bombardments as well as numerous bombing and strafing attacks from RFC aircraft. Most significantly on the long-term outcome of the battle, the German units in Flesquieres successfully halted two British tank battalions, knocking out dozens of the slow-moving vehicles with 77-mm field guns in the direct-fire mode at close range as the tanks crossed over the ridgeline. Of concern to the British commanders was the fact that 179 tanks out of the 378 tanks assigned a combat mission had been put out of action in the first day of the battle; a 47-percent attrition rate. More than 100 were lost due to mechanical failures or ditching in trenches with 65 having been destroyed by German artillery.[55] The loss of these tanks would be a major reason for the subsequent loss of momentum the British experienced in the subsequent days of the battle.

Notwithstanding the German defense of Flesquieres, by the end of the first day of the attack the British III and IV Corps had advanced to a depth of 9,000 yards, captured numerous villages, crossed the St Quentin Canal, and taken more than 4,000 prisoners and 100 artillery pieces. British casualties had been light in comparison, soldier morale was extremely high, and a breakthrough of the Hindenburg Line seemed likely the following day.

None of this would have been possible if it were not for the stalwart leadership of Brigadier General Tudor and the skill demonstrated by the officers and men of the Royal Artillery, the Royal Engineers, and the aircrew of the RFC. Tudor's concept for the overall plan of attack against Cambrai and his insistence on using predicted fires to achieve the element of surprise, as well as the precision and accuracy of the guns and howitzers of the Royal Artillery, proved to be the critical factors that set the conditions for the success the tanks and infantry achieved on the first day of the attack at Cambrai.[56]

Conclusion

The British continued the attack toward Cambrai on 21–22 November believing that they had weakened the German forces to the point that a breakthrough into open country could be achieved with one more combined attack by the tanks and infantry. Then it would be the turn of the five cavalry divisions to exploit the breech. Unfortunately, for Field Marshal Haig and General Byng's Third Army, the Germans proved once again that they might bend but they would not break.

After consulting Byng, Haig made the decision to continue the attack beyond the agreed upon 48 hours, with the aim of capturing the villages of Fontaine and Bourlon, two German strongpoints northwest of Cambrai. These attacks failed primarily due to a lack of reinforcements and exhaustion on the part of the attacking brigades. On 27 November, Haig was forced to use several of his cavalry divisions as dismounted infantry to repulse local German counter-attacks. Unknown to Haig and Byng and their staffs, German reinforcements had begun to arrive in the Cambrai area as the battle started, much sooner than the British commanders had anticipated. With casualties mounting by the day to unsustainable levels, Haig made the decision to consolidate the gains achieved and prepare the Flesquieres Ridge for defense. On 30 November, the Germans launched a counter-attack across the entire Cambrai sector, and in the course of a week recovered most of the ground they had lost on the first day of the battle. By the time the battle ended, the fighting at Cambrai had involved nearly 20 British divisions, a quarter of the British forces on the Western Front.[57]

Within the military revolution that occurred during the First World War, Cambrai is considered to have been the genesis of a combined arms revolution in military affairs. More importantly from a fires perspective were the lessons learned that would become doctrine within the Royal Artillery and the British Army to ensure a complementary relationship between fires and maneuver through the conduct of detailed planning and synchronization for the integration of fires. The development of field artillery operations, as well as the organizational force structure required to ensure the maneuver force was adequately supported by fires, was also a major lesson learned from Cambrai that the Royal Artillery analyzed and assessed for application in future large-scale ground combat operations.

In the first week of the battle the British had achieved a tactical success but they could not overcome the resilience of the German Army and its response, which prevented the British from achieving an operational victory. Not until August 1918, during the Second Battle of Amiens, were the British able to effectively apply the lessons learned from Cambrai and defeat the German Army in France and Belgium four months later. A significant factor which contributed to the final victory was the role of the artillery whose relationship with the maneuver forces had not changed but was redefined. No longer was the artillery's primary purpose the destruction of enemy obstacles or machine guns; instead it was to

Figure 2.4. Royal Field Artillery (RFA) 18-pounder setting up in new position, 1917. Photo courtesy of Imperial War Museum, Q5171.

destroy or neutralize enemy artillery. It could also focus more effort to the conduct of the deep battle.[58]

The use of predicted fires to neutralize, suppress, or destroy, what today is identified as high-payoff and high-value targets, as the attack begins ensures the element of surprise and that the initiative remains with the attacking maneuver force. The predicted fire technique developed by Tudor would become doctrine within the British, French, German, and American artilleries before the war ended. It survives today in artillery doctrine around the globe.

Finally, and perhaps most importantly to the conduct of present and future field artillery operations in large-scale combat operations, are the five requirements for accurate fire: 1) accurate target location and size; 2) accurate firing unit location; 3) accurate weapons and munitions information; 4) accurate meteorological information; and 5) accurate computational (gunnery) procedures, all of which were developed and put into practice by the Royal Artillery during the Battle of Cambrai.[59]

The tasks and systems that are the foundation of the fires warfighting function in today's US Army, specifically the delivery of fires, the integration of Army, joint and multinational fires, and the conduct of targeting can be traced to the lessons learned by the Royal Artillery during the Battle of Cambrai over 100 years ago. The doctrinal concepts of preparatory fires, counter-fire, suppression fires for gaining and maintaining fire superiority, as well as the inclusion of fixed wing air support as identified in Army

Doctrine Reference Publication (ADRP) 3-09, *Fires*, and Field Manual (FM) 3-0, *Operations*, also evolved from the techniques and tactics used by the British artillery at Cambrai.[60] The lessons learned from a battle fought over 100 years ago provide many valuable lessons for today's combined arms leaders as the Army prepares for large-scale combat operations in today's operational environment.

Notes

1. Bryn Hammond, *Cambrai 1917: The Myth of the First Great Tank Battle* (London: Weidenfeld & Nicolson, 2008), 68–69. See also Gary Sheffield, *Forgotten Victory: The First World War—Myths and Realities* (Headline Book Publishing, 2001), 181.

2. Jack Sheldon, *The German Army at Cambrai* (London: Pen & Sword Books, Ltd. 2009), 1.

3. Alexander Turner, *Cambrai 1917: The Birth of Armoured Warfare* (Oxford: Osprey Publishing Company, 2007), 10.

4. Hammond, *Cambrai 1917,* 193. See also Wilfrid Miles, *History of the Great War: Military Operations France and Belgium: The Battle of Cambrai* (1948; repr., Nashville, TN: The Imperial War Museum and The Battery Press, 1991), 88.

5. Bryan Cooper, *The Battle of Cambrai* (New York: Stein and Day Publishers, 1968), 14.

6. J.H. Johnson, *Stalemate: The Real Story of Trench Warfare* (London: Rigel Publications, 1995), 182.

7. Drew Middleton, *Cross-Roads of Modern Warfare: Sixteen Twentieth-century Battles that Shaped Contemporary History* (New York: Doubleday & Company Inc., 1983), 51. On the debate between Military Revolutions and Revolutions in Military Affairs see Scott Stephenson, "The Revolution in Military Affairs: 12 Observations on an Out-of-Fashion Idea," *Military Review* 90, no. 3, May–June 2010, 38–46; Michael J. Thompson, "Military Revolutions and Revolutions in Military Affairs: Accurate Descriptions of Change or Intellectual Constructs?" University of Ottawa, accessed 2 May 2018, http://artsites.uottawa.ca/strata/doc/strata3_082-108.pdf; MacGregor Knox and Williamson Murray, eds., *The Dynamics of Military Revolution, 1300–2050* (Cambridge: Cambridge University Press, 2001); and Jonathan A. Bailey, "The First World War and the Birth of the Modern Style of Warfare" in the *Dynamics of Military Revolution,* eds. Knox and Murray (Cambridge: Cambridge University Press, 2001), 132–53.

8. Bailey, "The First World War and the Birth of the Modern Style of Warfare," 132.

9. General Sir Martin Farndale, *History of the Royal Regiment of Artillery, Western Front 1914–1918* (Dorchester, England: The Dorset Press, 1986), 258. Specifically, the five requirements for accurate fire identified by the US Army Field Artillery can be traced back to the Royal Artillery's considerations of the use of artillery on the Western Front, 1914–1918: 1) Accurate target location and size; 2) Accurate firing unit location; 3) Accurate weapons and munitions information; 4) Accurate meteorological information; and 5) Accurate computational procedures. See Department of the Army, Field Manual (FM) 3-09, *Field Artillery Operations* (Washington, DC: 4 April 2014), 1-41.

10. J.P. Harris, *Men, Ideas and Tanks: British Military Thought and Armoured Forces, 1903–1939* (Manchester, UK: Manchester University Press, 1995), 62–67.

11. Kenneth Macksey, *Tank versus Tank: The Illustrated Story of Armored Battlefield Conflict in the Twentieth Century* (New York: Crescent Books, 1991), 16.

12. Harris, *Men, Ideas and Tanks,* 67.

13. Harris, 66–67. See also Gary Sheffield and John Bourne, eds., *Douglas Haig: War Diaries and Letters 1914–1918* (London: Weidenfeld & Nicolson, 2005), 229–31.

14. Bryan Cooper, *The Ironclads of Cambrai* (New York: Stein and Day Publishers, 1968), 58.

15. Cooper, 60.

16. The most prominent exceptions include: Farndale, *History of the Royal Regiment*, 216; Harris, *Men, Ideas and Tanks,* 108; Turner, *Cambrai 1917;* Hammond, *Cambrai 1917.*

17. Hammond, *Cambrai 1917,* 66.

18. Hammond, 78.

19. Hammond, 78.

20. Dale Clarke, *British Artillery 1914–19* (Oxford: Osprey Publishing, 2004), 3–4.

21. The principle of Quick-Firing or QF meant that the artillery piece had a hydrostatic buffer and recuperator system that absorbed the recoil after the weapon fired. The piece returned to its original firing position while the carriage remained stationary and the gun remained aligned on its target. Just as important, Quick-Firing also enabled an increased rate of aimed fire because of the gun's stability. The first artillery piece to possess this system was the French 75-mm field gun introduced in 1897 that became the mainstay artillery weapon of the French Army in the First World War.

22. Farndale, *History of the Royal Regiment*, 1.

23. In the Royal Artillery, guns were identified by the weight of their projectile e.g. 18-pounder. Howitzers were identified by the diameter of their projectile in inches (4.5-inch).

24. Clarke, *British Artillery 1914–19,* 8–9.

25. Clarke, *British Artillery 1914–19,* 9–10.

26. Shelford Bidwell and Dominick Graham, *Fire Power: British Army Weapons and Theories of War 1904-1945* (London: George Allen & Unwin Publishers Ltd., 1982), 10. See also Boyd L. Dastrup, *King of Battle: A Branch History of the US Army's Field Artillery* (Fort Monroe, VA: United States Army Training and Doctrine Command, 1993), 148.

27. Hammond, *Cambrai 1917,* 30. At Le Cateau the RHA and RFA had 38 guns captured and most of these gun crews were killed, wounded, or captured. Noted Royal Artillery historian, General Sir Martin Farndale would state that "Le Cateau was an artillery battle fought with 20th Century weapons by men used to 19th Century methods."

28. Paddy Griffith, ed., *British Fighting Methods in the Great War* (London: Frank Cass, 1996), 24.

29. Griffith, 24.

30. Griffith, 24.

31. Air Historical Branch, *The Royal Air Force in the Great War* (1936, Reprint, London: Department of Printed Books, The Imperial War Museum, 1996), 25.

32. Air Historical Branch, 26

33. Hammond, *Cambrai 1917,* 34.

34. The BEF General Staff produced numerous pamphlets during the war that incorporated lessons learned from each battle. In December 1916, a month after the end of the Battle of the Somme, the General Staff issued "Co-Operation of Aircraft with Artillery." The pamphlet addressed command and control issues as well as best practices for directing artillery from the air. The principles identified evolved into accepted doctrine by both the RFC and the RA for the remainder of the war.

35. Paddy Griffith, *Battle Tactics of the Western Front: The British Army's Art of Attack 1916–1918* (New Haven: Yale University Press, 1994), 139–40.

36. Griffith, 139–40.

37. In 1915, the Royal Artillery suffered a major shortage of ammunition, which resulted in the "Shell Scandal" that nearly brought down the British government.

38. Farndale, *History of the Royal Regiment,* 158.

39. Griffith, ed., *British Fighting Methods,* 35. See also Bidwell and Graham, *Fire Power,* 110.

40. Bidwell and Graham, *Fire Power,* 110.

41. Bidwell and Graham, 110.

42. Hammond, *Cambrai 1917,* 67–68.

43. Hammond, 105. See also Farndale, *History of the Royal Regiment,* 218.

44. Farndale, *History of the Royal Regiment,* 219.

45. Turner, *Cambrai 1917,* 29.

46. Hammond, *Cambrai 1917,* 216–21.

47. Farndale, *History of the Royal Regiment,* 219.

48. Of the 476 Mark IV tanks involved in the Battle of Cambrai, 378 were considered Fighting Tanks organized in nine battalions of 42 tanks each. Fifty-four tanks were to serve as supply tanks towing sledges with additional fuel and ammunition to resupply the fighting tanks. Thirty-two were given the mission of pulling the barbed-wire obstacles away after the lead echelon of tanks crushed the obstacle belts. An additional nine tanks were assigned as wireless communication vehicles to assist with command and control (one per tank battalion), and the remaining tank was assigned the task of carrying telephone cable from Third Army Headquarters to assist in keeping the higher headquarters informed of what was occurring on the front lines of the attack. Wilfrid Miles, *The Official History of Military Operations in France and Belgium, 1917, Volume 3: The Battle of Cambrai* (London, His Majesty's Stationery Office, 1948), 28.

49. Anthony Livesey, *Great Battles of World War I* (New York: MacMillan Publishing Company, 1989), 149.

50. Farndale, *History of the Royal Regiment,* 222.

51. Field Marshal von Hindenburg, *The Great War*, Charles Messenger, ed. (London: Greenhill Book, 2006), 156. See also Sheldon, *The German Army at Cambrai*, 303. Crown Prince Rupprecht, commander of Bavaria's Army Group in the Cambrai sector stated "The [British] offensive achieved complete surprise. . . . Our forces discounted the imminence of a major offensive because there had not been any increase in artillery fire. . . . Without a heavy artillery bombardment it seemed that an attack could be ruled out completely."

52. Sheldon, *The German Army at Cambrai*, 312.

53. Farndale, *History of the Royal Regiment*, 222.

54. Hammond, *Cambrai 1917,* 124–25.

55. Cooper, *The Ironclads of Cambrai*, 135.

56. John Pimlott, ed. *The Hutchinson Atlas of Battle Plans: Before and After* (Oxford: Helicon Publishing, 1998), 56–57.

57. Pimlott, ed., 62.

58. Jonathan A. Bailey, "British Artillery in the Great War," in *British Fighting Methods in the Great War,* 37–38.

59. Department of the Army, FM 3-09, 1-41–1-44.

60. Department of the Army, Field Manual (FM) 3-0, *Operations* (Washington DC: October 2017), 2-45–2-47.

Chapter 3
The Influence of Electronic Warfare on Operational Maneuver*
Major David M. Rodriguez

Editor's Introduction: Field Manual (FM) 3-0, Operations (2017), is the capstone doctrine on unified land operations describing how Army forces—as part of a joint team—will shape operational environments, prevent conflict, conduct large-scale ground combat, and consolidate gains against a peer threat. Though then-Major Rodriguez wrote this monograph on the influence of electronic warfare on operational maneuver nearly 30 years ago, the information is still relevant today and will be in the future as well. Technology and its applications for the conduct of warfighting is changing at an ever-expanding rate. The challenge that military professionals face for adapting to and incorporating emerging technologies has and will be difficult. Rodriguez' analysis of how technological advancements in the area of electronic warfare influenced military operations in the 1973 and 1982 mid-east wars between Israel and several near peer threats, provides us a historical case study on a critical topic for Army leaders to study and learn from. When the next conflict starts, the US Army may be at a disadvantage in the area of electronic warfare. Our adversaries will use cyberspace and electronic warfare to support their military operations. To mitigate this threat, the US Army will rely on both cyberspace and electronic warfare counter-measures as well as the best means to use our own offensive capabilities to assist in the defeat of a peer or near-peer threat.

Electronic warfare is a field where technology improves capabilities rapidly. Warfare in the electromagnetic spectrum began in World War I with rudimentary communication interceptions. It has progressed with such speed from then to now, that an argument can be made that the effect may be decisive. Chris Bellamy emphasizes that the 1982 Operation Peace for Galilee, "was not the first war in which electronic warfare featured prominently, but it demonstrated how electronic weaponry has become pivotal on the modern battlefield."[1] The dramatic increase in technological capability to influence war creates the current dynamic environment of electronic warfare.

The influence of electronic warfare is felt through the three levels of war: strategic, operational, and tactical. This chapter limits the analysis to the operational level of war, specifically, the influence of electronic warfare on operational maneuver. The purpose of the chapter is to determine how exploitation of electronic warfare capabilities support operational maneuver by ground forces to the operational depth of an opposing force.

The importance of the operational level of war in our doctrine was reintroduced in the 1982 Field Manual (FM) 100-5, *Operations,* and re-affirmed in the 1986 version. Operational maneuver is a major part of the operational level of war. Its purpose is to seek a decisive impact on the campaign by gaining advantage of position to exploit tactical success to achieve theater objectives.[2]

The Sinai Campaign in 1973 and the Bekaa Valley Campaign in 1982 are historical experiences analyzed to illustrate the impact of electronic warfare technology on operational maneuver. These experiences in the Middle East indicate that electronic warfare significantly enhances the ability to execute operational maneuver. However, it is evident that the risk of conducting an operational deep attack with maneuver forces is considered high because of survivability and sustainability issues.

After evaluating these historical examples, this paper will analyze future operational concepts designed to win control of the electromagnetic spectrum. The impact these concepts have on the ability to execute deep maneuver will be examined. The increasing relevance of electronic warfare on future operations is included.

The Theory of Operational Maneuver and Its Relation to Current Doctrine

The theory and importance of operational maneuver can be traced to the military theorist, Antione-Henry Jomini. He defines two types of decisive points: geographical objective points and objective points of maneuver. Both points, if attained, can lead to operational results. Objective points of maneuver are the basis for operational maneuver.[3]

The geographic objective point may be defined as: "an important fortress, the line of a river, a front of operations which affords good lines of defense or good points of support for ulterior enterprises."[4] Jomini further states that during offensive action, the geographical objective point is terrain which, if possessed by the attacker, will compel the enemy to make peace.[5] Compelling the enemy to make peace is one effect that can be attained by operational maneuver.

The other objective point is the objective point of maneuver. "Objective points of maneuver, in contradistinction to geographical points of maneuver, derive their importance from, and their positions depend upon, the situation of the hostile masses."[6] Jomini goes on to discuss the objective points of maneuver as points which relate to the destruction of the enemy army.[7] Thus, destruction of the enemy army is also an effect attained by operational maneuver.

The operational effects can therefore be defined as those that have a decisive impact on major operations or a campaign. According to Jomini, the two methods of attaining this are seizure of a piece of terrain that compels the enemy to make peace and destruction of the enemy army. The results therefore correspond to a given time and location relative to the enemy in terms of ability to force him to make peace due to positional disadvantage or loss of a major portion of its army.

Tracing Jomini's concepts to FM 100-5 (1986 edition) will illustrate his influence on current and future doctrine. FM 100-5 states: "Operational maneuver seeks a decisive impact on the conduct of a campaign. It attempts to gain advantage of position before battle and to exploit tactical successes to achieve operational results."[8] The decisive impact and operational results equate with Jomini's discussion relating to operational effects.

Another example of the operational effect of maneuver is the actual defeat of an enemy. Effective maneuver "continually poses new problems for the enemy, renders his reaction ineffective, and eventually leads to his defeat."[9] This technique also illustrates a means of producing an operational effect. The ability to conduct operational maneuver on the modern battlefield demands tremendous coordination of effort. "Leaders combine maneuver, firepower, and protection capabilities available to them in countless combinations appropriate to the situation."[10]

As situations become more complex due to the rapidly changing environment of modern war, the commander's ability to conduct operation maneuver is critical. The importance of firepower to operational maneuver is clearly stated in FM 100-5. Firepower supports friendly operational maneuver by damaging key enemy forces or facilities, creating delays in enemy movement, complicating the enemy's command and control, and degrading his artillery, air defense, and air support. At the operational level, firepower can also disrupt the movement, fire support, command and control, and sustainment of enemy forces.[11]

Offensive electronic warfare enhances the firepower effect by disrupting movement, fire support, command and control, and sustainment of enemy forces.[12] Electronic warfare used in conjunction with firepower is a large contributor to the tremendous effects all firepower can have while supporting operational maneuver. Electronic warfare support to the fire-power dynamic is increasing in importance on the modern battlefield and will continue to increase in the future.[13]

Protection is another dynamic of combat power that is integral to operational maneuver. FM 100-5 explains: "They (operational commanders) protect the force from operational level maneuver and concentrated air support. Air superiority operations, theater wide air defense systems and protection of air bases are important activities associated with maximizing combat power."[14]

Electronic warfare is a major player in each of these areas. The increasing role of ground based missiles in air defense roles is becoming a technological battle for control of the electromagnetic spectrum. The rapidly changing technological capabilities of electronic warfare systems make this battle for protection of the maneuver force a question of who possesses the latest technology and can effectively employ it. The important role electronic warfare has in support of operational maneuver will be the framework for the remainder of the paper.

Electronic Warfare Doctrine

FM 100-5 clearly specifies the purpose of electronic warfare: "Electronic warfare uses the electronic spectrum to deceive the enemy, locate his units and facilities, intercept his communications, and disrupts his command, control, and target acquisition systems at critical moments."[15] FM 100-6 goes somewhat further by establishing the electromagnetic spectrum, "electronic warfare is military action to determine, exploit, reduce, or prevent hostile use of the electromagnetic spectrum."[16]

The staff responsibility for the conduct of electronic warfare is assigned to the operations officer and the communications officer. FM 100-5 declares: "The G-3 or S-3 has the overall responsibility for electronic warfare, but focuses his primary effort on offensive electronic warfare. The G-2 or S-2 develops targets for interception jamming or destruction. The communications electronics officer manages defensive electronic warfare."[17] This methodology divides responsibility between offensive and defensive missions among different staff sections. Electronic warfare directly supports the commander's concept of the operation. FM 100-5 states electronic warfare assets should be integrated by the commander into his concept of operation. FM 100-5 emphasizes: "Commanders should treat electronic warfare assets much as he treats artillery assets. Electronic warfare is conducted concurrently at both the operational and tactical levels, and these efforts must be synchronized with each other and with other activities—maneuver, fire, and air support to obtain maximum benefit."[18] Thus our doctrine places a heavy emphasis on electronic warfare as one of the elements of combat power.

The defensive application of electronic warfare includes electronic counter-countermeasures (ECCM) and electronic warfare countermeasures (ECM). ECCM are passive measures to protect command, control, and communications (C3) systems against enemy activities. ECM can be used to transmit through enemy jamming or jam enemy signal intelligence systems to screen and prevent enemy intercept.[19]

The offensive components of electronic warfare are electronic support measures (ESM) and active electronic countermeasures CECM). ESM provides information for jamming, deception, targeting, and tactical employment of combat forces. ECM is a nonlethal attack of the enemy's command, control, and communication systems.[20]

Electronic warfare is an important player in deception activities: "Careful integration of electronic deception with visual, sonic, and olfactory actions is critical to the successful projection of a deception story."[21] Electronic deception uses either manipulative electronic deception (MED) or imitative electronic deception. MED is the passing of false data among friendly forces to deceive enemy signal intelligence capabilities. Imitative electronic deception is the imitation of the enemy's own electromagnetic radiation to deceive or confuse them.[22]

Due to the distinctive mission, scarce equipment resources and training problems, an integrated concept for electronic warfare employment is difficult to implement. FM 100-5 puts electronic warfare concepts in the current perspective: "plans should reflect the relative scarcity of electronic warfare weapons, their limitations, and the transient nature of their effects."[23] This transient nature of effects may or may not be true when considered in an integrated concept. The transient effects can be turned into permanent effects when combined with maneuver, firepower, protection, and intelligence. Control of the electromagnetic spectrum is a new mission. The services are like any large organization when it comes to assimilating changes, so the changes come slowly. The scarce equipment resources make it difficult to train and learn the difficult art of coordinating the effects of electronic warfare systems.

Lessons from the 1973 Mideast War

The origins of the 1973 war can be traced to the 1967 war. The defeat of Egypt and subsequent occupation of the Sinai by Israel were unacceptable to the Egyptians. Egypt prepared to regain the lost territory as soon as possible.

During the time between the 1967 and 1973 wars, Egypt had to find an answer to the superiority of the Israeli Air Force. Contrastingly, the Israelis believed that: "Having learned the lessons of the 1967 war, the Egyptians would not embark upon a new war until they felt capable of striking at Israeli airfields and neutral using the Israeli air force."[24]

However, assistance came from the Soviet Union in the form of modernized equipment. Modernization of Egyptian equipment began in 1970 to offset the Israeli Air Force's air superiority. The new equipment included more air superiority aircraft and, more importantly, surface to air missiles and electronic equipment:

> Through February and March (1970), in great secrecy their (Soviet) men and equipment began to arrive: 80 MIG-21 interceptors; 27 battalions of surface to air missiles (SAMS); banks of electronic equipment to counter that carried aboard the enemy intruders (Israeli); four MIG-25 high-altitude reconnaissance aircraft and the crews to man them.[25]

This is the first time that air superiority was countered by anything but more aircraft. The Israeli Air Force was to be dealt with by the creation of one of the densest missile "walls" in the world, composed of a mixture of various types of Soviet ground to air missiles SAM-3, and SAM-6, in addition to conventional anti-aircraft weapons, which would provide an effective umbrella over the planned area of operations along the Suez Canal. This would to a very considerable degree neutralize the effects of Israeli air superiority over the immediate field of battle.[26] The Egyptian ability to neutralize the Israeli Air Force was the goal for acquiring new equipment from 1970–1973.

Due to the equipment and the primary coverage area of the ADA umbrella, the Egyptian air defense system was defensively oriented:

> For static defense they might prove adequate (though we still did not have SAM batteries to protect every target), but they could provide no air cover for an offensive operation especially over the open landscape of the Sinai.[27]

The Egyptians understood the defensive orientation but were limited in what they could resource. The important thing was to establish an area in which they possessed the freedom to move equipment, arms and men. This enabled them to concentrate forces prior to the battle with little to no interference by the Israelis. This also allowed them to achieve surprise when the attack commenced.

The ability to concentrate undetected enhances the ability of a force to execute operational maneuver. Though the Egyptians did not conduct an operational deep attack, they did establish a relatively safe area to mass:

> We had guessed that they (Israelis) would try to knock out our SAM radars, which were set back some ten miles west of the canal by using strike air to ground missiles . . . we had devised electronic means of countering strike and were quite keen to test them . . . the missiles fell hopelessly short. Clearly we were beginning to establish a cordon sanitaire east of the canal too.[28]

This cordon sanitaire became a safe area in which to move, mass, and support major maneuver forces.

Engagements which subsequently occurred between the Egyptian air defense systems and the Israeli Air Force point out the effectiveness of modern electronic warfare. After the initial engagements it was becoming clear "that victory in any such conflict would go to whoever happened to have the more sophisticated electronic detection, jamming, and counter-jamming devices."[29] The level of sophistication and the new employment methods enabled the Egyptians to gain surprise and the early advantage.

The Israelis were basically caught unprepared the first day of the war:

> Poor electronic intelligence before the war left the Israeli Air Force unprepared and it sustained heavy losses in the first few days. However, it then quickly managed to develop countermeasures to suppress the radar, which controlled most of the air defense systems.[30]

It was in the interim between the Israeli's initial surprise and their counter-reaction that Egypt was able to tactically maneuver forces successfully.

The Egyptians, through the use of a missile umbrella supported with heavy electronic warfare assets, had established a limited zone of control where they could maneuver. Later, when the Egyptians attempted to maneuver outside of this zone, the Israeli Air Force and armored forces enjoyed success. "That they (Egyptians) had been justified in limiting themselves to the area covered by the missile umbrella was proved to them when the Israeli Air Force twice destroyed their advancing forces pushing southwards along the Gulf of Suez."[31] This example illustrates a strong link between air superiority operations and ability to maneuver.

The Israeli Air Force was not the only beneficiary of the turning tide in the air and missile war:

> On the west bank of the Suez Canal, an unusual example of mutual coordination emerged between the advance of ground-forces and the Israeli Air Force. As the armored forces on the west bank of the canal destroyed one surface-to-air missile battery after another, the Israeli Air Force gained a freer hand and became a major factor in supporting the advancing Israeli forces.[32]

In this example, which came after some initial successes by the Israeli Air Force that weakened the air defense umbrella, the ground forces directly supported then air superiority fight.

The relationship of air superiority to operational maneuver of heavy conventional forces is one of dependency. This was initially brought to light by Erwin Rommel from his experience against the Allies in North Africa. Rommel stated:

> During the day, practically our entire traffic—on roads, tracks, and in open country—is pinned down by powerful fighter-bomber and bomber formations, with the result that the movement of our troops on the battlefield is almost completely paralyzed, while the enemy can maneuver freely.[33]

Future developments in equipment and doctrine are continuing to support this premise. With the arrival of the missile age, the battle for air superiority became a totally joint air-ground effort as illustrated in the 1973 war. The electronic warfare impact on intelligence, protection, firepower, and leadership were enormous during the 1973 Mideast War. The impact was particularly important for Egyptian intelligence, due to the large influx of modern equipment:

> The Soviets had reorganized the Egyptian intelligence system and had provided it with modern, sophisticated equipment for all forms of electronic warfare. Radio interception, electronic surveillance and locating equipment were all introduced and attained a satisfactory standard of operation . . . the Arabs also benefited from Soviet surveillance over Israel by means of electronic intelligence and satellites.[34]

This new equipment was instrumental in gaining an advantage over the Israelis. As the Egyptians trained and learned with this new equipment, they also improved their own doctrine.

As the capabilities of this equipment became understood, the Egyptians knew they would have to adjust their own doctrine to improve and better protect their force. Examples of this include employment of radar and variety of air defense systems employment ·techniques: "to prevent the Israelis acquiring the locations and number of air defense radars by electronic intelligence (ELINT), the radars deployed forward to cover the initial assault over the Suez Canal were kept silent until the assault began."[35]

Examples of the air defense systems employment techniques included: use of different frequency bands which changed rapidly to minimize the effect of jamming; pulse; continuous wave and infrared homing radar to increase the difficulty of defeating both; and changes in radar positions to minimize the extent of Israeli ELINT.[36] "Some of the radar tracking systems also had the ability to track optically so that operations could continue even in a high ECM environment."[37] The electro-optics option was a simple fix to the technological battle of electronic warfare. Unfortunately, there are limitations such as visibility and shorter ranges of electro-optics that decrease its effectiveness.

The impact of electronic warfare on the firepower dynamic of combat power during the 1973 war was also dramatic. The preponderance of SAMS was the most important. "Each of these weapons (SAMS) possessed different electronic guidance characteristics, which complicated the application of electronic countermeasures."[38] This electronic warfare advancement was specifically used to enhance the Egyptian air defense umbrella while degrading the Israeli air support. This led directly to the Israeli Air Force's inability to support maneuver initially. The Egyptians capitalized on this and supported their initial attack by sound employment of SAMS. The Egyptian intent from the start was to cover their front line "in such a way that Israeli air intervention would have little or no effect on the initial stages of the attack, and would allow the Arab preponderance in artillery, troops, and armor to be concentrated fully at the point of attack."[39] This is a direct application of electronic enhanced firepower to support maneuver that was successful.

The impact on command and control was a race to integrate new technology. Lieutenant General Saad El Shazly, Egyptian Chief of Staff declared: "Our major innovations lay in training, technique, and determination; I was nevertheless constantly looking for any device that might help us."[40] The increased role of new technology as well as the development of training and techniques to improve combat capabilities is clearly evident from this example.

The major lessons learned with respect to electronic warfare in the 1973 war were numerous. These include: the importance of missiles, the synergism between air defense and air superiority, the role electronic warfare plays in concentrating major forces, and the air-ground coordination required to win the air-superiority fight.

Electronic guidance systems and the tremendous number of SAMS the Egyptians were able to employ ushered in the complete arrival of the missile age. The importance of this will have effects on all future conflicts in air, land, and sea operations. This also points out the technological battle between opposing forces as each attempts to counter the effectiveness of their opponent's weapons systems. The ranges of the missiles also increased significantly. The standoff capabilities of air, land, or sea based missiles increases the dependence on electronic means to provide early warning and tracking for destruction of these munitions prior to impact.

The link between air superiority and air defense was developed further. Ground based air defense systems are now more capable of directly influencing the air superiority battle than was ever imagined prior to this time. "The bulk of the Israeli losses (aircraft) were caused by missiles and conventional anti-aircraft fire, with honours roughly even between the two, particularly during close support missions."[41] This increasing effect of air defense systems requires a relook at the effect of air power in the future. The ability to gain air superiority will be degraded by the air defense systems and the pursuit of local air superiority will become more important.

The role electronic warfare plays in the ability to concentrate forces is extremely vital. The Egyptian plan to provide an electronic and air defense umbrella along its front lines is an excellent example. This umbrella helped them to move and to concentrate major forces while denying the Israelis the ability to observe. This provided the Egyptians with an opportunity to surprise the Israelis. The ability to protect concentrating forces at the point of attack is a key aspect of operational maneuver. The Egyptian success, though not used to launch a deep attack, is directly applicable to operational maneuver.

Air-ground cooperation to win the air superiority fight was also important. The Egyptians enjoyed success in the initial stages of the war because the umbrella was a combined air-ground effort. The Israeli response of aircraft was unsuccessful. After the Israelis recovered by upgrading their electronic countermeasures and coordinating closer with maneuver forces, the tide turned. The resultant air-ground coordination was effective against the Egyptian forces. Ground forces greatly assisted the fight for air superiority and the air forces assisted the maneuver of the ground forces.

Lessons from the 1982 Mideast War

The Bekaa Valley campaign in 1982 had a profound impact on the future of electronic warfare to support operational maneuver. The influence of air superiority and synchronized maneuver on the battle is important. The analysis will center on one day, 9 June 1982, during which electronic warfare played a prominent role. A general description of the events of that day follows:

> Just an hour after the attack started, the defenders (Syria) knew they were in big trouble. It was June 1982, and Lebanon's Bekaa Valley was a hornets nest of Soviet supplied surface-to-air missiles. They could, their Syrian operators thought, hurl up a lethal wall of firepower against any attacking aircraft. Instead, they hardly got off a shot. Radar seeking missiles honed in on 29 supposedly secret sites, blowing them away while gleeful Israeli officers sitting in situation rooms across the border watched the action on television. A masterstroke of warfare had left the skies controlled by the attackers, and Israel's friends and enemies alike wondered how they'd done it.[42]

The results provided Israeli ground forces the freedom to maneuver to drive the Syrians out of the Bekaa Valley.

The Israeli preparations for the Bekaa Valley Campaign are key to understanding the results. Armed with the lessons of the 1973 war, the Israelis prepared for the next war. Their essential preparations included acquisition of new high technology equipment, extensive intelligence preparation of the battlefield, and the integration of battlefield requirements to win control of the electromagnetic spectrum.

Acquisition of new equipment kept Israel at the forward edge of technological development from 1973–1982. This new equipment included remote piloted vehicles (RPVs) that were used in surveillance, target designation, jamming, and monitoring roles.[43]

Another major acquisition was the EC-707 aircraft which can be configured for communications intelligence, electronic intelligence, and jamming roles.[44] Anti-radiation and TV guided munitions both air and ground launched were particularly effective at attacking radar.[45] Another important equipment upgrade was the state of the art electronic warfare equipment carried on Israeli aircraft. These include jammers, chaff/flare dispensers and threat warning systems.[46] As shown, the Israelis were not going to be upstaged by not keeping abreast with technological advancements, especially in the realm of electronic warfare.

The Israeli intelligence preparation of the battlefield was a key to the successful operation. "They spent 12 months studying Syrian air defenses in the Bekaa Valley and along the Syrian/Lebanese border."[47] Information gained included electronic intelligence on SAM guidance radars, frequencies, and accurate locations of the majority of radar.[48] This extensive effort was profitable for two reasons: Israeli technology and Syrian ineptness in employing the SAMS.

The Israeli emphasis on winning control of the electromagnetic spectrum was exceptional. This thorough preparation paid dividends on the afternoon of 9 June. The control and sequence of the operation indicates a tremendously synchronized operation that was executed flawlessly. The scale and coordination of effort for the raid were unparalleled in modern warfare. "The Bekaa missile raid was a textbook example of modern day electronic: warfare."[49]

The Syrian preparation for the Bekaa Valley Campaign was a story of problems.The biggest problem, as with Egyptian use in the 1973 war, was the immobile layout of SAMS. "The Syrians used mobile missiles in a fixed configuration; they put the radars in the valley instead of the hills."[50] This enabled the Israelis to pinpoint their locations prior to the attack. The poor operational security of the Syrians made them susceptible to the vast Israeli collection efforts, most of which was electronic intelligence.

The Israeli operational plan to win the electronic warfare battle was an integrated concept from start to finish. First, RPVs were flown over the battlefield to stimulate the SAM radar sites. Following this, both RPVs and the EC-707 gathered information about the radars as they tracked the RPVs. Jamming began to blind the radars as well as the command and control nets. A coordinated attack occurred from air and ground launched anti-radiation missiles along with conventional artillery fires. Target assessment was accomplished by RPVs to include the first phase.[51]

The second phase followed as the Syrian Air Force began their defensive counter air operation. The Israelis jammed Syrian ground control radar and communications nets, preventing any coordinated attacks against the Israeli planes. The result was a loss of 24 aircraft on the Syrian side with no losses to the Israelis. Aerial dog fights continued the next day with similar results.[52]

Technology had enabled commanders to centralize control of the battle. As stated earlier, Israeli operations officers watched the Bekaa Valley raid on TV monitors. Though not much is written about the command and control of the operation, it is clear that it was a very high headquarters that provided the detailed plan and very centralized command:

> The control and direction of such an operation, and the orchestration required for all elements involved, is highly complex, and thus despite the very sophistication of the equipment, the human element still remains a dominant one.[53]

The effect on operational maneuver by the electronic warfare dominated air battle was tremendous. "This new development (victory over the missiles) now enabled the Israeli forces to take advantage of Israel air power and to dominate the battle-field,"[54] The Israeli Armored Forces were now able to maneuver under protection of the Israeli Air Force. Ben-Gal's corps broke through and was able to advance up the Bekaa Valley. The corps penetrated to the operational depth of the Syrian forces who committed their operational reserve, the Syrian 3rd Armored Division. The 3rd Armored Division was interdicted and became engaged directly by Ben-Gal's corps on 11 June, when the Syrians agreed to a cease fire.[55] The Israelis had maneuvered to a position that had afforded them the opportunity to destroy the Syrian force. In Jomini's terms, they had reached the operational point of maneuver that motivated the Syrians to quit the field in the eastern area of operations.

The importance of the fight for air superiority and its relationship to operational maneuver were lessons learned from the 1973 war. The Israelis knew that they could concentrate forces under an air umbrella augmented by electronics. They also realized that the ability to maneuver large armored forces even in difficult terrain was dependent on air superiority. This knowledge was applied in the Bekaa Valley in 1982 to effectively conduct operational maneuver.

Electronic warfare had a marked impact on the 1982 war. The Israelis were able to gain real-time intelligence. Smart munitions and anti-radiation munitions contributed to firepower. Control of the air was coordinated by an advanced electronic warfare supported operation. This allowed armored forces to move freely and also protected them from Syrian maneuver. The exploitation of offensive electronic warfare paralyzed the Syrian command structure resulting in a loss of control and unresponsive actions to counter Israeli maneuver.

The use of drones gave Israeli commanders access to near real-time intelligence:

> The field commanders benefited from almost instant intelligence, which facilitated their task of reaching immediate decisions. It is clear that the very effective development of reconnaissance drones, produced over recent years by Israeli industry, has played an important part in the success of battlefield intelligence.[56]

The use of electronic intelligence was important during both the intelligence preparation of the battlefield and during the Bekaa Valley operation. In both situations the Israelis gained such a relative advantage over the Syrians, that this played a significant role in their success.

The use of smart munitions and anti-radiation munitions enhanced the effect of firepower, as the batteries "were probably attacked with sophisticated air-launched 'smart' weapons. Such weapons are highly accurate and some can be launched from well beyond the reach of SAMS."[57] As noted in a July 1982 *New Republic* article:

> These weapons are quite effective, but can be countered in part by turning off the radar. What the Israelis reportedly did was modify the guidance systems of these missiles so that even if the target radars are turned off, the missile will continue straight to the last source of radar pulses.[58]

The exploitation of the electromagnetic spectrum was effective in enhancing firepower as exemplified by the devastating effect of these munitions.

The protection required when moving heavy units around today's lethal battlefield is an important requirement to support operational maneuver. Protection from opposing force maneuver is key and the Israeli Air Force accomplished this during the offensive maneuvers in the Bekaa Valley:

> The Israeli Air Force was successful in interdicting and in preventing reinforcements from reaching the battlefield, as when a brigade of the Syrian 3rd Armored Division was caught in a narrow defile and badly mauled.[59]

The electronic warfare assets assisted in detecting this force and were the main reason air superiority over the Bekaa Valley could be maintained.

The employment of offensive electronic warfare to disrupt Syrian command and control was highly successful: "Prior to and during the attack, the Syrians claim that their entire radar net was both decoyed and reconnoitered by RPVs and subject to extensive jamming generated by airborne Boeing 707 stand-off platforms, ground stations, and dedicated

A-4 Skyhawk aircraft."[60] This paralyzed the Syrian command structure, which could offer no adequate response.

Another related effect on command and control was the result the Bekaa Valley attack had on the Syrian high command:

> The destruction of this doctrinal theory, knocked the Syrian command off balance, as it was clear, as they threw air units desperately into battle, thus incurring additional heavy air losses that they were urgently seeking a reply to a situation for which they had not planned.[61]

The Syrian command lost the initiative midday on 9 June, and they were unable to recover it throughout the war. The shock that sent the Syrians reeling was reminiscent of the effect the blitzkrieg had on Germany's Second World War opponents in 1939-1940.

Lessons learned in the 1982 Bekaa Valley Campaign are applicable to a wide range of electronic warfare, air superiority, and operational maneuver issues. The technological impact of electronic warfare is quickly changing employment concepts. The fight for the Bekaa Valley "was one between the complex technological systems, including the most modern and highly sophisticated air control and electronic communication equipment."[62] Acquiring new electronic warfare equipment and more importantly integrating improved operational concepts throughout the force occupies a critical role in the preparations for the next war.

Electronic warfare, when integrated with other warfighting systems, can be the decisive factor in enabling one to maneuver operationally. The success of the fight to defeat the SAMS and gain air superiority over the valley was the first step. After this, a combined air-ground operation actually carried out the maneuver, "the first move was to strike with heavy air attacks, the only major air action in nine days combined with artillery and armor."[63] This type of operation forced the Syrians to fight defensively and withdraw before they were destroyed.

The operational commander's concept of operation must integrate electronic warfare. The entire operation on 9 June was dominated by the battle for the electromagnetic spectrum. This will not always be the most important factor in the future, but its potential effect cannot be downplayed. It seems evident from the 1982 war that if electronic warfare is not integrated into the concept of operation, the operational commander is inviting trouble.

The potential of unmanned vehicles in the future is limitless. The RPV's capacity to be used as a platform for a wide range of capabilities is inviting.

In addition to communications, intelligence, jamming, and radar decoy, the Israelis also used them as a weapons platform. "At least one SAM-8 was destroyed by a RPV configured with an ammunition payload."[64] The only limiting factor to employing RPVs seems to be lack of imagination.

The speed and lethality of modern combat was graphically illustrated over the Bekaa Valley. In less than an hour, the SAMS were destroyed. The fight for air superiority lasted less than two days. In 16 days the Israelis moved the Syrians to the northern entrance of the Bekaa Valley and destroyed significant aircraft, air defense systems and Syrian forces. The effect of this operational maneuver compelled the Syrians to make peace.

Conclusions: The Future Direction of Electronic Warfare to Enhance Operational Maneuver

Several conclusions that are critical to future large-scale combat operations can be drawn from experience in the mid-east wars. First, the battle for control of the electromagnetic spectrum must be won to effectively conduct operational maneuver. Second, military doctrine must keep pace with improving technologies. Third, near real-time intelligence increases the speed of the commander's decision-making cycle. Technology is increasing the difficulty of effectively employing electronic warfare capabilities, and the risk of being caught short in electronic warfare capabilities can be decisive in future operations.

Coordination of the fight for control of the electromagnetic spectrum, air superiority, and operational maneuver are inseparable in the missile age. This has made air-ground cooperation an even more crucial link than in the past. Control of the electromagnetic spectrum which includes denial of the enemy's free use of it, is critical to war now. Without control, our ability to gain air superiority for even limited periods of time is questionable. The side that wins the electronic warfare battle will possess advantages in the air superiority fight that will be nearly impossible to overcome.

Gaining air superiority is critical to maintaining the ability to execute operational maneuver. The ability to concentrate forces, maneuver forces freely, and adequately protect the force must be accomplished for successful operational maneuver to occur. Because air superiority depends on the ability to control the electromagnetic spectrum, these capabilities are interdependent.

The effectiveness of operational firepower depends in many ways on electronic warfare capabilities. Without effective offensive and defensive capabilities, the air force will be hard pressed to deliver operational fires.

The increased dependence on electronically guided missiles also makes forces vulnerable. If these guided missiles are electronically defeated, numerous air, sea and ground launched long range missiles will contribute little to operational fires.

Protection of forces depends heavily on electronic warfare capabilities. The Egyptian umbrella in the 1973 war and the destruction of the Syrian umbrella in 1982 are perfect examples of the protection dynamic in war. The Egyptian defensive umbrella provided protection for their forces. As the umbrella was degraded, air support became the means of protection. In 1982, the Syrian air defense umbrella was quickly destroyed and Israeli air superiority again became the means of protection.

Operational leadership is becoming more and more dependent on intricate communications systems. Destruction of these means even for short periods of time could be critical. The effect one hour had on the Syrian high command on 9 June exemplifies this well. From this day forward, they were in a reactive mode and could not recover. Despite a fairly good showing at the tactical level, the Syrians could not regain the initiative operationally.

Military doctrine and operational concepts must keep pace with improving technologies. The risk of not doing this could be operational surprise. The emphasis in this area by the Russians can be seen in the following passage:

> Hundreds of Russian experts and advisors rushed to Syria within days of the air battles, because once again as in 1969, in Egypt in the war of attrition, the system defending the Soviet empire had been tested by the Israeli Air Force and found wanting. The Soviets will inevitably provide a reply to Israel's technological solutions, but the results of the air battles in the Bekaa Valley have given them much cause for concern.[65]

NATO, and the United States in particular, is as interested as the Russians. In future large-scale combat operations the cost of being upstaged by new technologies will be great. But it is not only the technology that provides input into the equation. Research and development cycles, and more importantly, training and preparation for employing new concepts are time consuming processes.

The impact of near real-time intelligence provided by electronic warfare has decreased the decision cycle in modern combat. This can have a dramatic effect on the speed of modern combat. Major General Doyle E. Larson in discussing one role of electronic warfare intelligence states: "The sensor information needed for C3CM [Command, Control, and Communications Countermeasures] execution must be available at the lowest level within 15 seconds of collection. This is a tough goal for us to reach, but one which is within our technological capability."[66]

The technological impact is increasing the difficulty of effectively using electronic warfare capabilities. The cost of fielding this type of equipment is almost prohibitive. Budgetary constraints complicate the problem. The focus on physical destruction or "hard kill" weapons normally increases while "soft kill" electronic weapons take a back seat.[67]

The expertise necessary to operate and maintain new electronic warfare weapons is increasing. The impact on operational maneuver is tremendous. We must exploit the increasing capabilities of electronic warfare to successfully execute operational maneuver. The decisive effect of operational maneuver is within our grasp. A synchronized air-ground fight for control of the electromagnetic spectrum will be a major factor in the future.

Implications

Education of operational commanders is becoming more difficult due to the increasing complexity of electronic weaponry. Battle for control of the electronic spectrum has no service boundaries. It is truly a joint fight. The capabilities of each service must be understood to develop a coherent concept of operation or campaign plan. The many new electronic warfare capabilities in each service make attaining the required technical knowledge increasingly difficult.

The problem of developing new operational concepts for integrating electronic warfare into future doctrine is twofold. General William E. Depuy, with respect to the US Army, stated:

[They are] not yet comfortable with Electronic Warfare. The senior leaders have little firsthand experience and thus little confidence or skill in its use and tend to leave it, unintegrated, in the hands of specialists. The specialists, in turn, are faced with a tradition and structure of secrecy and compartmentalization—a hangover in part from the days of ULTRA.[68]

The ability to implement innovative uses of the technology is seen as limited to the "specialists" who are kept abreast of technological improvements. This is a dangerous situation that must be overcome.

Another implication related to electronic warfare is the mission command warfighting function enabling a commander to balance the art of command and the science of control in order to integrate the other warfighter functions. "There are real-time television monitors at division, corps, and territorial headquarters, which may indicate an inclination in the Israeli Army to centralize command at higher levels."[69] This could be critical to operational leadership in the future. Mission commands tends to lead initiative at lower levels of command. On the other hand, limited electronic warfare assets difficulty in employing them on the scale of the Israelis in the Bekaa Valley requires centralization.

The ability of mission command must be closely analyzed as future technological developments occur. The mission command issue and susceptibility to electronic warfare problem go hand in hand. Continual dependence on technology that increases centralization of command and control without regard to protective countermeasures would be disastrous. The balance is tenuous at best, and the opportunity for miscalculations is high, as history has so effectively demonstrated.

Electronic warfare is changing the environment of modern war. We must be prepared to adapt quickly as new technologies are developed. The electromagnetic spectrum is now as important as the air, land, and sea dimensions of battle. Control of this spectrum is essential to conduct effective operational maneuver. These case study examples of electronic warfare and the ever changing environment require further studies of our past to enable our large-scale combat operations in the future.

Notes

* Major David M. Rodriguez, "The Influence of Electronic Warfare on Operational Maneuver," School of Advanced Military Studies Monograph, US Army Command and General Staff College, 22 May 1989.

1. Chris Bellamy, *The Future of Land Warfare* (New York: Croom Helm, 1987), 31.

2. Department of the Army, Field Manual (FM) 3-0, *Operations* (Washington, DC: 2017), 12.

3. Baron De Jomini, *The Art of War* (Westport, CT: Praeger Publishers, 1977), 88–89.

4. Jomini, 89.

5.. Jomini, 88.

6. Jomini, 88.

7. Jomini, 89.

8. Department of the Army, Field Manual (FM) 100-5, *Operations* (Washington, DC: 1982), 12.

9. Department of the Army, FM 100-5, 12.

10. FM 100-5, 11.

11. FM 100-5, 13.

12. Department of the Army, Field Manual (FM) 34-1, *Intelligence and Electronic Warfare Operations* (Washington DC: 1987), 1-3.

13. David Bolton, editor, "The Challenge of Electronic Warfare." *Whitehall Paper No.1* (London: Her Majesty's Stationary Office, 1986), 10.

14. Bolton, 13.

15. Bolton, 54.

16. Department of the Army, Field Manual (FM) 100-6, *Large Unit Operations* (Washington, DC: 1987), 3-12.

17. Department of the Army, FM 100-5, 54.

18. FM 100-5, 54.

19.. Department of the Army, FM 34-1, 1-3.

20. FM 34-1, 1-4.

21. Department of the Army, Field Manual (FM) 90-2, *Tactical Deception* (Washington, DC: 1978), 2-16.

22. FM 90-2, 2-16–2-17.

23. Department of the Army, FM 100-5, 54.

24. Chaim Herzog, *The Arab-Israeli Wars* (New York: Random House, 1984), 227.

25. Lieutenant General Saad el Shazly, *The Crossing of the Suez* (San Francisco, CA: American Mideast Research, 1980), 13.

26. Herzog, *The Arab-Israeli Wars*, 227.

27. Shazly, *The Crossing of the Suez*, 21–22.

28. Shazly, 81.

29. Shazly, 15.

30. Bolton, *The Whitehall Paper No. 1*, 11.

31. Herzog, *The Arab-Israeli War*, 310.

32. Chaim Herzog, *The War of Atonement* (New York: Little Brown & Company, 1975), 274.

33. B.H. Liddell Hart, editor, *The Rommel Papers* (New York: Harcourt & Brace, 1953), 476–477.

34. Herzog, *The War of Attonement*, 274.

35. Bellamy, *The Future of Land Warfare*, 222–223.

36. Bellamy, 222–223.

37. Bellamy, 223.

38. Herzog, *The Arab-Israeli Wars*, 307.

39. Herzog, 307.

40. Shazly, *The Crossing of the Suez*, 76.

41. Herzog, *The Arab-Israeli Wars*, 311.

42. Jim Schefter, "Stealthy Robot Planes," *Popular Science*, October 1987, 64.

43. Martin Streetly, "The Israeli Experience: A Lesson in Electronic Air Combat," *Jane's Defense Weekly*, August 1985, 319.

44. Streetly, 316.

45. Streetly, 317.

46. Streetly, 317.

47. Bolton, *Whitehall Paper No. 1*, 11.

48. Bolton, 11.

49. Richard A. Gabriel, *Operation Peace for Galilee* (New York: Hill & Wang Publishers, 1984), 98.

50. Marshall Lee Miller, "The Soviet Air Force View of the Bekaa Valley Debacle," *Armed Forces Journal International*, June 1987, 54.

51. Bolton, *Whitehall Paper No. 1*, 11.

52. Gabriel, *Operation Peace for Galilee*, 99.

53. Herzog, *The Arab-Israeli Wars*, 366.

54. Herzog, 348.

55. Herzog, 349.

56. Herzog, 364–365.

57. W. Seth Carus and Stephen P. Glick, "The Battle of Lebanon: The Aerial Assault," *The New Republic,* July 1982, 16.

58. Carus and Glick, 16.

59. Herzog, *The Arab-Israeli Wars*, 366.

60. Streetly, "The Israeli Experience: A Lesson in Electronic Air Combat," 317.

61. Herzog, *The Arab-Israeli Wars*, 365.

62. Herzog, 366.

63. Gabriel, *Operation Peace for Galilee*, 109.

64. Gabriel, 99.

65. Gabriel, 366.

66. Doyle E. Larson, "Controlling the Electromagnetic Spectrum," *The Marine Corps Gazette*, October 1983, 49.

67. Bolton, *Whitehall Paper No. 1*, 35–36.

68.. Bellamy, *The Future of Land Warfare*, 240.
69. Gabriel, *Operations for Galilee*, 195.

Chapter 4

Firepower and Breakthrough in the Meuse-Argonne: 1 November 1918

Lieutenant Colonel (USAF-Retired) Mark E. Grotelueschen

If we are to be economical with our men, we must be prodigal with guns and ammunition.[1]

—Major General Charles P. Summerall
Commanding General, V Corps

The first phase of the Meuse-Argonne campaign, which began on 26 September 1918, was a demonstration of the modest *initial* success that could be achieved in a prepared large-scale assault. However, that offensive also clearly showed the problems and loss in efficiency that the attacking units experienced during subsequent assaults. Considering the tremendous strength of the German positions opposing his army, General John J. Pershing's plans for his initial attack in the first phase of the offensive were exceptionally optimistic. The attack orders directed his forces to advance some 16 kilometers within two days and break through the enemy's main line of resistance, the *Kriemhilde Stellung* of the Hindenburg line, at the far end of the deep two-day advance. While the attack on 26 September began well along much of the front, with the leading units of many divisions pushing forward as far as 7 kilometers on the first day, once the infantrymen advanced beyond the range of their supporting artillery the progress slowed, then stopped, and the casualties rose. In a few instances, most notably in the sector of the green 35th Division, over-extended and disorganized infantry battalions were unable to hold their advanced positions, and were thrown back by German counterattacks.[2] In every case, the attacking divisions soon proved unable to advance despite suffering serious losses in their efforts. Three divisions in the center of the line—the 35th, 37th, and 79th—each had to be replaced after less than a week of fighting, but even then, the new divisions, including such experienced units as the 1st, 32nd, and 3rd, found progress slow, and the price high.[3] Finally, on 14 October, after weeks of painfully slow, forward progress, the Army reached the initial objectives it had set for 27 September.[4] While determined and skillful German resistance in terrifically challenging terrain explains much of the First Army's difficulty, weaknesses with its own fire support effort also contributed.

The first phase of the First Army's offensive in the Meuse-Argonne suffered from three major problems in its employment of artillery. First, plans called for the infantry to continue its initial attack all the way to distant objectives that were surely going to be beyond the range of the supporting artillery.[5] Pershing and his staff were clearly counting on their infantry being able to successfully carry those distant objectives with little or no artillery support. Second, the attacking corps and divisions attempted to make such a quick, deep penetration without using one of the most tactically decisive weapons of the German Army's spring offensives—gas. Smothering the defending forces with tons of gases of all types was an integral part of each one of Germany's spring offensives in 1918.[6] Pershing also included a massive gas bombardment in his initial plan for the 26 September attack. Unfortunately, the American Expeditionary Forces (AEF) could not secure all the gas shells that it needed to fully carry out the plan. Additionally, the decision as to when, where, and how to use the gas that was available was left to the corps and division commanders. However, due to unfamiliarity with the weapon, these commanders had an almost inexplicable fear of enemy retaliation with gas—inexplicable because the commanders surely knew that the massive use of gas had become standard practice by the German Army in 1918. That fear, coupled in some inexperienced units with an inflated expectation of what the infantry could accomplish on its own, led many unit commanders to disregard Pershing's ideas for employing gas.[7] A third problem was that the army and corps artillery groups were not used to maximum effect in either counter-battery against the German guns, or in directly supporting the infantry advance with an additional rolling barrage. Due to the expectations of many high-ranking AEF officers that aggressive infantrymen would be able to make successful attacks without the support of heavy artillery, and the fear that the use of heavy guns in an infantry support role would lead to a rash of friendly fire incidents, the corps and army guns were prohibited from firing on positions close enough to the advancing infantry to be of any practical use to them.[8]

The Reorganization of First Army

However, from mid-October until the end of the month, the American First Army focused on preparing for its next massive assault, to take place on 1 November—an attack that would prove to be its final major offensive of the war.

Lieutenant General Hunter Liggett, who replaced Pershing as commander of the First Army on 16 October, made changes tailored to solve the problems that had plagued the first two phases of the offensive. He also ensured that experienced units served to spearhead the attack, most notably, the 2nd Division, which had recently completed one of the most impressive offensive feats of the year when it seized Blanc Mont Ridge in early October while part of the French Fourth Army. By late October it was moving towards the front lines in the Meuse-Argonne, where it would join the 89th Division to form the V Corps.

Meanwhile, the 2nd Field Artillery (FA) Brigade, which had been supporting the 36th Division along the Aisne River, was finally recalled to rejoin the 2nd Division on 28 October, and it took up firing positions behind

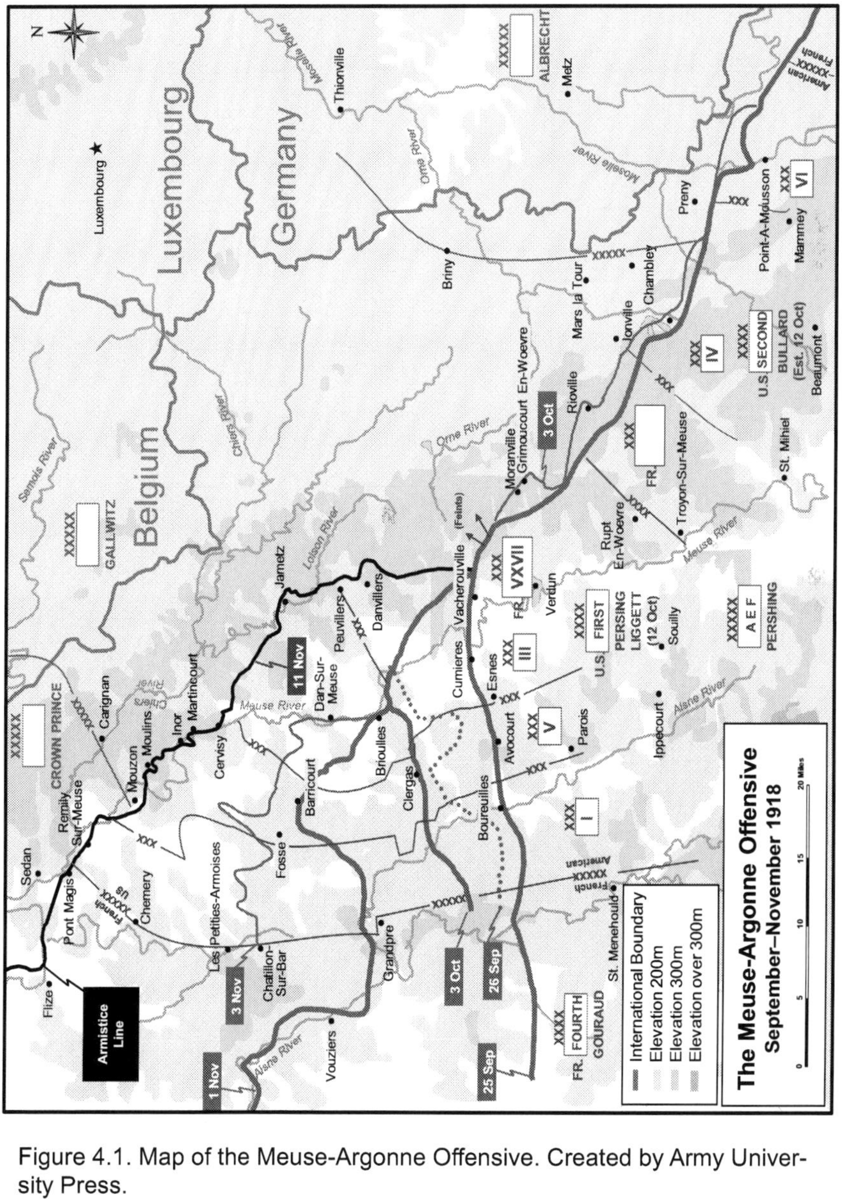

Figure 4.1. Map of the Meuse-Argonne Offensive. Created by Army University Press.

its infantry brigades in the Meuse-Argonne sector two days later. By then plans for the attack on 1 November were almost finalized. Brigadier General Albert J. Bowley, the 2nd FA Brigade commander, left Colonel Joseph R. Davis from the 15th Field Artillery (FA) in command of the artillery brigade which was still with the 36th Division north of Blanc Mont, and had joined General Lejeune to aid him in the last stages of the planning effort.[9] As early as 25 October, the division had produced a "Tentative Plan of Attack," and the infantry brigade, regimental, and battalion commanders were able to study the plan and reconnoiter the ground.[10]

General Liggett assigned the 2nd Division to Major General Charles P. Summerall's V Corps which held the lines in the center of the American First Army. Unlike the previous attacks in this campaign, the plan of attack for 1 November did not call for all divisions in line to make as deep a penetration as possible. The V Corps was directed to make a 9-kilometer-deep penetration to seize the heights of Barricourt Ridge, while the other two corps, the I Corps on the left and the III Corps on the right, were to make supporting attacks only. The 2nd Division was to advance through two intermediate objectives, each followed by a-30 minute rest, before taking the final "First Day" objective. Subsequent attacks on following days by all three corps were to drive the enemy north of the Meuse River.[11]

Figure 4.2. Major General Charles P. Summerall.
Photo courtesy of US Army Center of Military History.

These plans, and the supporting artillery fire-plans, were developed in a series of conferences held at V Corps Headquarters which were attended by the corps and division commanders, their chiefs of staff, all chiefs of artillery, and the division machine-gun officers.[12] While previous attacks often counted on the infantrymen to fight their way forward, this attack, more than any other large-scale

AEF or 2nd Division attack of the war, put its faith in massive amounts of well-coordinated firepower.

This was especially true in V Corps, where Summerall, an artilleryman and former artillery brigade commander, ordered that "fire superiority, rather than sheer man power be the driving force of the attack."[13] With the full support of General Liggett, army and corps planners addressed each of the three major artillery problems that had plagued the earlier phases of the campaign. First, the plans called for the supporting artillery to fully cover the attacking troops all the way through the first day's final objectives. Of equal importance was the fact that all of the main lines of enemy resistance scheduled to be assaulted on the first day were within a few kilometers of the jump-off positions and were therefore well within range of all the supporting artillery.[14] Second, unlike previous attacks, AEF artillery was to subject the enemy to a very heavy gas bombardment, in some places beginning as much as two days before the actual assault. The plan called for the use of gas, specifically persistent mustard gas, to systematically neutralize the large German artillery groups on each flank, so as to protect the main thrust of the V Corps from the crushing fire that had previously come from the enemy guns in those positions.[15]

Last, the heavy guns of the army and corps batteries were to be extensively involved in providing accompanying fire for the infantry. In previous attacks the use of heavy guns in the infantry support role had been confined to firing concentrations on known or "suspected" enemy positions, and always well ahead of the infantry they were supposed to be supporting. For the 1 November attack, Liggett removed this restriction and directed the "complete use of artillery."[16] His First Army planners therefore programmed the use of army and corps guns in an infantry support role, allowing them to fire their concentrations on a rolling barrage schedule that kept the fire always within 1,000 meters of the attacking infantry throughout their advance.[17]

The V Corps Fire Support Plan

In V Corps, Summerall divided the fire support plan into four periods: the time preceding the preliminary bombardment, the preliminary bombardment itself, the covering fire for the infantry's initial assault, and the support of the infantry during "subsequent stages of the advance." The first period covered several days and included the firing of gas, shrapnel, and high explosive shells by all calibers on "all enemy organizations, batteries, and routes of communication." During this time, American gunners would fire short but intense artillery barrages from all guns two or three times a day, so that the defending German troops, who fully expected a continuation of the offensive, would not be sure when the real assault was starting and would be "trained" to respond more slowly when it did come. Additionally, AEF artillerymen would use this period to carry out a carefully scheduled and concealed registration of those artillery pieces already in their positions.[18]

The fire-plan called for the actual preliminary bombardment to last only two hours, but it was to be accomplished at the maximum rate of fire for each gun. According to the corps commander, the very short preparation was driven by the amount of available ammunition, "as ammunition could not be procured for a maximum rate of fire during a longer period," and Summerall believed it "better to deliver fire at a maximum rate than to employ slow fire over a longer period."[19] This line of reasoning was right in step with much of the most current and effective artillery practices of war, such as the short German bombardments of the spring offensives and the "hurricane bombardments" of the British Expeditionary Force (BEF). As for targeting, batteries of 75-mm howitzers were to hit the enemy front lines and specifically identified German units. The 155s were to hit certain towns, woods, and all known and suspected machine-gun nests. Other corps and army guns were to neutralize enemy batteries.[20] To add to the maelstrom, 255 machine guns would fire coordinated barrages into the German positions opposite the 2nd Division.[21]

One important innovation was made to this preparation. Some infantry attacks in previous phases of the offensive had been met immediately by heavy enemy machine-gun fire. Often this delayed the infantry's advance so much that it caused them to lose contact with their rolling barrage. Research into the problem showed that German machine gunners had been noting the short limit of the artillery fire during the preparation and then moved into shell holes far enough into "No Man's Land" to avoid the incoming shells. These troops were ready and waiting with their machine guns when the infantry assault finally came. To catch these forward machine gunners, prior to the initial infantry assault of 1 November, the gunners supporting the 2nd Division spent the last ten minutes of the preparatory bombardment firing a heavy standing barrage that was drawn back 200 yards from the previous short limit. During this barrage, the leading assault troops moved up as close to the standing barrage as possible, so that they could hit the first enemy positions within moments of the barrage's first lift forward.[22]

After the start of the infantry attack the focus of nearly all the firepower in the corps was on covering the infantry attack. The rate of advance of the rolling barrage was tailored to match the type of terrain facing the infantry: 100 meters every four minutes on open ground, 100 meters every six minutes up steep slopes, and 100 meters every eight minutes through woods. Two batteries in each light battalion (75mm) were to shoot high explosive shells, and the third was to superimpose shrapnel fire on the whole battalion sector, firing 200 meters ahead of the batteries shooting the high explosive. Other guns were dedicated to fire smoke shells throughout the barrage. The 155s were directed to fire "a series of standing barrages, lifting as the infantry advances so as to fall at least 500 meters beyond the rolling barrage."[23] Following each infantry objective the rolling barrage was to halt, and the 155s were to shoot "heavy concentrations" on "all enemy organizations" within 2 kilometers of the new front line. Batteries of eight-inch howitzers were designated to further intensify this accompanying fire by adding another layer to the barrage, 500 meters ahead of the 155s, when the barrage rolled through certain strong points and wooded areas. The order made it clear that those army and corps guns not assigned specific counter-battery missions were to continue supporting the infantry advance all the way through the third and final objective of the first day.[24]

To accomplish this massive fire-plan, the 2nd Division received more artillery augmentation than in any previous attack. In addition to its own guns, it would have the support of two other divisional artillery brigades, the 1st FA Brigade of the 1st Division and the 67th FA Brigade of the 42nd Division (a total addition of four 75-mm regiments and two 155-mm regiments). The 2nd Division also received the dedicated support of 2 batteries of 8-inch howitzers and 3 batteries of 105-mm guns, and would share with the 82nd Division to their right some 17 batteries of 155-mm howitzers and 21 batteries of 155-mm guns from the corps and army artillery groups. All told, the infantrymen of the 2nd Division would be supported by more than 300 guns and howitzers.[25]

Command of the three brigades of divisional artillery was given to the ranking artillery commander, General George G. Gatley from the 67th FA Brigade. However, more than with any other attack by the 2nd Division, the plans issued by the Corps Chief of Artillery, in this case Brigadier General Dwight E. Aultman, had carefully scripted all artillery actions, even to the point of detailing exactly when each divisional artillery battalion would displace forward and to what position it was to move. Two hours after the infantry began their attack, the 2nd FA Brigade was to begin its movement forward by echelon, one battalion advancing at a time. The forward batteries were then to pick up the barrage, or otherwise support the infantry attack, after the first objective was reached. While exact forward positions were listed in the plan, the guiding principal was that "batteries were to be pushed as far forward as the tactical situation permits." The plan also directed that "previous to 'D' day," the 67th FA Brigade was to take up positions "as far advanced as compatible with conservation of the material and replenishment of ammunition," so that it would be sure to have the capability of firing the entire barrage without advancing.[26] In fact, General Gatley procured enough of the long distance 1917 Model "D" shell to enable both the 67th and 1st FA Brigades to fire the barrage all the way through the final objective without having to advance their batteries.[27]

The divisional plan also had an additional measure of flexibility in its rolling barrage, which was inserted to limit the damage that would result from one of the more common problems in previous American attacks. The attack order stated that "should the infantry at any time be unable to keep up with the barrage, the barrage may be recalled to some well established line, to rest there until the infantry lines are adjusted."[28] This was, of course, easier to write into an attack order than to accomplish in the midst of an attack that was, by definition, not going well, but it does represent an important attempt to solve an all too common problem.

As at the AEF's previous offensive at St. Mihiel, the corps instructions called for accompanying guns to be used in the attack. Aultman directed that "batteries or single guns will be detailed, after consultation with Division and Infantry Brigade Commanders, to accompany the advance of the infantry, for the purpose of firing on Machine Gun nests."[29] In this regard, the divisional plan specified that one battalion each from the 12th and 15th FA Regiments were "to be prepared to move forward for close support of the infantry as soon as the advance of the infantry warranted it."[30] However, just as at St. Mihiel, the leadership of the 2nd Division had no intention of breaking up these battalions and assigning the pieces directly to individual infantry battalions. While still subject to requests for fire from any infantry unit, these battalions were to remain assigned to and under the control of their respective artillery battalion, regimental and brigade commanders.[31]

All told, it was the most comprehensive firepower employment plan that the 2nd Division, or any other AEF division, had ever seen. Everything was in place well in advance of the jump-off time, which was set for 0530 on 1 November. During the artillery preparation, which began promptly at 0330, all the guns assigned to the corps opened up on their German targets, namely batteries and those infantry positions that were able to deliver fire upon American infantry at their starting positions. Eighty gas projectors also fired lethal chemicals on known machine-gun nests, observation posts, and suspected enemy machine-gun positions in no-man's land. Ten minutes before H hour (the designated time to start), the standing barrage was put down in front of the German forward positions, as was a thick smoke screen to hide the American infantry moving up to the barrage. At 0530 the barrage rolled forward, and the attacking infantry battalions of the 2nd Division began their advance, assisted by one company of 15 tanks.[32]

The Attack

Three regiments moved forward simultaneously, with the leading battalions of the 6th Marine, 5th Marine, and 23rd Infantry Regiments covering the 4-kilometer-wide divisional front. The 9th Regiment advanced in support. Reports from across the front agree that the first German positions "did not offer a great deal of resistance." On the right, the 23rd Regiment "followed the barrage closely," cleared out the enemy strong points in the Bois de Hazois, and reached the first objective at the scheduled time.[33] At this point the divisional front narrowed, and the 23rd Regiment moved to the left and took a support position behind the two Marine regiments. After the 30 minute rest at the first objective, the Marines continued the advance, meeting only slight enemy resistance, and taking "one objective after another on scheduled time." At the third and final objective the Marines consolidated their positions and sent patrols forward to the "exploitation line."[34] The 9th and 23rd Regiments dug in behind them for the night.

The first day's attack was an unequivocal success; the division had broken through the enemy's main line of resistance, advanced 9 kilometers, and had suffered light casualties.[35] It was another well-executed set-piece attack, like the 1st Division's assault of Cantigny in May, the 2nd Division's seizure of Vaux in July, and the initial phase of the First Army's attack on the St. Mihiel salient in September. On 1 November, the 2nd Division took all of its assigned objectives without any serious difficulties. Strategically, the division had achieved one of the main objectives of the campaign, as the German Army's critically important Metz-Sedan railroad line had been brought within range of heavy artillery fire. Regarding the one-day advance of his division, Lejeune proudly claimed that it fundamentally changed the remainder of the offensive. For the Germans, the attack changed their defensive plan from one of "stubborn resistance, in a prepared position, to one of a series of holding engagements."[36] For the Americans, the operation changed "from that of a prepared attack, with a defined objective, to one of exploitation of a success already gained."[37]

For the second time in less than a month, the artillery had proven itself more than equal to the tasks assigned it in the initial attack. The infantry was even more impressed with the artillery support of the 1 November assault than they were for the support of the first attack at Blanc Mont. The acting commander of the 3rd Brigade, Colonel Robert O. Van Horn, claimed that the preliminary preparation "was the most intense and best executed of any preceding any attack of the brigade [sic]."[38] Brigadier General Wendell C. Neville, commanding the 4th Brigade, credited the "thorough" preparation with causing the withdrawal of a portion of the German forces.[39] The counter-battery effort also appears to have been successful, as some reports stated that the German artillery response was "weak" or "light," and others did not even deem it worthy of mention.[40]

As for the artillery fire accompanying the assault, a commander in the 3rd Brigade claimed that the "resistance of the enemy was shattered by the intensity and rapidity of the barrage fire" and that it was "most effective." Colonel Stone of the 23rd Infantry Regiment reported that "the initial attack was marked by a brilliant coordination of arms, the artillery laying down an absolutely smothering barrage which the infantry followed closely. . . . Attention must again be called to the wonderful work of our artillery in the first fighting. Our troops have never advanced behind a more perfect barrage."[41] These reports are confirmed by the commander of the tank company that accompanied the initial assault. Captain C. H. Barnard reported that when his tanks advanced at "H" hour, they found that "the artillery work had been so thorough that there was very little wire to be cut and practically no machine gun resistance except for an isolated gun here and there which they destroyed."[42]

The 2nd FA Brigade also appears to have been very successful in moving forward during the initial attack. As early as 0745, General Bowley reported to the corps headquarters that his first batteries were moving forward "as per the schedule."[43] By 1230, the advance battalions were in forward positions firing the rolling barrage, and the other light battalions had been in motion for hours. The first battalion of 155s was on the road forward at 1000, and the other two were advancing before 1700. Every gun in the brigade was therefore in a forward position in time to guard the day's gains throughout the first night. While the 1st FA Brigade also moved forward that evening, the 2nd Division did lose the support of the 67th FA Brigade, as that brigade was returned to its parent division.[44] This meant that by the beginning of the first night of the offensive, the division had already lost one third of its divisional artillery strength.

On the night of 1 November, V Corps ordered the 2nd Division to pre-pare to change directions and advance due west, in order to make a flank attack on the German forces opposing the American division on its left. However, early the next morning the corps changed its mind and directed the division to continue advancing to the north. Due to these changes in or-ders, the division made no advance until that night.[45] After passing through the 4th Brigade, the 3rd Brigade formed its regiments in one long column of twos, with advance and flank guards, and made a bold advance under cover of darkness and rain some 3 kilometers to the "exploitation line" given in the first day's orders. The night march took the regiments through the Bois de Folie, which was still laced with German soldiers performing a rear-guard mission. By 0600, 3 November, the brigade was on its objec-tive and was ready to continue the attack. Six hours later it had advanced another 4 kilometers, and found itself facing a German defensive position that was supported by artillery and *Minenwerfers* (trench mortars), at the south edge of the Bois de Belval.[46]

Although the supporting batteries from Colonel Davis's 15th FA had just moved to more advanced positions that day, the 3rd Brigade had no trouble arranging for fire to be brought on the German positions. Colonel Van Horn reported that the supporting guns from the 15th FA "shot up the resistance with good effectiveness."[47] After blasting the edge of the woods, the artillery fired a rolling barrage of sorts that advanced along a road

Figure 4.3. US Army 108th Field Artillery in action during the Meuse-Argonne campaign, October–November 1918. Photo courtesy of US Army Center of Military History.

through the woods, concentrating its fire to cover just 200 yards on each side of the road. That evening the 9th and 23rd Regiments again formed into columns of two and followed an advance guard through the woods, advancing some 6 kilometers that night. By midnight on 3 November, the leading elements of the division were some 8 kilometers ahead of the divisions on their flanks. The success of the night march also proved the disorganization rampant in the forward German units at that time. Whole groups of German officers and soldiers were captured while sitting in well-lit farm houses, or while asleep in the woods, all totally unaware of the depth of the American advance.[48]

Finally, on the morning of 4 November, the Germans were able to piece together a strong line of resistance with well-organized machine-gun nests, 2 kilometers south of the town of Beaumont. When Colonel James C. Rhea, the new commander of the 3rd Brigade, realized his forces were up against a formidable enemy position, on difficult ground, with both flanks exposed, he reported the situation to General Lejeune, who ordered the brigade to continue the advance. Rhea claimed that he had just one battalion from the 15th FA in position to support the attack. While the attack succeeded in breaking the German line and in continuing the advance for about a kilometer, Rhea said it was only accomplished "at the expense of heavy casualties, the losses being in the neighborhood of 1,000 casualties, with a high percentage killed."[49]

Why was there so little artillery support available for this particular attack? The division was in its fourth day of continuous operations, during which it had by this time advanced more than 20 kilometers. The division was straining its logistical elements to the limit, and the constant rain made that strain much worse. Rhea stated that the roads in his sector "were at first almost impassable, and after November 3rd were entirely impassable."[50] The artillery, and all of its ammunition, had to make its way forward either cross-country or by using the congested roads in other divisional sectors. A divisional inspector reported that all roads in the 2nd Division's sector were "axle deep in mud," and that he had personally witnessed a team of "22 horses hitched to one gun and they could just move it in the mud."[51]

A second factor contributing to the lack of artillery support was that on 4 November the 4th Brigade moved out of its support role to advance into the divisional sector not covered by the 3rd Brigade's night marches. Therefore, the Marine brigade was using the batteries of Lieutenant Colonel John A. Holabird's 12th FA to support that movement.[52] The 1st FA Brigade had been returned to its parent division that day as well, which meant that while the leading infantry battalions for the 1 November attack had the dedicated support of more than three whole artillery brigades, just three days later the assaulting infantry units were reduced to scraping together as many guns as they could get from their one supporting regiment of light guns and half of the 17th FA.

To make matters worse, division inspectors had reported to the Inspector General of the AEF, and through him to Major General Summerall, that the 2nd Division did not properly employ "accompanying guns" during the initial assault, as per the corps order. Pressured to rectify this irregularity, General Lejeune ordered that as of 3 November, accompanying artillery was to be detailed to the infantry, with two guns going to each battalion in the front line.[53] Therefore, those guns were probably not available to the regimental artillery commander at a time when he was called on to provide the greatest possible concentration of fire.

On 4 and 5 November, both infantry brigades pressed towards the Meuse River, and the German forces opposing them fought rear-guard actions to enable the greatest number of German troops and materiel to get behind their new line of resistance across the river. From 6 to 10 November, the infantry brigades improved their positions on the west bank of the Meuse, all the while being subjected to heavy German artillery fire from across the river. The artillery brigade also established gun positions in preparation for supporting an eventual crossing of the river.[54]

Finally, late on 9 November, General Lejeune complied with corps directives and ordered his troops to cross the Meuse in two places on the following night. General Neville was ordered to command a crossing force composed of troops from two V Corps divisions, the 2nd and 89th Divisions. Neville requested that the orders be changed to allow for a daytime crossing at just one location, since he was convinced of the strength of the German positions on the east bank and because he had "little artillery with which to support even one crossing." The requests were denied.[55] The 12th FA and four batteries of the 17th FA were to support the northern crossing near Mouzon, which was thought of as the main effort. The 15th FA, along with the other two batteries of 155s, were assigned to the southern crossing near Letanne. The crossings were attempted at 2130, preceded by an hour-long artillery preparation. At Mouzon, the responding German fire was so strong that the engineers and infantrymen could not even get the temporary bridges across. At Letanne, the German gunners were slower in identifying the crossing point and three battalions from the two attacking divisions were able to fight their way across the foot bridges and establish positions east of the river. However, the casualties sustained in these "surprise" attacks were heavy; General Summerall even called them "excessive."[56] Within hours of the crossing the armistice took effect, and the war was over. The 2nd FA Brigade had fired its last shell of the war.[57]

The attack of the 2nd Division in the third phase of the Meuse-Argonne campaign was viewed by many in the AEF as being the most successful American attack of the entire war. In eleven days it advanced some 29 kilometers, captured more than 1,700 prisoners and 105 artillery pieces, and suffered 3,299 casualties.[58] However, just as with the previous offensives, an operational analysis demonstrates that the division, the V Corps, and the First Army, showed both its strengths and its weaknesses at different parts of the campaign.

There can be no doubt that the preliminary bombardment was effective, as noted above. The decision to pull back the barrage for the last ten minutes of the preparation demonstrated an ability to adapt to the changing tactics of the enemy, and may have been an important measure of the success of the initial assault.[59] Another factor crucial to the success of the attack was the use of massive quantities of gas in the preparatory bombardment to neutralize both German batteries and infantry strong points. Rexmond Cochrane, in his analysis on the American use of gas in the Meuse-Argonne, asserted that "the gas plan for the final assault [on 1 November] was the best that could have been devised, and it succeeded exactly as planned."[60]

Despite these achievements, probably the most significant innovation made in the final attack was the massive, overpowering rolling barrage that incorporated both heavy and light artillery throughout its execution. While the 2nd Division, and the AEF in general, had previously used heavy guns to fire in concentrations in advance of the 75-mm rolling barrage, the goal of that fire had always been to "soften-up" known or suspected obstacles that the infantry was eventually going to meet. The attack on 1 November was the first to incorporate the heavy guns into a comprehensive infantry support fire-plan that had as its goal the neutralization of "only those positions from which fire could be delivered upon our infantry at that moment."[61] The use of this "thick" barrage was the result of a victory by those in the AEF who were convinced that, regardless of what General Pershing thought the infantryman could accomplish with just his rifle and bayonet, "the assault battalions must be covered by artillery and machine gun fire in all stages of the advance."[62] The results achieved by the 2nd Division and the entire V Corps on 1 November attest to the effectiveness of that principle.

Of course, covering the infantry attack with fire was much easier to arrange on the first day of the attack, and the 2nd Division proved the necessity for overwhelming fire-power again in the later stages of the attack by demonstrating the costs of not being able to provide it. Just as at Blanc Mont in early October, the number of guns assigned to the division became smaller and smaller as the attack progressed. When situations arose in which the attacking infantry needed strong, concentrated artillery support, as occurred with the 3rd Brigade on 4 November and to the 4th Marine Brigade in its attempt to cross the Meuse, the divisional artillery brigade was often unable to provide adequate support on its own. This insufficient artillery support was not caused solely by a reduction in available firepower, but also by the compression in the amount of time allowed to properly prepare and coordinate the firepower that was assigned. For the Meuse crossings, senior officers in the division attempted to secure the use of allied aircraft to get updated photographs of the new German defenses so that the fire-plan for the attack would adequately suppress enemy fire. Colonel Dan Moore, who replaced Bowley as commander of the artillery brigade, asserted that "if photos had been available for the preparation of the attack for the crossing of the Meuse, a much more intelligent bombardment of the enemy's machine gun and battery positions might have been undertaken, and the crossing probably would have been a success at Mouzon."[63] The lack of time and resources available to adequately support infantry attacks in the "exploitation" phase were factors that caused the 2nd Division trouble throughout the war.

The use of "accompanying guns" was one innovative attempt to provide artillery support to the infantry attacking in the "exploitation" phase. However, when General Aultman, the Chief of Artillery for V Corps, reported that the 2nd Division could only make "little use" of its accompanying guns and that "they were of no value to the artillery" during the period they were parceled out to the infantry, it was an all too common description of the use of accompanying guns by American units.[64] Clearly, Lejeune and Bowley shared a dislike for accompanying guns and were convinced that despite the problems of attempting to employ masses of artillery after the initial assault, it was better to maintain a system that enabled the possibility of concentrating a "more effective volume of fire . . . on any point desired" than to break up the guns and hope that they would be used to provide some support at critical points in the attack.[65] Colonel Moore, Bowley's replacement, closed his operations report for the Meuse-Argonne campaign by asserting that attacking divisions get the "best results from artillery by placing artillery support in the hands of the artillery regiment and battalion commanders, who follow the advance closely and solve the problems of enemy resistance through direct liaison with the infantry."[66] However, keeping all the guns "close" and the liaison "direct" was easier said than done, and the division never fully met either challenge.

The infantry regiments of the 2nd Division made much better use of a different innovation to reduce their susceptibility to enemy firepower in the "exploitation" phase of the attack. The night marches were clearly an attempt by the attacking infantry to continue to make aggressive advances in the midst of the enemy, without having to measure their own firepower against that of the enemy. It was a brilliant and bold tactic, and each maneuver surely saved many lives and much hard fighting. However, it is also clear that such a tactic would have been suicidal just one month earlier had it been tried at Blanc Mont, or just about anywhere else on the Western Front. From 3 November on, the German forces in the Meuse-Argonne were disorganized and frantically attempting to withdraw to a position east of the river, and that is what allowed the night marches to be such a success.[67] It is important to realize that even though the German forces were in the midst of a rather disorganized withdrawal, they still were able on two occasions to confront the advancing forces of the 2nd Division and inflict heavy casualties on them.

Nevertheless, the German forces that were hurled back some 9 kilometers during the initial assault on 1 November were, while tired and depleted, neither disorganized nor seriously considering a withdrawal. Those forces were resoundingly defeated by a 2nd Division force that proved, once again, that it could deliver an extremely effective set-piece attack. It was only in the later stages of the "exploitation" that the 2nd Division showed that it still was battling the troubles caused by a doctrine that was ill-suited to its area of expertise. Even at the end of the war, Pershing's query from 8 August was still very pertinent to AEF operations in the "exploitation" phase of any attack--perhaps they were *still* "losing too many men," and perhaps the doctrine Pershing relied on deserved a share of the blame.[68]

In its three final attacks, at St. Mihiel, Blanc Mont, and the Meuse-Argonne, the 2nd Division positively demonstrated what it had given strong hints of at Vaux and Soissons—that it could execute limited, set-piece attacks with great success. It succeeded against determined defenders who were in strong defensive positions, and did so without suffering excessive casualties. It even proved capable of successfully executing these attacks despite being given insufficient time to prepare (e.g. at Blanc Mont) and having the divisions on its flanks make unimpressive supporting advances (e.g. Blanc Mont and Meuse-Argonne). What also emerged, most notably in the final two offensives, was a desire on the part of the senior divisional officers to break from official AEF doctrine and fight for limited objectives by maximizing the use of artillery. On the negative side, the division struggled to make successful attacks after the initial assault. Though the division may have been inclined to hold its new lines and make preparations for additional artillery-centered, set-piece attacks, the French and American high commands each compelled it to press ahead. These follow-on attacks nearly always led to excessive casualties, while yielding unimpressive gains.

Conclusion

What are the lessons to be gained from this case-study of large-scale combat operations waged a hundred years ago? First, combat doctrine, and the operational plans based on it, must match the capabilities of the units that will have to conduct the operations. Whether there are, as General Pershing believed, unchanging "essential principles of war" or not, a mismatch between unit capabilities and official doctrine can be disastrous.[69] However, when operational plans properly consider the actual capabilities of the combat units that are expected to carry out the attacks, even relatively inexperienced units—and in the fall of 1918, nearly all AEF units were relatively inexperienced by modern standards—can achieve remarkable results. Second, unit commanders, at all levels, must be willing to innovate and adapt in order to succeed on the modern battlefield, even if that means choosing what works best over doctrinal orthodoxy. Third, despite the desire to keep the pressure on the enemy and drive forward until his forces collapse, sometimes it may be wiser to pause and allow one's own forces to regroup.

During his time as First Army commander, General Pershing attempted to push the enemy to the breaking point by conducting three weeks of nearly non-stop attacks. By mid-October, his forces were bloodied, worn out, disorganized, and unable to conduct large-scale combat operations efficiently. While the defending Germans were hard-pressed, the front-line American forces lacked the power to conduct even attritional warfare effectively, much less force a breakthrough. Lieutenant General Liggett wisely chose to stop these inefficient attacks and give his forces time to refit and reorganize. The remarkable success of the First Army's attack on 1 November shows that Liggett chose wisely, and that certain AEF units, such as the 2nd Division and the V Corps, had learned how to succeed on the modern battlefield.

Notes

1. Major General Charles P. Summerall, "Comments by the Corps Commander upon the Operations of the Fifth Army Corps," in V Corps Historical File, Entry 1118, RG 120, NA.

2. This chapter includes excerpts from Mark E. Grotelueschen, *Doctrine Under Trial: American Artillery Employment in World War I* (Westport, CT: Greenwood Press, 2001). For a detailed study on the case of the 35th Division, see Robert Ferrell, *Collapse at Meuse-Argonne: The Failure of the Missouri-Kansas Division* (Columbia, MO: University of Missouri Press, 2004).

3. Of the initial nine divisions that attacked on 26 September, three had to replaced within the first week, and four lasted just eight days. Casualties for these divisions were: 35th: 6,006 in six days; 91st: 4,768 in eight days, 37th: 3,060 in five days, 79th: 3,529 in five days. American Battle Monuments Commission, *American Armies and Battlefields in Europe* (Washington, DC: US GPO, 1992), 327–28.

4. David F. Trask, *The AEF and Coalition Warmaking*, (Lawrence, KS: University Press of Kansas, 1993), 122–23, 149.

5. Allan R. Millett, *The General* (Westport, CT: Greenwood Press, 1975), 399.

6. The German Army used gas extensively in the 1918 spring offensives to neutralize both enemy infantry and artillery. In the Chemin des Dames offensive, 50 percent of the three million artillery rounds fired on the first day were gas rounds. See David T. Zabecki, *The German 1918 Offensives: A Case Study in The Operational Level of War* (Routledge, 2006).

7. "The failure to use gas in the Argonne and on the 5th Corps front in the opening assault were therefore major blunders," according to Rexmond Cochrane, *The Use of Gas in the Meuse-Argonne Campaign, September-November 1918*, Study #10, *US Army Chemical Corps Historical Studies: Gas Warfare in World War I* (Army Chemical Center, Maryland, 1958), 90. While Cochrane asserted that there was no sign of any shortage of gas shells for the First Army, Colonel Conrad Lanza, the Chief of Operations for the First Army Artillery during the campaign, claimed that plans to use great quantities of gas shell "had to be abandoned due to the fact that nothing like the amount of gas shell asked for could be had." See Conrad H. Lanza, *The Army Artillery, First Army* (United States, s.n., no date), ii. This undated typescript unit history was commissioned by the War Department, and is held at the U.S. Army Military History Institute, Carlisle Barracks, PA. The testimony of General Charles P. Summerall, a division and corps commander in the campaign, supports Lanza's claim. He stated that "the Corps was at all times anxious to fire large quantities of non-persistent gas and the amount of gas so fired was only limited by the supply that could be obtained." See Major General Charles P. Summerall, "Comments by the Corps Commander upon the Operations of the Fifth Army Corps," 4, V Corps Historical File, Entry 1118, RG 120 NA.

8. Conrad H. Lanza, "The Artillery Support of the Infantry in the A.E.F" *Field Artillery Journal* (January–March, 1936): 70–71.

9. "Report of Operations During the Period Nov. 1st to Nov. 11th," HQ 2nd FA Brigade, 26 December 1918, Folder 15, 2nd Division files, G-3 Reports, AEF/GHQ, Entry 270, RG 120, NA; Lieutenant William D. Bickham and Major William Burr, "Second Field Artillery Brigade History," 22, undated typescript, 2nd FA Brigade Historical File, Entry 1246-11.4, RG 120, NA.

10. The division received the first drafts of the First Army and V Corps plans on 24 October, Oliver Spaulding and John W. Wright, *The Second Division: American Expeditionary Force in France, 1917–1919* (New York: The Hillman Press, 1937), 198; "Report of Operations, 3rd Brigade from October 17, 1918 to 2nd Nov, 1918," Folder 50, 2nd Division files, G-3 Reports, AEF/GHQ, Entry 270, RG 120, NA.

11. Field Orders No. 88, First Army, AEF, 27 October, 1918, in Department of the Army, *United States Army in the World War* 9 (Washington, DC: GPO, 1948), 333–49 (hereafter *USAWW*).

12. Major General Charles P. Summerall lecture, "Recent Operations from the Standpoint of Employment of Artillery with Particular Reference to Co-operation between the Infantry and the Artillery," 5, to the ACAS, on 16 December 1918, in Folder 14, ACAS Files, Entry 371, RG 120, NA.

13. Field Order No. 101, V Corps, 28 October, 1918, in US Army, 2nd Division, *Records of the Second Division (Regular)* 1 (Washington DC: Army War College, 1924), (hereafter *RSD*).

14. The farthest main line of resistance (south of the Meuse) for the Germans was the *Freya Stellung*, which was within 6 kilometers of the 2nd Division's jump-off position and as close as 4 kilometers to the 89th Division's front lines.

15. Cochrane, *The Use of Gas*, 4.

16. Lanza, "Artillery Support," 75.

17. Lanza, 75.

18. Major General Charles P. Summerall lecture, "Recent Operations from the Standpoint of Employment of Artillery with Particular Reference to Co-operation between the Infantry and the Artillery," 1-2, to the ACAS, on 16 December 1918, in Folder 14, ACAS Files, Entry 371, RG 120, NA.

19. See Summerall lecture, "Recent Operations from the Standpoint of Employment of Artillery with Particular Reference to Co-operation between the Infantry and the Artillery," 1–2, to the ACAS, on 16 December 1918, in Folder 14, ACAS Files, Entry 371, RG 120, NA.

20. Operations Order No. 5, "Plan of Attack," Artillery HQ, V Corps, 29 October, 1918, V Corps Historical File, Entry 1118, RG 120, NA.

21. This number comes from General Lejeune. How many machines guns were involved throughout the whole of V Corps front is not known. John A. Lejeune, *The Reminiscences of a Marine* (Philadelphia, PA: Dorrance, 1930), 384.

22. Spaulding and Wright, *The Second Division*, 199–200.

23. Operations Order No. 5, "Plan of Attack," Artillery HQ, V Corps, 29 October 1918, V Corps Historical File, Entry 1118, RG 120, NA.

24. Operations Order No. 5, "Plan of Attack," Artillery HQ, V Corps, 29 October, 1918, V Corps Historical File, Entry 1118, RG 120, NA.

25. Summerall stated that the 2nd Division had 236 divisional guns, the 89th Division had 208 guns, and that they shared 152 corps guns, including the dedicated army groups that were put under corps direction. This was spread on an eight kilometer front, giving the corps an artillery density of one 75-mm gun for each 29 meters, a 155-mm or 8 howitzer for every 39 meters, and a 105-mm or 155-mm gun for every 69 meters of front. The division also had a battery (12) of six-inch Newton Mortars, and a number of gas projectors. Memo, Summerall to Deputy Chief of Staff, AEF, 5 January 1919, V Corps Historical File, Entry 1118, RG 120, NA; Operations Order No. 5, "Plan of Attack," Artillery HQ, V Corps, 29 October, 1918, V Corps Historical File, Entry 1118, RG 120, NA.

26. Operations Order No. 5, "Plan of Attack," Artillery HQ, V Corps, 29 October, 1918, V Corps Historical File, Entry 1118, RG 120, NA.

27. Spaulding and Wright, *The Second Division*, 200.

28. Field Order No. 49, HQ the 2nd Division, 0700, 31 October 1918, 2nd Division Historical File, Entry 1241-32.1, RG 120, NA.

29. Operations Order No. 5, "Plan of Attack," Artillery HQ, V Corps, 29 October, 1918, V Corps Historical File, Entry 1118, RG 120, NA.

30. "Report of Operations, 2nd FA Brigade," Folder 15, 2nd Division files, G-3 Reports, AEF/GHQ, Entry 270, RG 120, NA.

31. "Report of Operations, 2nd FA Brigade," Folder 15, 2nd Division files, G-3 Reports, AEF/GHQ, Entry 270, RG 120, NA.

32. Each battery in the first battalion of the 12th FA fired 400 rounds at enemy strong points and forward positions. "Report on advance of 1st Btn, 12 FA, Nov. 1," Folder 9, 2nd Division files, G-3 Reports, AEF/GHQ, Entry 270, RG 120, NA; Summerall lecture, "Recent Operations from the Standpoint of Employment of Artillery with Particular Reference to Co-operation between the Infantry and the Artillery," 1–2, to the ACAS, on 16 December 1918, in Folder 14, ACAS Files, Entry 371, RG 120, NA; "Report of Operations from Sept. 26th to Nov. 8th, 1918," HQ V Corps-Artillery, 14 November, 1918, V Corps Historical File, Entry 1118, RG 120, NA; Memo, "Projected Use of Gas Troops," 26 October 1918, 2d Battalion, First Gas Regiment, to V Corps Commander, Folder 14, 2nd Division files, G-3 Reports, AEF/GHQ, Entry 270, RG 120, NA; Spaulding and Wright, *The Second Division*, 200.

33. "Report of Operations, 3rd Brigade from 17 Oct. 1918 to 2 Nov. 1918," Folder 50, 2nd Division files, G-3 Reports, AEF/GHQ, Entry 270, RG 120, NA.

34. "Operations Report, 4th Brigade, Marines, 24 Oct.–11 Nov.," Folder 87, 2nd Division files, G-3 Reports, AEF/GHQ, Entry 270, RG 120, NA.

35. General Neville, whose Marine battalions served as the assault troops for all three first day objectives, estimated that his brigade suffered casualties of just five percent of the forces engaged on that day. Lejeune reported that "the prisoners taken exceeded the losses sustained on that day." "Operations Report, 4th Brigade, Marines, 24 Oct.–11 Nov.," Folder 87, 2nd Division files, G-3 Reports, AEF/ GHQ, Entry 270, RG 120, NA; "Report of Operations, 3rd Brigade from Oct. 17,

1918 to 2 Nov. 1918," Folder 50, 2nd Division files, G-3 Reports, AEF/GHQ, Entry 270, RG 120, NA; "Operations Report of the 2d Division," *RSD*, vol. 1.

36. "Operations Report of the 2d Division."

37. "Operations Report of the 2d Division."

38. "Report of Operations, 3rd Brigade from Oct. 17, 1918 to 2 Nov. 1918," Folder 50, 2nd Division files, G-3 Reports, AEF/GHQ, Entry 270, RG 120, NA.

39. "Operations Report, 4th Brigade, Marines, 24 Oct.–11 Nov.," Folder 87, 2nd Division files, G-3 Reports, AEF/GHQ, Entry 270, RG 120, NA.

40. No unit in the 3rd Brigade even mentioned German artillery fire during this attack. "Records of Telephone Messages Sent and Received, Nov. 1st to Nov. 11th, inclusive," V Corps Historical File, Entry 1118, RG 120, NA; "Operations Report, 4th Brigade, Marines, 24 Oct.–11 Nov," Folder 87, 2nd Division files, G-3 Reports, AEF/GHQ, Entry 270, RG 120, NA.

41. "Report of Operations," 3rd Brigade, Nov. 2–11 and "Report of Operations, Nov. 1–11, 23d Infantry," 27 November 1918, found in "Report of Units of 2nd Division, Meuse-Argonne Offensive, No. 1-11, 1918," Folder 15, 2nd Division files, G-3 Reports, AEF/GHQ, Entry 270, RG 120, NA.

42. Of the 15 tanks that started with the 2nd Division, only six reached even the first objective. The rest either broke down, or were "hung up" in tank traps, ditches, or deep shell holes. The 4th Brigade said they were "ably supported by the tanks" while the 23rd Infantry claimed that the "tanks failed to keep up and were of little assistance." See "Report of Operations, 1st Provisional Tank Company, 1st Brigade Tanks," 1 November 1918, in 2nd Division Historical Files, Entry 1241-33.0, RG 120, NA; "Operations Report, 4th Brigade, Marines, 24 Oct.–11 Nov," Folder 87, 2nd Division files, G-3 Reports, AEF/GHQ, Entry 270, RG 120, NA; "Report of Operations, Nov. 1–11, 23d Infantry," 27 November 1918, found in "Report of Units of 2nd Division, Meuse-Argonne Offensive, No. 1-11, 1918," Folder 15, 2nd Division files, G-3 Reports, AEF/GHQ, Entry 270, RG 120, NA.

43. "Records of Telephone Messages Sent and Received, Nov. 1st to Nov. 11th, inclusive," V Corps Historical File, Entry 1118, RG 120, NA.

44. "Records of Telephone Messages Sent and Received, Nov. 1st to Nov. 11th inclusive," V Corps Historical File, Entry 1118, RG 120, NA; "Report of Operations during the Period Nov. 1st to Nov. 11th," HQ 2d FA Brigade, Dec. 26, 1918, Folder 15, 2nd Division files, G-3 Reports, AEF/GHQ, Entry 270, RG 120, NA.

45. "Operations Report," 2nd Division, *RSD*, vol. 1.

46. "Report of Operations," 3rd Brigade, Nov. 2–11, in "Report of Units of 2nd Division, Meuse-Argonne Offensive, No. 1-11, 1918," Folder 15, 2nd Division files, G-3 Reports, AEF/GHQ, Entry 270, RG 120, NA; Spaulding and Wright, *The Second Division*, 208, 210.

47. One battalion from the 17th FA had been assigned to the 15th FA for advanced operations on this day and took part in the shelling of the German positions in the woods. "Report of Operations, Nov. 1–11, 9th Infantry Regiment," 29 November 1918, Folder 15, 2nd Division files, G-3 Reports, AEF/GHQ, Entry 270, RG 120, NA; Spaulding and Wright, *The Second Division*, 208–09.

48. "Report of Operations," 3rd Brigade, Nov. 2–11, in "Report of Units of 2nd Division, Meuse-Argonne Offensive, No. 1-11, 1918," Folder 15, 2nd Division files, G-3 Reports, AEF/GHQ, Entry 270, RG 120, NA; "Operations Report," 2d Division, *RSD*, vol. 1.

49. "Report of Operations," 3rd Brigade, Nov. 2–11, in "Report of Units of 2nd Division, Meuse-Argonne Offensive, No. 1-11, 1918," Folder 15, 2nd Division files, G-3 Reports, AEF/GHQ, Entry 270, RG 120, NA.

50. "Report of Operations," 3rd Brigade, Nov. 2–11, in "Report of Units of 2nd Division, Meuse-Argonne Offensive, No. 1-11, 1918," Folder 15, 2nd Division files, G-3 Reports, AEF/GHQ, Entry 270, RG 120, NA.

51. "Report of Operations," 3rd Brigade, Nov. 2–11, in "Report of Units of 2nd Division, Meuse-Argonne Offensive, No. 1-11, 1918," Folder 15, 2nd Division files, G-3 Reports, AEF/GHQ, Entry 270, RG 120, NA; Report of 14 November 1918, in Inspection Reports of Armies, Divisions and Corps, Entry 590, RG 120, NA.

52. "Operations Report, 4th Brigade, Marines, 24 Oct.–11 Nov," Folder 87, 2nd Division files, G-3 Reports, AEF/GHQ, Entry 270, RG 120, NA.

53. "Report of Operations from Sept. 26th to Nov. 8th, 1918," HQ V Corps-Artillery, 14 November, 1918, V Corps Historical File, Entry 1118, RG 120, NA; Report of Colonel J. C. Johnson, Inspector General, "Operations and Conditions, 2d and 89th Divisions, V Corps, 1–3 Nov. 1918," and Memo, Major General A. W. Brewster, AEF Inspector General to V Corps Commander, subject: "Use of Artillery 2nd Division," both in Artillery folder, Entry 590, RG 120, NA.

54. "Report of Operations during the Period Nov. 1st to Nov. 11th," HQ 2d FA Brigade, Dec. 26, 1918, Folder 15, 2nd Division files, G-3 Reports, AEF/GHQ, Entry 270, RG 120, NA; "Report of Operations," 3rd Brigade, Nov. 2–11, in "Report of Units of 2nd Division, Meuse-Argonne Offensive, No. 1-11, 1918," Folder 15, 2nd Division files, G-3 Reports, AEF/GHQ, Entry 270, RG 120, NA; "Operations Report, 4th Brigade, Marines, 24 Oct.–11 Nov," Folder 87, 2nd Division files, G-3 Reports, AEF/GHQ, Entry 270, RG 120, NA.

55. "Operations Report," 2d Division, *RSD*, vol. 1; "Operations Report, 4th Brigade, Marines, 24 Oct.–11 Nov," Folder 87, 2nd Division files, G-3 Reports, AEF/GHQ, Entry 270, RG 120, NA; Spaulding and Wright, *The Second Division*, 219–20.

56. Memo, Summerall to Deputy Chief of Staff, AEF, 5 January 1919, 6, V Corps Historical File, Entry 1118, RG 120, NA.

57. "Operations Report, 4th Brigade, Marines, 24 Oct. –11 Nov," Folder 87, 2nd Division files, G-3 Reports, AEF/GHQ, Entry 270, RG 120, NA; Spaulding and Wright, *The Second Division,* 219–20.

58. Again, the ABMC total for casualties is slightly lower, 3282; the figure in the text is taken from the report of 2nd Division Commander (Major General John A. Lejeune), to Assistant Chief of Staff, G-3, GHQ, AEF, Subject: "Operations Information," 30 December 1918, in Reports and Other Records Regarding the History of AEF Units, Divisional Skeleton Histories, Entry 443, RG 120, NA.

59. The US 80th Division, on the left flank of the 2nd Division on 1 November, was stopped immediately by machine guns that had slipped beyond the artillery preparation and rolling barrage. The division inspector who investigated the poor first day showing of that division reported that they should have done just what their neighbors to the right did. Memo for Inspector General, AEF, titled "Observations with 1st and 5th Corps," 8 November 1918, in "Inspection Reports of Armies, Divisions, and Corps," Entry 590, RG 120, NA.

60. Cochrane, *The Use of Gas*, 91.

61. Summerall, "Recent Operations from the Standpoint of Employment of Artillery with Particular Reference to Co-operation between the Infantry and the Artillery," lecture to the ACAS on 16 December 1918 in Folder 14, ACAS Files, Entry 371, RG 120, NA, 2–4.

62. Summerall, 2–4.

63. Colonel Moore replaced General Bowley on 3 November, as the latter was promoted to be the Chief of Artillery for VI Corps; "Report of Operations during the Period Nov. 1st to Nov. 11th," HQ 2d FA Brigade, 26 December 1918, Folder 15, 2nd Division files, G-3 Reports, AEF/GHQ, Entry 270, RG 120, NA.

64. General Lejeune said much the same thing when he asserted that "no material advantage was gained" by his employment of accompanying guns. He was convinced that "more satisfactory results are obtained when all of the artillery remains under the control of the Artillery Commander and the 37mm. and Stokes mortars are used to best advantage by the infantry." Memo for Inspector General (IG), AEF, 8 November 1918, subject: "Observations with First and Fifth Corps with respect to Artillery in recent operations," Entry 590, RG 120, NA; "Report of Operations," "Report of Operations from Sept. 26th to Nov. 8th, 1918," HQ V Corps-Artillery, 14 November 1918, V Corps Historical File, Entry 1118, RG 120, NA.

65. General Bowley told an Inspector General official that he "did not believe in this use of accompanying guns." Report of Colonel J. C. Johnson, Inspector General, "Operations and Conditions, 2d and 89th Divisions, V Corps, 1–3 Nov. 1918," and Memo, Major General A. W. Brewster, AEF Inspector General to V Corps Commander, subject: "Use of Artillery 2nd Division," both in Artillery folder, Entry 590, RG 120, NA.

66. "Report of Operations during the Period Nov. 1st to Nov. 11th," HQ 2d FA Brigade, 26 December 1918, Folder 15, 2nd Division files, G-3 Reports, AEF/GHQ, Entry 270, RG 120, NA.

67. Spaulding and Wright, *The Second Division*, 210.

68. Pershing is quoted in James W. Rainey, "Ambivalent Warfare: The Tactical Doctrine of the AEF in World War I," *Parameters*, Journal of the US Army War College, September 1983, 41.

69. Pershing issued official documents during the war stating that "the essential principles of war have not changed," and that "the fundamental principles governing the conduct of fire for field artillery remain essentially unchanged." See *USAWW*, 3: 316–17, 326.

Chapter 5

The Division Artillery: Linking Strategy to Tactics in Operations Desert Shield/Storm

Major Lincoln R. Ward

In 2016, with his initial message to the force, Chief of Staff of the Army General Mark Milley established readiness as the top priority for the US Army. Within the field artillery branch, the implication was how to achieve the highest level of readiness, while also preparing for ground combat against a near peer competitor. Additionally, the deterioration of the field artillery in the 12 years of persistent low-intensity conflict created a sense of urgency within the Army that spawned the reestablishment of the division artillery.

This chapter will identify how the division artillery can achieve the Chief of Staff's strategic guidance, specifically the objective of readiness "through the arrangement of tactical actions in time, space, and purpose."[1] Operations Desert Shield and Storm, show the evolution of doctrine, organization, and employment of field artillery against a near peer competitor. The conduct of these operations demonstrated several of the tenets of unified land operations, which "describes the Army's approach to generating and applying combat power in campaigns and operations."[2] Specifically, the elements displayed were flexibility, lethality, adaptability, and synchronization. The division artillery acts as an operational artist, while within modularity, there is no advocate for ensuring that subordinate field artillery units are getting the manning, training, and employment that prepares them for future conflict.

In April 2014, the Army re-established the division artillery, a brigade level field artillery headquarters. Its stated mission, not yet codified in doctrine but outlined in a Fires Center of Excellence white paper, is to "fight fires for the division" and to "provide training certification standardization of all field artillery units in the division."[3] This is further outlined in the US Forces Command (FORSCOM) Division Artillery implementation order addressing declining proficiency levels, the ability to mass and synchronize since the advent of modularity in 2003, and the decline of artillery skills as a result of "in lieu of" missions in support of the Global War on Terror.[4] In 2015, the Army suspended the phased reestablishment of the division artillery. This decision has caused uncertainty and confusion about the role of the division artillery. Research findings and historical context demonstrate that the role of the division artillery will continue to be the link connecting the Chief of Staff of the Army's strategic guidance to tactical action.[5]

Division Artillery's Role in Large-Scale Combat Operations

In draft US Army doctrine, the role of the division artillery is to facilitate the training, manning, and equipping of field artillery battalions, as well as ensure the professional development of field artillery Soldiers and leaders.[6] In future conflict, specifically in large-scale combat operations against a near peer adversary, the division artillery will be vital in synchronizing and delivering accurate and timely fires.

Historical case studies illustrate the role and effectiveness of division artilleries in both large-scale combat operations and as a part of stability operations. Operation Desert Shield and Operation Desert Storm provide an invaluable case study in the train up, organization, and employment of fires in support of large-scale combat operations. An analysis of the Air-Land Battle doctrine used during these two operations is also integrated with the case study. This framework shows how the division artillery can take the strategic guidance from the Chief of Staff of the Army and translate the guidance to tactical action, improving readiness and effectively preparing for future combat operations.

The historical case studies also demonstrate the evolution of doctrine, organization, and employment of field artillery against a near peer competitor. This is the framework in which General Milley has framed his strategic guidance to the Army to be prepared for ground combat with a near peer competitor.[7] The Battles of Operation Desert Shield and Storm demonstrated several of the tenets of unified land operations, which "describes the Army's approach to generating and applying combat power in campaigns and operations."[8] Specifically, the elements displayed were flexibility, lethality, adaptability, and synchronization. Flexibility is defined as employment of a versatile mix of capabilities, formations, and equipment for conducting operations.[9] The employment of field artillery in Operation Desert Storm displayed lethality, which in this context "is the capacity for physical destruction, which is fundamental to all other military capabilities."[10] Adaptability in this case refers to "a willingness to accept prudent risk in unfamiliar or rapidly changing situations, and an ability to adjust based on continuous assessment."[11] Finally, both operations displayed synchronization or "the arrangement of military actions in time, space, and purpose to produce maximum relative combat power at a decisive place and time."[12]

A review of current trends is necessary to tie the historical case study to the current state of the field artillery. Current refers to that time since the beginning of operations in Afghanistan, the 2003 invasion of Iraq, and the advent of the modular Brigade Combat Team in 2003.[13] The deterioration of the field artillery in the 12 years of persistent low intensity conflict between 2004 and the present has created a sense of urgency within the Army that spawned the reestablishment of the division artillery as a brigade level headquarters. The conclusion and recommendations will demonstrate how

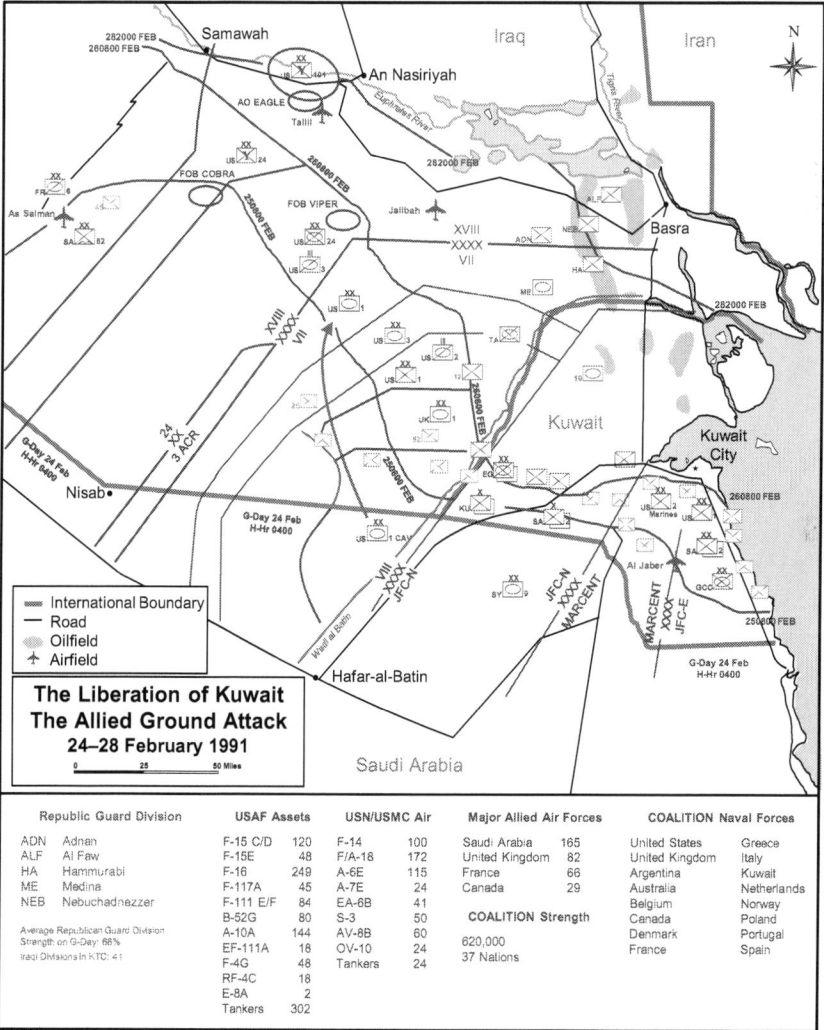

Figure 5.1 Operation Desert Shield/Desert Storm. Map courtesy of US Military Academy, West Point/created by Army University Press.

the division artillery will achieve the Chief of Staff's strategic guidance, specifically the objective of readiness "through the arrangement of tactical actions in time, space, and purpose."[14] The division artillery is the operational artist, whereas within modularity, there is no advocate for ensuring that subordinate field artillery units are getting the manning, training, and employment that prepares them for future conflict.[15]

Analysis of the role of artillery during Operations Desert Shield and Desert Storm is separated into three sections. The analysis highlights the preparation for deployment, the use of artillery in preparation for the ground offensive, and finally for the attack of Iraq itself. Each phase is examined in terms of the elements of operational art, unified land operations, and the AirLand Battle doctrine. Using this context demonstrates how the division artillery headquarters conducted operational art. This case study is being used for several reasons: to examine the successful employment of field artillery against a near peer competitor, to identify the factors that enabled the linking of tactical actions to operational and strategic objectives, and to pull forward best practices for how to best train, prepare, and employ field artillery in the future.

Training and Organizing for Desert Shield/Desert Storm

Operation Desert Shield, the preparation and buildup of forces in the Saudi Arabian desert, followed by Operation Desert Storm, which began with the offensive into Iraq, were the result of the August 1990 Iraqi invasion of its southern neighbor Kuwait. At the time, Iraq had the fourth largest military in the world, numbering over one million men. Its organization and doctrine reflected its ties to the British Empire as well as with its main supplier of arms, Russia, and was formed into seven corps-sized elements, with four of the corps oriented to the south, toward Saudi Arabia and in Kuwait.[16] Each mechanized corps not only had a robust armored force, but also contained a substantial indirect fire capability. Each corps contained a brigade of artillery, numbering between 70 and 140 medium artillery pieces. The overall numerical artillery advantage was exacerbated by the generally overall greater ranges possessed by the Iraqi artillery systems.[17] Overall strength of direct support artillery was some 3,300 pieces along with some 300 more longer ranging multiple launch rocket systems. Complicating matters was the capability for the Iraqi army to employ chemical munitions with its artillery assets.[18]

The threat of the use of chemical weapons and the large number of Iraqi artillery drove training and emphasized the importance of US artillery. Across the deploying force, division artilleries led training of all subordinate artillery battalions, which created a familiarity between the subordinate units and facilitated interoperability within the units. Firing, logistical, and communications operations were all standardized within the subordinate artillery units within a given division artillery.[19] By standardizing operations, subordinate artillery units would later be able to provide flexible support to any of the maneuver units based on the enemy threat or friendly mission. For maneuver commanders, the level of support could be counted on, regardless of artillery unit. This, in effect, reduced some of the fog and friction that Clausewitz famously points out happens in war.[20]

One example to indicate commonality across the force stems from the 3rd Armored Division Artillery, who would later help spearhead the VII Corps attack into Iraq. By focusing on command post exercises with its subordinate battalions, it was able to create a shared understanding of the processes and procedures needed to provide accurate and timely fires in support of the division. The division artillery commander noted that the "training exercises proved highly invaluable in getting all available artillery assigned to the force field artillery headquarters working together prior to deployment."[21] The common training and familiarity greatly aided in employment the of the division artillery which was "responsible for recommending the fires organization for combat and positioning all units organic to, assigned to, and supporting the maneuver force commander."[22] This would prove fortuitous once operations began in facilitating flexibility, mass, and tempo that led to the overwhelming success of US forces. This training can arguably be traced back to the way of thinking seen in Brigadier General Leslie McNair as a division artillery commander in 1937, and guidance from McNair as Army Ground Forces commander in 1943. Almost 50 years later, the doctrine had become firmly ingrained.

The first tenet of unified land operations that was met during the division artillery training and preparation for deployment was flexibility.[23] This common understanding and familiarity enabled commanders at each level to tailor their force, specifically field artillery units, to achieve the mission, weight the main effort, and have the confidence that they would receive the lethal effects to face a severely reduced enemy. This flexibility, which could be translated to the AirLand Battle imperative of agility, was defined as "the ability of friendly forces to act faster than the enemy, [which] is the first prerequisite for seizing and holding the initiative. Such greater quickness permits the rapid concentration of friendly strength against enemy vulnerabilities."[24] Achieving the AirLand Battle imperatives would have been considered critical considering the nature of the enemy that coalition forces were preparing to face during Operation Desert Shield.

Preparations

As the overall war plans developed, the US Army portion of the coalition would attack with two corps abreast, conducting a flanking maneuver on the Iraqi defenses into Iraq.[25] Additionally, a corps sized coalition led by the First Marine Expeditionary Force (1MEF) was to attack into Kuwait itself.[26] To reduce the Iraqi forces and mitigate some of the risk of being overmatched by sheer numbers of armored forces and artillery, the coalition waged an extensive air campaign. The air campaign was extremely effective at reducing and demoralizing Iraqi forces and engaging strategically important targets deep within Iraq. Artillery, along with rotary wing support, was used for setting the conditions for the close fight, specifically the initial breach of the Iraq border defensive belt. An effective tactic used to prepare for the ground offensive was the artillery raid. Overall, the organization, training, and finally the execution would demonstrate that the division artillery was the level of command that would link strategy to tactical action.

Artillery raids were employed to reduce enemy artillery, mitigating the threat of both conventional and chemical munitions. Each division artillery demonstrated its proficiency prior to the invasion by facilitating the numerous artillery raid operations along the Iraq international border. The artillery raid involved sending artillery units forward, into range of their known targets and massing fires. Prior to execution, the division artillery facilitated these raids by deconflicting airspace with Army aviation and other air assets. In order to prevent being engaged by enemy artillery, US artillery would displace after every barrage was fired. Division artillery radar and dedicated firing units stood by, ready detect to engage Iraqi artillery counter-fire. These artillery raids had devastating effects on the enemy, one report stating that 97 of 100 howitzers within an Iraqi division had been destroyed by massed fires.[27] On 13 February, the 1st Cavalry Division Artillery massed an entire attached multiple launch rocket system battalion, destroying 24 Iraqi targets with more than 300 rockets, all in less than five minutes.[28]

The tremendous effects of this tactic would not have been possible without the organization of the artillery within the division artillery. As outlined previously, the fires force headquarters, doctrinally, had the responsibility for ensuring the training and readiness of all artillery organizations as well as "recommending the fires organization for combat and positioning all units organic to, assigned to, and supporting the maneuver force commander."[29] The effectiveness of the artillery raid is also indicative of extending operational reach prior to conducting the ground offensive."[30] To achieve the desired surprise with the artillery raid, a significant amount of synchronization was required. The division artillery set the conditions for successful artillery raids through standardized training. During planning and execution, the division artillery managed the movement, observation, target observation and sustainment capabilities of the subordinate battalions.

Additionally, by reducing the enemy forces prior to the invasion, the tactical actions facilitated the attainment of an operational level decisive point.[31] In this case, Army Central planners had "assumed that the proper level of attrition was roughly 50 percent of the Iraqi armor and artillery, including 90 percent of the tanks and guns at the breach sites."[32] Thus, the critical factor was the destruction of enemy forces prior to commencing the ground offensive. Prior to the invasion, the 3rd Army intelligence cell assessed that 53 percent of Iraqi artillery and 42 percent of the Iraqi armor had been lost.[33]

Finally, the artillery raids demonstrated phasing and transitions. This usually "involves a change of mission, task organization, or rules of engagement. Phasing helps in planning and controlling and may be indicated by time, distance, terrain or an event."[34] In this case, artillery units dis-

Figure 5.2. 1st Battalion, 9th Field Artillery conducting fire mission in Iraq, February 1991. Photo courtesy of Lieutenant Colonel Bill Pitts.

played their flexibility as they transitioned between massing fires on Iraqi forces prior to the ground offensive to providing direct support to maneuver units. The ability to organize quickly into a mobile artillery task force, maneuver within range of enemy targets, synchronize massed artillery fire to destroy the enemy, and quickly return to the supported maneuver formation is a testament to the collective training, communication, and standardization prior to deploying.

The artillery raids conducted by coalition forces prior to the ground attack exemplify the AirLand Battle Doctrine during Operations Desert Shield and Storm. Specifically, when planning for or conducting offensive operations "firepower exploits maneuver by neutralizing the enemy's tactical forces and destroying his ability and will to fight. Firepower may also be used independent of maneuver to destroy, delay, or disrupt uncommitted enemy forces."[35] Additionally, the artillery raids conducted prior to the invasion exemplify the doctrinal imperative that "engagements must be violent to shock, paralyze, and overwhelm the enemy force quickly. They must be terminated rapidly to allow the force to disperse and avoid effective enemy counterstrikes."[36]

The Attack

Actions once US forces crossed into the Iraqi defensive zone once again demonstrated that the training, organization, and execution of the division artillery was the tactical headquarters which could link strategy to tactics. Once the attack into Iraq began early on the morning of 23 February 1991, field artillery continued to play a significant role in the success of the US forces. Units displayed the skill they had gained in training and continually demonstrated flexibility as the offensive proceeded. The offensive began as the 2nd Armored Cavalry Regiment (2nd ACR) entered Iraq as a covering force for the two corps which were the main effort. As the spearhead for offensive into Iraq, the 2nd ACR depended heavily on artillery to mitigate the superior numbers of Iraqi forces. Intelligence reports indicated 2nd ACR would encounter the elite Republican Guard, which possessed its most formidable weapon, the T-72 tank.[37] To mitigate the risk of facing the Republican Guard, the regiment, in addition to considerable air support, was augmented with an entire field artillery brigade. This flexibility enabled the 2nd ACR to conduct 30 minutes of preparation fires with an entire brigade to "suppress or destroy Iraqi observation posts located in several bunkers and observation towers."[38] The 30-minute artillery barrage on the Iraqi positions along the border crushed enemy morale.

Three separate division artilleries coordinated targeting of numerous Iraqi command and control, artillery, and sustainment nodes in order to eliminate the possibility of enemy forces disrupting the offensive. The 3rd Army battle damage estimate reported that all 100 Iraqi artillery pieces that 2nd ACR initially faced were indeed destroyed.[39] Throughout the entire operation, the 30 minutes of artillery preparation involved more than 350 artillery pieces. Three field artillery brigades supported breaching operations, firing more than 11,000 rounds and 414 rockets. This massed fire destroyed more than 50 Iraqi tanks, 139 other armored vehicles, and 152 artillery pieces.[40]

As the 2nd ACR maneuvered, its supporting division artillery tailored artillery support based on the enemy situation template, which was surprisingly accurate. After the initial breach of the Iraqi defense, 2nd ACR received light contact throughout its 64-kilometer movement on the first day of the ground offensive. When the regiment did receive enemy contact, it was quickly suppressed and neutralized by responsive field artillery support.[41] The support on the first day of the offensive enabled and exemplified the AirLand Battle dynamic of maneuver in that actions demonstrated "the means of concentrating forces at the critical point to achieve the surprise, psychological shock, physical momentum, and moral dominance which enable smaller forces to defeat larger ones."[42] As demonstrated with the artillery raids, the execution of the artillery units in support of 2nd ACR also displayed the fundamentals of firepower as described in AirLand Battle, by facilitating "maneuver by suppressing the enemy's fires and disrupting the movement of his forces. Firepower exploits maneuver by neutralizing the enemy's tactical forces and destroying his ability and will to fight."[43] This was clear as enemy infantry, in entrenched positions, were engaged with US artillery, resulting in "numerous enemy prisoners of war surrendering."[44]

Into the second day of the ground offensive, the weather took a turn for the worse with poor visibility due to dust and haze, severely restricting the employment of close air support. This made the role of the field artillery even more critical as 2nd ACR continued its movement toward the Iraqi premier force, its Republican Guard. Again, the division artillery seamlessly increased artillery support to lead elements is the regiment approached the elite Iraqi unit. AirLand Battle prescribed that "priority of support should change automatically when the commander shifts his main effort."[45]

This not only demonstrated flexibility, but also the AirLand Battle imperative of depth. The doctrine stated, "through the use of depth, a commander obtains the necessary space to maneuver effectively; the necessary time to plan, arrange, and execute operations; and the necessary resources to win."[46] Despite the challenges presented with the poor weather and corresponding reduction in air support, once the Republican Guard was engaged, field artillery fires had a devastating effect. According to the battle damage assessments over a brigade's worth of enemy armored vehicles were destroyed. This is remarkable given the supposed maneuverability of Iraqi armored forces, and the general inability for field artillery to have effects on moving targets.[47]

While the 2nd ACR saw the majority of the action during the initial 48 hours of the invasion of Iraq, the remaining two corps followed and prepared to become the main effort of the operation. Field artillery units were continuing to demonstrate their agility as the corps maneuvered in division columns. Artillery commanders continually reallocated forces to weight the main effort within the division columns, in this case the elements most likely to make contact with enemy forces.[48] Despite minimal enemy contact the agility prepared the divisions "for the rapid concentration of friendly strength against enemy vulnerabilities."[49]

Figure 5.3. US Field Artillery Multiple Launch Rocket System (MLRS) conducting fire mission. Photo courtesy of Morris Swett Digital Collections & Archives, Fires Center of Excellence, Fort Sill, Oklahoma.

Analysis and Conclusion

Intelligence reported that 43 Iraqi divisions prepared to defend along its border, organized into four corps. Despite their overwhelming numerical superiority, the Iraqi army was woefully overmatched and defeated soundly in a little more than four days of ground combat. The coalition force was prepared to face a much more determined enemy.[50] Specifically, the field artillery exemplified the tenets and imperatives of the current doctrine, AirLand Battle. The field artillery heeded "integrating fire support into operations, the most important considerations are adequacy, flexibility, and continuity."[51] They carried out their doctrinal imperatives due to the integrated training led by each division artillery, which had begun long before being notified of deploying. Notification of the deployment focused their training, creating a sense of urgency that enhanced unit cohesion.[52]

Upon arriving in theater and preparing for ground combat, fires facilitated by the division artillery displayed flexibility by reducing enemy defenses with numerous artillery raids. This satisfied the imperative that "engagements must be violent to shock, paralyze, and overwhelm the enemy force quickly. They must be terminated rapidly to allow the force to disperse and avoid effective enemy counterstrikes."[53] The artillery raids completely neutralized the threat of artillery delivered chemical munitions during the initial attack into Iraq and vastly reduced the conventional artillery threat. This undoubtedly had a huge psychological benefit to the coalition forces as one of had neutralized one of the enemy's most dangerous tools. Finally, the division artilleries continually adjusted the task organization of their subordinate units to provide the maximum available support to maneuver elements in contact or probable contact with the enemy. The AirLand Battle imperative which states "priority of support should change automatically when the commander shifts his main effort," though simply stated, takes quite a bit of foresight, common training and understanding, and effective communication.[54] This is exemplified as at one point on the third day of the advance through Iraq, when the 3rd Armored Division Artillery massed fires from three artillery battalions to destroy both an enemy bunker system and the supporting artillery that was a part of the bunker's defense.[55] By the end of the ground offensive, American field artillery had fired more than 58,000 rounds, helping to drive Iraq out of Kuwait.[56]

Overall, the performance of the field artillery was a testament to the training, habitual relationships within each division artillery, their subordinate units, and the comprehension and application of their current doctrine. These units displayed their readiness as a key part of the coalition force as it closed with, destroyed, and achieved a decisive victory over the Iraqi forces. When looked at through the lens of operational art, the division artilleries which participated in Operations Desert Shield and Desert Storm were the organizations that ensured that artillery was the decisive arm, "enabling the achievement of operational and strategic objectives through tactical action in time space and purpose."[57] This will become important to remember as the US Army shifts its focus from counterinsurgency operations to multi-domain operations and an operational environment where the US Army may be challenged by a near peer threat with superior technological capabilities. Using historical case studies as a guidepost, such as Operations Desert Shield/Desert Storm, the US Army Field Artillery must be organized, equipped and trained to demonstrate flexibility, adaptability, synchronization, and lethality if it is to successfully accomplish cross-domain fires in future large-scale ground combat operations.

Notes

1. Mark Milley, 39th Chief of Staff of the Army, "Initial Message to the Army," August 2015, accessed 7 July 2016, https://www.army.mil/e2/rv5_downloads/leaders/csa/Initial_Message_39th_CSA.pdf.

2. Milley.

3. US Army Fires Center of Excellence, *DIVARTY White Paper*, May 2014, 14.

4. US Army Forces Command, *US Army Forces Command Division Artillery Implementation Order*, 9 April 2014, 2.

5. Historically known as "non-divisional units," or what are now known as Field Artillery Brigades, will not be discussed. They generally consist of Multiple Launch Rocket System (MLRS) battalions and High Mobility Artillery Rocket System (HIMARS) battalions. Field Artillery Brigades generally support a corps or field army. The principal missions of non-divisional artillery were the neutralization or destruction of hostile artillery (counterbattery fire), destruction of hostile defenses, long-range interdiction fire, and reinforcement of division artillery fires. This mission has generally remained unchanged between World War II and today.

6. Fires Center of Excellence, *DIVARTY White Paper*, 32.

7. Mark Milley, "Initial Message to the Army."

8. Department of the Army, Army Doctrine Publication (ADP) 3-0, *Operations* (Washington, DC: 2016), 7.

9. ADP 3-0, 8.

10. Army Doctrine Reference Publication (ADRP) 3-0, *Operations* (Washington, DC: 2016), 1-11.

11. ADRP 3-0, 3-10.

12. ADRP 3-0, 3-15.

13. With the modular Brigade Combat Team came the reduction of several brigade level headquarters historically associated with a US division, including the division support command and the division artillery. The intent was to, as the name implies, make brigades modular, self-contained organizations. While the Brigade Combat Team performed well when conducting stability/counterinsurgency operations, the unintended consequence of the deactivation of division artilleries across the army resulted in the atrophy of skills and proficiency of artillerymen and artillery units to perform their military occupational skills and mission essential tasks.

14. Department of the Army, ADRP 3-0, 2-1.

15. "Who we are" United States Army Field Artillery School," accessed 16 October 2016, http://sill-www.army.mil/USAFAS/who-we-are.html. The Field Artillery Branch and the Field Artillery School, headquartered at Fort Sill, Oklahoma, have the shared responsibility for basic and mid-level training for Field Artillery Soldiers. Within the scope of the division artillery, they also contribute to generating and revising field artillery doctrine and gather and disseminate lessons learned from across the force.

16. Theresa Kraus and Frank Schubert, *The Whirlwind War: The United States Army in Operations Desert Shield and Desert Storm,* (Washington, DC: US Army Center of Military History, 1995), 133–34.

17. Kraus and Schubert, 135–36. Iraqi tube artillery consisted of at least six different variants, ranging from 100-mm to 160-mm caliber rounds. For context, artillery less than 100-mm is considered light, 100-mm to 210-mm is medium-caliber, and greater than 210-mm is considered heavy artillery. A common Iraqi artillery piece was the G5, with a range of 39 kilometers. This range exceeded the 30-kilometer maximum range of the M109A2 self-propelled "Paladin", the most common howitzer within the US armored divisions.

18. Kraus and Schubert, *The Whirlwind War,* 135; Kevin M. Woods and Michael R. Pease, *The Mother of All Battles: Saddam Hussein's Strategic Plan for the Persian Gulf War* (New York, NY: Naval Institute Press, 2008), 60.

19. US Army, Third Armored Division Artillery *Historical Summary*, 1991, 2.

20. Carl von Clausewitz, *On War*, ed. Michael Howard and Peter Paret (Princeton, NJ: Princeton University Press, 1984), 101.

21. Third Armored Division Artillery, *Historical Summary*, 2.

22. Department of the Army, Field Manual (FM) 3-09, *Field Artillery Operations and Fire Support* (Washington, DC: 2014), 1-6; Fires Center of Excellence, *DIVARTY White Paper*, 32.

23. Department of the Army, Army Doctrine Publication (ADP) 3-0, *Operations*, 7. Flexibility is "the ability to employ a versatile mix of capabilities, formations, and equipment for conducting operations."

24. Department of the Army, Field Manual (FM) 100-5, *Operations* (Washington, DC: 1986), 16.

25. Robert Scales, *Certain Victory: The US Army in the Gulf War* (Fort Leavenworth, KS: US Army Command and General Staff College Press, 1994), 132.

26. Woods and Pease, *The Mother of All Battles*, 6.

27. Kraus and Schubert, *The Whirlwind War,* 165.

28. US Army Field Artillery School (USAFAS), "Redleg Update," USAFAS PAO, 2017, 22.

29. Department of the Army, FM 3-09, 1-6; Fires Center of Excellence, *DIVARTY White Paper*, 32.

30. Department of the Army, Joint Publication (JP) 3-0, *Operations*, 4-5. Operational reach is "the distance and duration across which a joint force can successfully employ military capabilities."

31. Department of the Army, *ADRP 3-0,* 4-4. Decisive point is "a geographic place, specific key event, critical factor, or function that, when acted upon, allows commanders to gain a marked advantage over an adversary or contribute materially to achieving success."

32. Kraus and Schubert, *The Whirlwind War,* 167.

33. Richard M. Swain, *Lucky War: Third Army in Desert Storm* (Fort Leavenworth, KS: US Army Command and General Staff College Press, 1994), 204.

34. Department of the Army, ADRP 3-0, 4-7.

35. Department of the Army, FM 100-5, 12.

36. FM 100-5, 24.

37. Scales, *Certain Victory,* 223.

38. 210th Field Artillery Brigade, *Summary of Significant Events: Operation Desert Storm* (New York, NY: Department of the Army, March 1991), 2.

39. Scales, *Certain Victory,* 226.

40. USAFAS, "Redleg Update," 22.

41. 210th Field Artillery Brigade, *Summary of Significant Events,* 3.

42. Department of the Army, FM 100-5, 12.

43. FM 100-5, 12.

44. 210th Field Artillery Brigade, *Summary of Significant Events,* 2.

45. Department of the Army, FM 100-5, 44.

46. FM 100-5, 16.

47. 210th Field Artillery Brigade, *Summary of Significant Events,* 1-3.

48. Third Armored Division Artillery, *Historical Summary*, 10.

49. Department of the Army, FM 100-5, 16.

50. Kraus and Schubert, *The Whirlwind War,* 133–135.

51. Department of the Army, FM 100-5, 44.

52. Third Armored Division Artillery, *Historical Summary*, 2.

53. Department of the Army, FM 100-5, 24.

54. FM 100-5, 44.

55. Third Armored Division Artillery, *Historical Summary*, 13.

56. USAFAS, "Redleg Update," 22.

57. Department of the Army, ADRP 3-0, 4-4.

Chapter 6

The Kasserine Pass Battles: Learning to Employ Artillery Effectively in Large-Scale Combat Operations

Major Jeffrey S. Wright

The US Army and the field artillery, following the conclusion of major combat operations in Iraq and Afghanistan in 2003, shifted focus to counterinsurgency and stability operations. While the wisdom gained remains important, leaders within the US Army acknowledge that it does not adequately prepare units for peer and near-peer threats. Some leaders even raised concerns that the artillery's focus on non-standard missions created an atrophy of traditional fires core competencies, reducing the ability to integrate with maneuver forces to meet future threats.[1] To combat this, the US Army and field artillery instituted several corrective actions, to include focusing combat training center rotations on decisive action and the re-establishment of the division artillery (DIVARTY) concept.[2] While improving training concepts and organizational structures remain important, it is critical that leaders reflect on historical examples that highlight challenges and successes in large-scale combat operations.

The Kasserine Pass battles in February 1943, the first major engagement between American and Axis forces in Africa during World War II, provide an opportunity to assess the US Army and artillery's ability to operate in large-scale combat operations. During such operations, commanders "conduct decisive action to seize, retain, and exploit the initiative" through multiple synchronized and simultaneous tasks.[3] Unable to seize and retain the initiative during the initial Axis offensive, American and Allied forces found success when they synchronized efforts "across the breadth and depth of their assigned AOs."[4] The successive defeats suffered in the initial battles resulted from fundamental flaws in Allied dispositions. These included artillery units—and the larger force as a whole—isolated on *djebels* (hills), dispersed too widely to provide mutual support, and generally unprepared for an attack by Axis forces. The success of the Allied defense in Kasserine Pass, in contrast, resulted from effective leadership, the establishment of a combined arms defense in depth, and a concentration of artillery linked by a fire direction center (FDC) and enabled by forward observers to disrupt the attack with rapid, accurate, and devastating massed fires.

A synthesis of joint and US Army doctrine provides a way to analyze the field artillery's effectiveness during the battles. These tools include two Principles of Joint Operations and two tenets of Unified Land Operations. *Mass* entails concentrating combat power effects "at the most advantageous place and time to produce decisive results," and requires "maximum massed fires when and where they are required."[5] *Maneuver* involves the "employment of forces in the operational area through movement in combination with fires to achieve a position of advantage," and requires artillery to "displace rapidly, keep pace with the supported force . . . and position as needed to support future operations."[6] *Flexibility* requires leaders to "adapt to conditions as they change and employ forces in a variety of ways" based on an accurate understanding of their operational environment, equipment, and unit.[7] Finally, the *synchronization* of the artillery with the rest of the combined arms team in time, space, and purpose allows "maximum relative combat power at a decisive place and time."[8]

The Road to the Kasserine Pass Battles

On 13 February 1943, the Allies in North Africa occupied dispersed positions along the Eastern Dorsal of the Atlas Mountains in Central Tunisia. Divided into three sections along a 250-mile front from the north Tunisian coast to El Guettar, the British First Army under Lieutenant General Sir Kenneth Anderson consisted of the British V Corps in the north, the French XIX Corps in the center, and the American II Corps under Major General Lloyd Fredendall in the south.[9] Allied Forces commander General Dwight Eisenhower told Anderson and Fredendall the day before the Axis offensive that he considered the Allied dispositions "as good as could be made pending the development of an actual attack and in view of the great value of holding the forward regions."[10] Despite Eisenhower's optimism, the Allies had struggled since their successful North African arrival.

After landing successfully in North Africa in November 1942, the Allies attempted to defeat Axis forces quickly in Tunisia and capture Tunis. Unfortunately, Axis forces prevented this due to their greater concentration of forces, better air cover, and shorter supply lines.[11] Failing to seize Tunis quickly in late 1942, the original aim of trapping Field Marshall Erwin Rommel's *Afrika Korps* in northern Libya between the First Army and General Sir Bernard Montgomery's Eighth Army could not occur. With General Juergen von Arnim's Fifth Panzer Army well positioned in northern Tunisia, Allied leaders recognized that Montgomery would need to drive Rommel west of Tripoli and into Tunisia.[12] Not content to remain idle in Tunisia while Montgomery attacked, Eisenhower planned an attack by II Corps against Rommel's western flank to inflict casualties on his forces, keeping them off balance while ideally breaking the Axis line of communication.[13] However, the scheduled date of attack (late January 1943) coincided with Montgomery's planned arrival in Tripoli, and fears of a German counterattack against the Americans while the First Army fixed the Fifth Panzer Army led Eisenhower to cancel the operation.[14] Rommel and his *Afrika Korps*, along with Fifth Panzer Army, seized the opportunity to strike in central Tunisia as Montgomery slowly advanced and the Allies gradually built up combat power.[15]

Multiple operations described as struggles "for the advantages of position and initiative" between Fifth Panzer Army and the Allies, specifically the possession of major passes in the Eastern Dorsal took place in January 1942.[16] Already in control of a corridor along the eastern Tunisian coast, the Germans conducted operations to capture additional passes to block future Allied advances and to threaten their lines of communication and supply bases.[17] The Fifth Panzer Army attacked the French XIX Corps successfully on three separate occasions, with poorly trained and equipped French soldiers receiving little support from nearby forces.[18] Throughout these operations, the Allies took several actions that set the stage for the Kasserine Pass battles.

Beginning in late January, Eisenhower instructed Anderson to keep the II Corps on the defensive and to hold the 1st Armored Division as a concentrated, mobile reserve pending Montgomery's arrival in Tunisia.[19] However, Eisenhower acquiesced to Fredendall's plan to conduct several raids with II Corps along the Allied southern flank.[20] Wanting to test newly arrived units of the 1st Armored Division, Fredendall instructed the division commander, Major General Orlando Ward, to establish three more combat commands in addition to Combat Command B (CCB) to perform various missions.[21] While a standard capability of the American triangular division at the time, the formation of combat commands offered great flexibility at the cost of increased complexity and reduced cohesion—significant risk during a division's first experience of combat. Ward soon found his division widely dispersed, with CCB supporting the French XIX Corps and Combat Commands A (CCA), C (CCC), and D (CCD) conducting unsuccessful operations between 24–30 January to seize Maknassy Pass and retain Faid Pass from Axis forces.[22] Instead of potentially controlling two key passes, the Allies held neither. With the 1st Armored Division instructed to "hold as much as possible of the forward areas" in preparation for a March offensive, II Corps found itself ill prepared to hold areas east of the Western Dorsal should the Germans attack—a dangerous situation with the arrival of Rommel's *Afrika Korps* in Tunisia on 4 February.[23] As Eisenhower received a briefing on 13 February, Brigadier General Paul

Robinett, commander of CCB, recommended that Eisenhower withdraw these II Corps units to better defensive positions as soon as possible.[24]

Artillery Integration at the Kasserine Pass Battles

As elements of the Fifth Panzer Army attacked Sidi Bou Zid in the early morning of 14 February, they confronted dispersed and isolated II Corps units. CCA, reinforced by the 168th Infantry Regiment of the 34th Infantry Division, occupied positions in and around Sidi Bou Zid that prevented artillery units from massing fires. Two artillery battalions—the 91st Field Artillery and 2nd Battalion, 17th Field Artillery—occupied exposed positions in the open plain east of Sidi Bou Zid, with two batteries of the 91st isolated from its parent battalion.[25] As Von Arnim's forces attacked from the Faid and Maizila Passes, they encircled II Corps units on two isolated hills and attempted to envelop Allied forces around Sidi Bou Zid.[26] While two of the three firing batteries of the 91st withdrew under pressure in support of CCA, the third outlying battery failed to displace in time and succumbed to German forces.[27] The 2nd Battalion, 17th Field Artillery no longer existed as a functioning combat unit after the initial encounter, losing every artillery piece in a German air attack after failing to displace in time.[28] Any hope of II Corps stopping the Axis assault would require a strong counterattack force.

The II Corps counterattack force sent to destroy the German attackers near Sidi Bou Zid and aid in the withdrawal of CCA on 15 February did not possess the artillery or maneuver strength to accomplish its mission. The Allies counterattacked with a weaker force, made up of CCC and only one armor battalion of CCB from the French XIX Corps sector.[29] Anderson refused to release all of CCB to Ward because he still expected the Axis main effort to attack farther to the north.[30] Only the understrength 68th Field Artillery battalion supported the counterattack force. Although not nearly enough artillery to support the operation, the 68th maneuvered and remained flexible by adapting to different forms of support well, providing counterbattery fires, close support fires directed by observers against enemy tanks, and even direct fire.[31] Despite valiant Allied efforts, Axis forces defeated the counterattack and forced II Corps to withdraw under pressure to the Western Dorsal.[32] With elements of the 5th Panzer Army seizing Sbeitla and the *Afrika Korps* seizing Gafsa and Feriana by 17 February, Axis forces positioned themselves for a final attack through the Western Dorsal passes and into the Allied rear areas of Central Tunisia.[33]

As II Corps and the French XIX Corps withdrew and reconsolidated along the Western Dorsal, Rommel received a directive to attack toward

Le Kef in the Allied rear areas.[34] To accomplish this task, Rommel sent the 21st Panzer Division north of Sbeitla to penetrate the Allied line at Sbiba as the *Afrika Korps* prepared to attempt a similar penetration via the Kasserine Pass to the southwest. Rommel positioned the 10th Panzer Division in a central position near Sbeitla to exploit success wherever the opportunity appeared.[35] As the Axis forces prepared their operations on 19 February, the Allies hurriedly massed infantry and artillery to defend the Sbiba and Kasserine Passes. Eight infantry battalions with three field artillery battalions in support prepared for the defensive operation in Sbiba

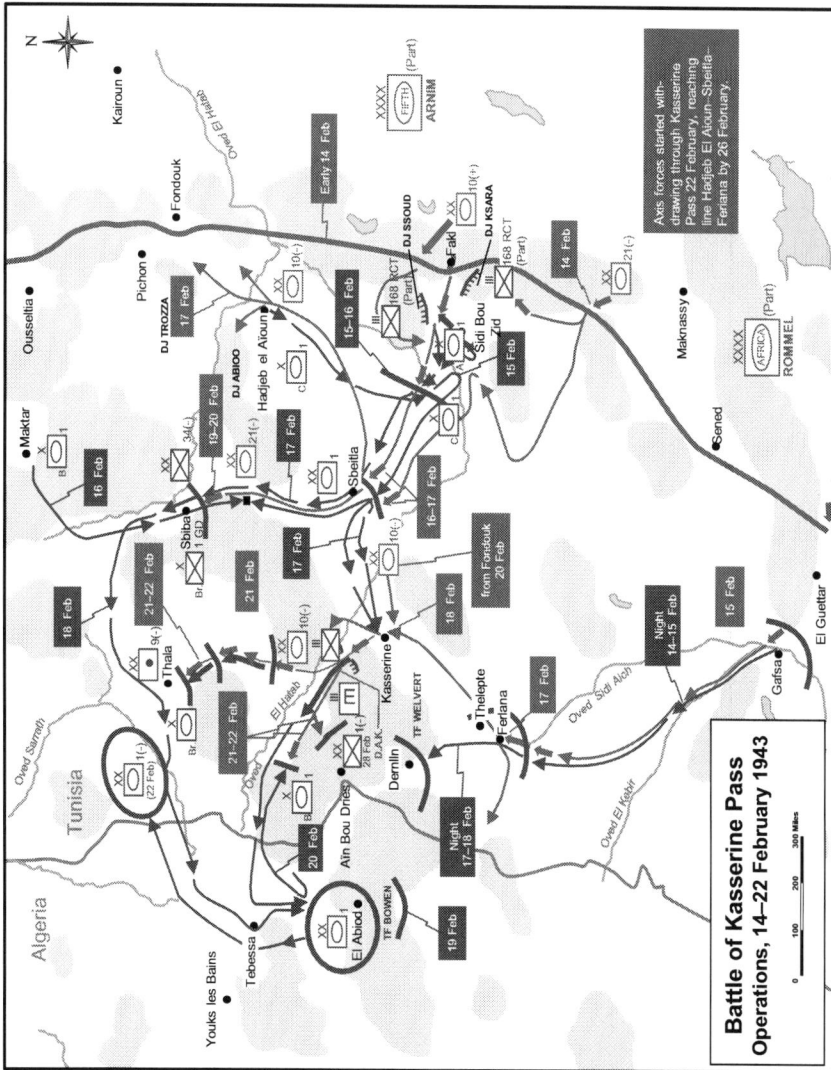

Figure 6.1. Kasserine Pass Battles. Map created by Army University Press.

Pass.[36] Concurrently, Colonel Alexander Stark situated his "Stark Force" of an infantry battalion, an artillery battalion, and an engineer regiment in defensive positions at the opening of the Kasserine Pass.[37] Success for the Allies would depend on how long they could delay the Axis offensive and how many units could arrive in time to serve as reinforcements.

As the 21st Panzer attacked Sbiba Pass, it confronted three well-prepared artillery battalions with more than 100 pre-planned targets along the likely attack route and multiple observers to adjust indirect fires.[38] As the attack on Sbiba failed to penetrate this defensive position of massed and synchronized fires, Rommel ordered the 10th Panzer to reinforce the *Afrika Korps* as it attacked the much smaller Stark Force in the Kasserine Pass.[39] As Stark's defense of the Kasserine Pass went into a second day on 20 February, Rommel ordered the 10th Panzer and *Afrika Korps* to conduct a "side-by-side attack," which finally enabled him to gain control of the pass on the evening of 20 February.[40] Allied senior commanders anticipated their inability to hold and repositioned units in defensive positions on either side of the Bahiret Foussana Valley, west of Kasserine Pass, to limit any Axis exploitation.

Anderson ordered the 16th Infantry Regiment and 7th Field Artillery Battalion of the 1st Infantry Division to block the Axis attack vicinity Bou Chebka on the northwest side of the valley.[41] Meanwhile, the British 26th Armored Brigade established defenses along Highway 17 on the northeast side of the valley while CCB established defensive positions at Djebel el Hamra, covering the passes to the Allied rear areas of Tebessa and Haidra.[42] The arrival of Allied reinforcements and commanders that knew how to employ them as part of a combined arms defense—Robinett and 1st Infantry Division commander Major General Terry Allen—meant that Rommel's forces would face solid defenses on 21–22 February.[43]

As Rommel's forces moved into the Bahiret Foussana Valley, Allied forces blocked their advance and prevented any attempt to exploit victory in the Kasserine Pass. Four artillery battalions supporting CCB and elements of the 1st Infantry Division delivered massed fires that contributed significantly to the defeat of Axis attempts to penetrate at Djebel el Hamra and Bou Chebka. Supporting CCB, the 27th Field Artillery alone fired over 2,000 rounds, while Colonel Clift Andrus—the 1st Infantry DIVARTY commander—synchronized counterattacks with fires from the 7th and 33rd Field Artillery battalions.[44]

On the northeast side of the valley, the 10th Panzer advanced toward Thala against the British 26th Armored Brigade. Possessing two batteries of artillery, the brigade withdrew twice to subsequent defensive positions before taking final defensive positions just south of Thala.[45] These retrograde operations provided time for the 9th DIVARTY under Brigadier General S. LeRoy Irwin to arrive, establish mutually supporting positions, and assist the British in defeating the German attack. Bringing with him three artillery battalions and two cannon companies, Irwin established a "three-mile arc" to deliver massed fires.[46] Rommel believed that the arrival of this additional artillery portended an impending counterattack and ordered all Axis units to withdraw from the Kasserine Pass on the night of 22 February.[47]

Analyzing Field Artillery Employment

While American artillery failed to mass fires effectively at the beginning of the Kasserine Pass battles due to poor unit dispositions preventing mutual support, II Corps weighted the main effort sufficiently with artillery during the defensive battles at Sbiba, Djebel el Hamra, Bou Chebka, and Thala. The failure to weight either the forces in vicinity of Sidi Bou Zid or the counterattack force caused one senior leader to write, "the concentration of artillery fire is a prerequisite of success."[48] The ineffective combat command structure of the 1st Armored Division contributed to the initial inability of supporting artillery to deliver massed fires. Excessively dispersed artillery units could not provide mutual support, particularly because the 1st Armored Division created two additional ad hoc combat commands, CCC and CCD.[49] Artillery battalions had the tools to mass, but senior leaders following the campaign recommended keeping the three division artillery battalions in mutual support, to employ artillery "as a battalion and not as separate batteries," and to maintain centralized control at the division-level in order to mass fires at the decisive point.[50]

Maneuverability can enable artillery to avoid counterbattery fire, enhance survivability, and ensure guns stay in supporting range of ground combat units. Senior artillery leaders participating in the battles stressed at the conclusion of the Tunisian Campaign the need for artillery units to improve survivability in order to support future combat operations effectively. Topics of discussion included multiple avenues of displacement, anti-tank operations, tube dispersion, and local security.[51] Some artillery units, like the 91st and 2nd Battalion, 17th Artillery, failed in this regard during the Battle of Sidi Bou Zid. Others, such as the 68th, effectively supported their maneuver brethren while maintaining survivability due to effective leadership and solid training.[52]

The Allies initially failed to demonstrate flexibility by refusing to withdraw the First Army from the Eastern Dorsal to better defensive posi-

Figure 6.2. A 105-mm howitzer and crew from B Battery, 33rd Field Artillery Battalion, prepare to fire at advancing German infantry during the Battle of Kasserine Pass, February 1943. Photo courtesy of US Army Center of Military History.

tions and await favorable weather and additional combat power. Flexible and adaptive leaders must possess "comfort with ambiguity and uncertainty," and an "ability to rapidly adjust while continuously assessing the situation."[53] Eisenhower acknowledged his unwillingness to change the plan based on knowledge of the operational environment after the war, "had I been willing at the end of November to admit temporary failure and pass to the defensive, no attack against us could have achieved even temporary success."[54] Such a willingness to change could have prevented the positioning of dispersed artillery units in non-mutually supportive positions before the Axis attack on 14 February. Only until successive defeats on 14–15 February did Anderson acknowledge the precariousness of the situation and order a withdrawal to the Western Dorsal. As the field artillery battalions reconsolidated and moved within mutual supporting distance, senior artillery leaders recognized they could employ their units according to doctrine to mass fires through FDCs and observed fires.

Finally, effective synchronization of artillery with other combat arms did not take place until the battles of Sbiba, Djebel el Hamra, Bou Chebka, and Thala largely because senior leaders familiar with synchronizing artillery with maneuver were not present to coordinate such actions. Two weeks before the Axis attack on Sidi Bou Zid, the 1st Armored DIVARTY commander took command of the improvised CCD, depriving the division of a senior artillery commander and his staff to synchronize fires effectively.[55] As senior artillery commanders (like Colonel Andrus of the 1st Infantry DIVARTY and Brigadier General Irwin of the 9th DIVARTY) arrived to coordinate artillery fires with maneuver forces around Bou Chebka and Thala, Allied forces exercised effective synchronization to defeat Axis attacks.

Conclusion

Initial employment of artillery in the Kasserine Pass battles suffered from the same problems as the larger Allied force. As Major General Ernest Harmon—the new 1st Armored Division commander following the battles—summarized in his Tunisian Campaign report, the division "was never employed as a unit except in the final phase . . . the division had arrived piecemeal and had been used piecemeal."[56] As commanders and leaders conduct decisive action during large-scale combat operations to seize, retain, and exploit the initiative, fires weight the decisive operation or main effort to ensure mission success. This remains particularly important at the commencement of large-scale combat operations, as there is a high probability that US Army forces will need to defend against an enemy with locally superior capabilities.[57] During future large-scale combat operations, successful employment of American field artillery requires an array of forces that sets the conditions to mass, flexibility by adapting to conditions as they change in the operational environment, maneuverability to gain an advantage, and synchronized action with maneuver forces to achieve greater effects. The initial attacks by Axis forces during the Kasserine Pass battles caught the II Corps unprepared to employ its excellent fire support system developed from sound, practical doctrine and procedures. As the operation progressed, II Corps learned from its mistakes and employed artillery to enable Allied victory.

Notes

1. Sean MacFarland, Michael Shields, and Jeffrey Snow, "White Paper: The King and I: The Impending Crisis in Field Artillery's Ability to Provide Fire Support to Maneuver Commander," White Paper, United States Army, 2007, 1.

2. Dennis Steele, "Decisive-Action Training Rotations: 'Old School Without Going Back in Time,'" *Army* (February 2013): 28-32; Scott R. Gourley "Return of Division Artillery Stokes the Fires," *Fires*, November–December 2014, accessed 18 May 2018, http://sill-www.army.mil/firesbulletin/current/06_Gourley.html.

3. Department of the Army, Field Manual (FM) 3-0, *Operations* (Washington, DC: 2017) 5-3.

4. FM 3-0, 5-5.

5. Joint Chiefs of Staff, Joint Publication (JP) 3-0, *Joint Operations* (Washington, DC: 2017) A-2; Department of the Army, Army Doctrine Reference Publication (ADRP) 3-09, *Fires* (Washington, DC: 2012) 1–9

6. Joint Chiefs of Staff, JP 3-0, GL-12; Department of the Army, ADRP 3-09, 1–9.

7. Department of the Army, Army Doctrine Publication (ADP) 3-0, *Operations* (Washington, DC: 2017) 10; Department of the Army, ADRP 3-09, 1–5.

8. Department of the Army, ADRP 3-09, 1–5.

9. Omar Bradley, *A Soldier's Story* (New York: Henry Holt and Company, 1951), 24.

10. George F. Howe, *Northwest Africa: Seizing the Initiative in the West, United States Army in World War II: The Mediterranean Theater of Operations* (Washington, DC: Office of the Chief of Military History, 1957), 405.

11. Carlo D'Este, *World War II in the Mediterranean* (Chapel Hill: Algonquin Books of Chapel Hill, 1990), 7–10; Gerhard Weinberg, *A World at Arms: A Global History of World War II* (New York: Cambridge University Press, 1994), 435.

12. Howe, *Northwest Africa,* 347; D'Este, *World War II in the Mediterranean,* 8, 12.

13. Howe, 349–50.

14. Howe, 353; US Military Academy, *The War in North Africa, Part 2 (The Allied Invasion)* (West Point: United States Military Academy AG Press, 1947), 24.

15. Weinberg, *A World at Arms,* 441–42, Howe, *Northwest Africa,* 349.

16. Howe, 386.

17. US Military Academy, *The War in North Africa, Part 2,* 23; Howe, 386; Orr Kelly, *Meeting the Fox* (New York: John Wiley and Sons, 2002), 149.

18. Kelly, 154; US Military Academy, 25–26; Rick Atkinson, *An Army at Dawn* (New York, NY: Henry Holt and Company, 2002), 308.

19. Howe, *Northwest Africa,* 384; Atkinson, *An Army at Dawn,* 305.

20. Atkinson, 305.

21. Kelly, *Meeting the Fox,* 155–56.

22. Atkinson, *An Army at Dawn,* 305–07, 310–12; Howe, *Northwest Africa,* 392.

23. Howe, *Northwest Africa,* 399; US Military Academy, *The War in North Africa,* 27–28.

24. Kelly, *Meeting the Fox,* 175.

25. Howe, *Northwest Africa,* 411; George F. Howe, *The Battle History of the 1st Armored Division* (Washington, DC: Combat Forces Press, 1954), 145; Kelly, 176–77.

26. Atkinson, *An Army at Dawn,* 340, 342; Bradley, *A Soldier's Story,* 25.

27. Howe, *The Battle History of the 1st Armored Division,* 146, 149.

28. Kelly, *Meeting the Fox,* 187–88; Atkinson, *An Army at Dawn,* 340; Howe, *Northwest Africa,* 412.

29. Atkinson, *An Army at Dawn,* 349; Howe, *Northwest Africa,* 418–19.

30. Howe, 416; Atkinson, 349.

31. Howe, *The Battle History of the 1st Armored Division,* 155–63.

32. Atkinson, *An Army at Dawn,* 352–53; Howe, *Northwest Africa,* 423–24.

33. Howe, 426–27.

34. Howe, 440–41.

35. Atkinson, *An Army at Dawn,* 369.

36. Howe, *Northwest Africa,* 442–43.

37. Howe, 442–443; Atkinson, *An Army at Dawn,* 366–67.

38. Howe, 452–53; Kelly, *Meeting the Fox,* 234; Atkinson, 378.

39. Atkinson, 378; Howe, 459.

40. Howe, 459; Atkinson, 372.

41. "A Factual Summary of the Combat Operations of the 1st Infantry Division in North Africa and Sicily During World War II (Extract)," in *Kasserine Pass Battles: Readings I, Part 2,* ed. Harold W. Nelson, Roger Cirillo (Washington, DC: US Army Center of Military History, 1993), 15–16.

42. Howe, *Northwest Africa,* 457–58.

43. Paul M. Robinett, "Combat Command B, 1st Armored Division, Operations Report, Bahiret Foussana Valley, 20–25 February 1943," in *Kasserine Pass Battles: Readings I, Part 2,* 2; Atkinson, *An Army at Dawn,* 379; Howe, *Northwest Africa,* 462–63.

44. Robinett, "Combat Command B," 2; Terry Allen, "1st Infantry Division, Summary of Activities, January–March 1943, and Division Commander's Notes," in *Kasserine Pass Battles: Readings I, Part 2,* 3.

45. Howe, *Northwest Africa,* 464–66.

46. Robert C. Baldridge, "How Artillery Beat Rommel After Kasserine," *Field Artillery,* May–August 2002, 49–50; Atkinson, *An Army at Dawn,* 385.

47. Atkinson, 385–87.

48. Headquarters, Thirteenth Armored Regiment to Commanding General, 1st Armored Division, 8 July 1943, Dwight D. Eisenhower Presidential Library, US Army: Unit Records, 1917–1950, 1st Armored Division, 1940–1946, Box 16, 1st Armored Division Misc. Staff Section Battle Lessons 1943.

49. D'Este, *World War II in the Mediterranean,* 10, 18; Kelly, *Meeting the Fox,* 155–56.

50. Headquarters, 27th Armored Field Artillery Battalion to Commanding General, 1st Armored Division, 16 July 1943, Dwight D. Eisenhower Presidential Library, US Army: Unit Records, 1917–1950, 1st Armored Division, 1940–1946, Box 16, 1st Armored Division Misc. Staff Section Battle Lessons 1943; Headquarters, 91st Armored Field Artillery Battalion to G3, 1st Armored Division, 10 July 1943, Dwight D. Eisenhower Presidential Library, US Army: Unit Records, 1917–1950, 1st Armored Division, 1940–1946, Box 16, 1st Armored Division Misc. Staff Section Battle Lessons 1943; "Lessons from Tunisian Campaign, 1943," in *Kasserine Pass Battles: Readings II, Part 3*, ed. Harold W. Nelson and Roger Cirillo (Washington, DC: US Army Center of Military History, 1993), 28; Boyd L. Dastrup, *King of Battle: A Branch History of the US Army's Field Artillery* (Fort Monroe: United States Army Training and Doctrine Command, Office of the Command Historian, 1992), 210–11.

51. 27th Armored Field Artillery; Headquarters, 1st Infantry Division to Commanding General, Allied Force Headquarters, 9 July 1943, Dwight D. Eisenhower Presidential Library, US Army: Unit Records, 1917–1950, 1st Infantry Division, 1942–1945, Box 756, 1st Infantry Division Reports on Combat Experience and Battle Lessons for Training Purposes; Headquarters, 68th Armored Field Artillery Battalion to Commanding General, 1st Armored Division, 10 July 1943, Dwight D. Eisenhower Presidential Library, US Army: Unit Records, 1917–1950, 1st Armored Division, 1940–1946, Box 16, 1st Armored Division Misc. Staff Section Battle Lessons 1943.

52. Howe, *The Battle History of the 1st Armored Division,* 162–65.

53. Department of the Army, Army Doctrine Reference Publication (ADRP) 3-0, *Operations* (Washington, DC: 2017), 3–9.

54. Atkinson, *An Army at Dawn,* 391.

55. Atkinson, 347.

56. Headquarters, First Armored Division to Commanding General, Allied Force Headquarters, 13 July 1943, Dwight D. Eisenhower Presidential Library, US Army: Unit Records, 1917–1950, 1st Armored Division, 1940–1946, Box 16, 1st Armored Division Misc. Staff Section Battle Lessons 1943.

57. Department of the Army, FM 3-0, 5-5.

Chapter 7
Operational Artillery in the Korean War
Major G. Kirk Alexander

Exhausted American Soldiers lined the Naktong River in a series of observation posts to provide early warning and to direct and adjust artillery fire missions to disrupt the next enemy attack. Mindful of every noise, no one could be sure where or when the North Koreans would attempt another attack the fragile Pusan Perimeter, the final effort to buy time to allow the United Nations (UN) to build up forces in Korea. The summer months and lack of rain had decreased the river depth to three feet in several areas, almost negating the river as a defensive obstacle. The Naktong River defenders were aware of these conditions and anticipated a large-scale North Korean attack. As expected, incoming artillery rained in on the men and broke the silence, a standard precursor to a North Korean attack. According to plan, fire support officers executed designated artillery and air targets on likely enemy crossing points to increase their responsiveness. The plan did not account for every aspect of the enemy's attack.

Forward observers, observation battalions and observation aircraft were all refining targets and adjusting calls for fire to compensate for this lack of predictability. Requests for indirect artillery support funneled into the fire support net monitored by the corps artillery headquarters. They maintained centralized control of all artillery units not under the control of the division to permit maximum integration of all available assets on the targets. Meanwhile, the artillerymen were at work slamming rounds into their howitzers and guns in an attempt to keep up with enemy offensive. The harsh Korean terrain thwarted any attempt to reposition the howitzers. Regardless, they delivered massive amounts of artillery at an alarming rate, sometimes exceeding the howitzer's physical capacity resulting in damage to the tubes. North Korean soldiers struggled to maintain their formations and crossing sites, immediately noting the accuracy and effectiveness of the volleys. Additionally, the North Koreans found their own artillery under intense bombardment, which limited their ability to continue to the attack. As the North Koreans began to disperse and retreat from the Naktong, they presented the UN's artillery forward observers with additional targets of opportunity. Divisional artillery battalions and close air support attempted to finish the rest of the enemy forces. Unfortunately, just as the artillerymen were about to deliver another destructive volley, their position was attacked by an infiltration force that had slipped through the line. Transitioning to direct fire mode, the artillerymen attempted to depress the tubes to engage dismounted enemy breaching the defensive wire. As enemy armor, artillery, and machine gun fire increased, the artillerymen abandoned their howitzers to take up defensive positions in nearby buildings. Ultimately, it was a lost cause. Forced to evacuate the firing point, the artillerymen left the howitzers to the North Koreans.[1]

This depiction is representative of a number of the conflicts that took place along the Pusan defensive line between 1 August 1950 and 1 September 1950. Primarily, it describes the employment of artillery in the defense against an enemy with seemingly limitless manpower. United States artillery in the Korean War was a mix of towed and self-propelled howitzers and guns that delivered projectiles up to 15 miles away upon designated targets.[2] The ability to employ these weapons at the most basic level hinged on the interaction of the three components of the artillery team: the observer that locates the target, the fire direction center that computes the data to engage the target, and the actual howitzer or gun team that executes the mission. Massed fires were concentrating the effects of more than one howitzer or gun on a single target. Artillery battalions of up to 18 howitzers could coordinate these effects on a single target internally. However, on a larger scale, synchronizing multiple battalions in this way added another level of complexity. These massed effects did not simply happen in the Korean War; extensive target planning, adequate command and control structures to coordinate efforts, and the flexibility to engage targets of opportunity with divisional and non-divisional artillery made them possible. Centralized control at the battalion and corps levels permitted the controlling authority to determine the most lucrative targets to engage with the full complement of artillery and close air support.[3] Additionally, the survivability of artillery battalions was critical to ensure the availability of all battalions at any time. Security of artillery forces was lacking in the beginning of the conflict. During the Pusan defense, North Korean forces overran the UN's artillery positions several times, but UN forces fought to regain lost ground with the infantry. By 1951, the artillery battalions corrected or mitigated the majority of the security concerns.[4] Despite the security shortfalls of the artillery in support of the Pusan Perimeter, operational artillery remained highly effective at repelling the human wave attacks of North Korean forces.[5]

The Korean War provides a unique window to examine the effective use of artillery in large-scale combat operations because of the unprecedented amount of artillery rounds fired per gun during the conflict.[6] At times, the US Army artillery fired five times the daily expenditure rates of World War II.[7] This heavy rate of fire was necessary because of a number of factors. The nature of defensive fires in protection of dispersed out-posts, particularly against the sheer number of North Korean and Chinese militants, forced the UN forces to make up for their lack of artillery units through increased rates of fire for long durations. Additionally, in order for the UN's counter-fire to be effective against heavily fortified static North Korean and Chinese artillery positions, it resorted to precision fires that used high volumes of artillery to destroy these positions.[8] Therefore, the UN forces had to evaluate their current methods for providing effective artillery support in response to these threats. During this process, leaders drew upon lessons from World War II, recommendations during the inter-war period, and adaptations during the Korean War conflict. In 2013, as the US Army reorganizes after ten years of counter insurgency warfare and looks at conducting multi-domain operations, it is time to reevaluate our current ability to provide massed artillery against a near peer threat during large-scale combat operations.

The Korean War: A Brief Synopsis

On 25 June 1950, North Korea launched an invasion across the 38th Parallel. US President Harry S. Truman almost immediately responded

Figure 7.1. Gun crew of B Battery, 61st Field Artillery Battalion, 1st Cavalry Division fire their 105-mm howitzer across the Naktong River on North Korean troops, 7 August 1950. Photo courtesy of US Army Center of Military History.

with the commitment of air and naval forces to support the Republic of Korea's defense. Two days later, the UN Security Council passed a resolution to aid in the defense of South Korea and President Truman (without consulting Congress) approved the deployment of two Army divisions from Japan to Korea. He failed to get a congressional declaration of war though Congress did little to stop the intervention. The North Korean assault continued and by 28 June, Kim Il Sung's forces seized Seoul, the capital of South Korea. General Douglas MacArthur, nominated as commander of UN military forces in Korea, committed Task Force Smith, an unprepared force of approximately 500 men to delay the North Koreans while a larger force deployed to Pusan. In the ensuing battle with North Korean forces, Task Force Smith lost half of its combat force and withdrew under pressure. Fortunately, the UN's air superiority provided a marked advantage to delay the north, but it became clear that a larger ground force would be required to stop the North Korean People's Army. The UN committed additional US divisions to reinforce the delaying action, but they were forced east of the Naktong River into the Pusan defensive perimeter.[9]

Holding firm within the Pusan Perimeter, UN forces under General MacArthur initiated an amphibious landing at Inchon on 15 September 1950 to regain Seoul and cut the supply lines of the North Korean forces in the south. This allowed the UN's forces to launch an offensive that eventually pushed North Korean forces back to the 38th Parallel. After crossing the 38th Parallel and conducting amphibious landings in the east, UN forces decimated remaining North Korean forces and reunited the peninsula. This prompted Chinese intervention, which launched three massive offensives against the UN forces and eventually recaptured Seoul in early January 1951.[10]

Over the next month, UN forces withdrew south of Wonju to Line D, approximately the 37th Parallel. Able to hold this line, the UN conducted several counteroffensives and stopped the Chinese Fourth Offensive in mid-February. Capitalizing on their momentum, the UN forces conducted two more offensives that recaptured Seoul on 14 March 1951 and re-established the UN front along the 38th Parallel. Two more offensive operations allowed the UN forces to move 30 miles north of the 38th Parallel to establish a defensive line along Phase Line Kansas to prepare for another Chinese offensive.[11]

The Chinese began their Fifth Offensive on 22 April 1951, resulting in some of the most extreme fighting of the Korean War. The offensive forced the UN forces back to No Name Line, but ultimately they held there. On 16 May 1951, the Battle of the Soyang River and other battles along the

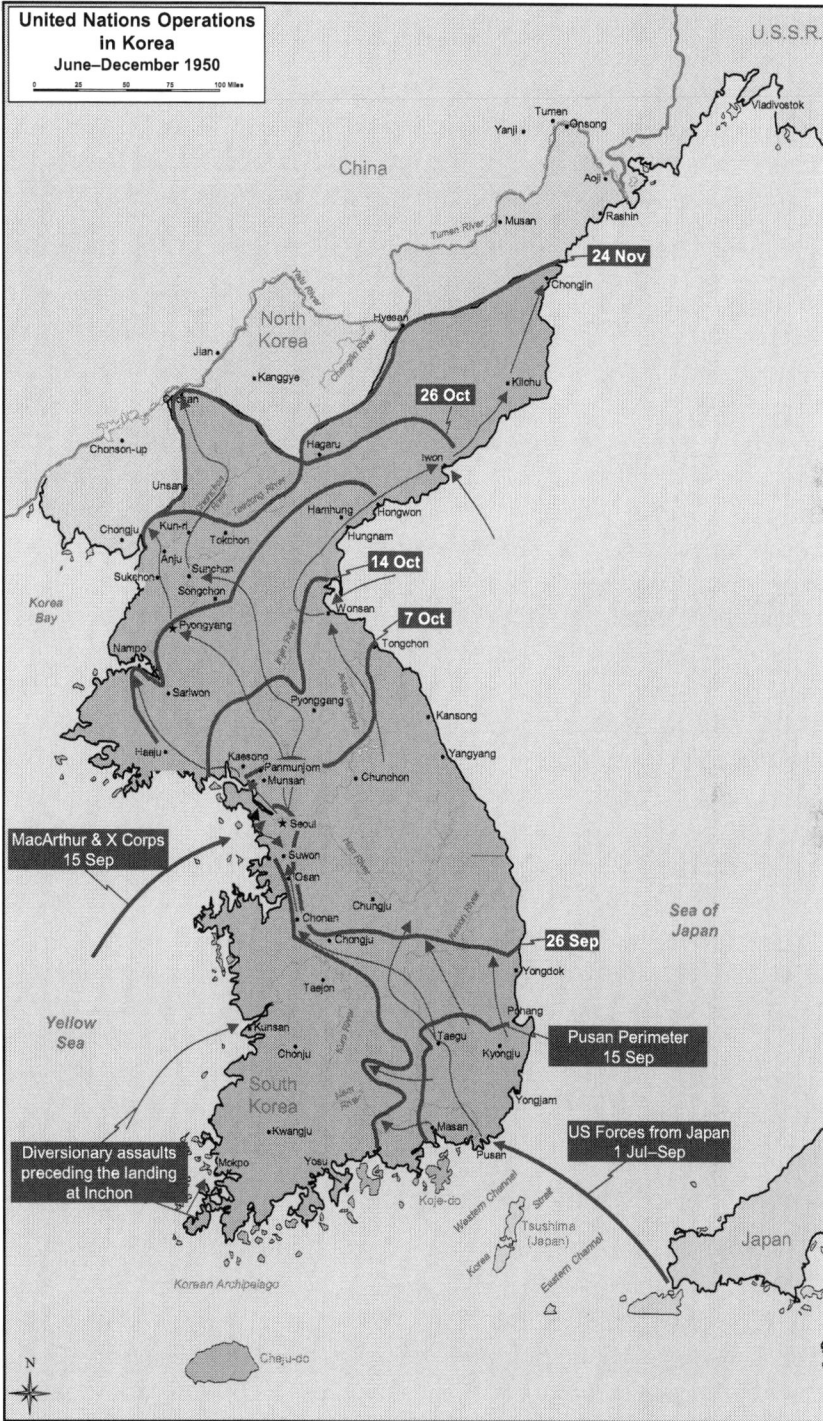

United Nations Operations
in Korea
June–December 1950

U.S.S.R.

Vladivostok

China

Tuman
Yanji   Onsong

Aoji

Tuman River   Musan   Rashin

24 Nov

Chongjin

North
Korea   Hyesan

Jian

Kanggye

26 Oct

Kilchu

Chonson-up

Hagaru

Iwon

Unsan

Hamhung   Hongwon

Chongju   Kun-ri   Tokchon   Hungnam

Anju   Sunchon   14 Oct

Sukchon   Songchon

Korea
Bay   Wonsan   7 Oct

Pyongyang   Tongchon

Nampo

Sariwon   Pyonggang

Kansong

Haeju   Kaesong   Yangyang

Panmunjom   Chunchon

Munsan

Seoul

MacArthur & X Corps
15 Sep   Suwon

Osan

Chunju   Sea of
Japan

Chonan

Chongju   26 Sep

Yongdok

Taejon

Pohang

Yellow
Sea   Kunsan   Taegu   Kyongju

Chonju   Pusan Perimeter
15 Sep

South
Korea   Yongjam

Kwangju   Masan   US Forces from Japan
1 Jul–Sep

Diversionary assaults   Mokpo   Pusan
preceding the landing   Yosu
at Inchon   Koje-do

Tsushima
(Japan)   Japan

Korean Archipelago

N

Cheju-do

Figure 7.2. United Nations operations, July–December 1950. Map recreated
by Army University Press, courtesy of the US Military Academy, West Point. 123

No Name Line forced the Chinese and North Korean forces to withdraw to the 38th Parallel by mid-May 1951. UN forces began a final summer offensive that pushed the Chinese and North Koreans back to beyond the Wyoming-Kansas Line where UN forces held on 22 June 1951. Negotiations for an armistice began at Kaesong, but took two years to complete. The final armistice signaled the end of active hostilities on 27 July 1953.[12]

The Fundamental Principles of using Artillery in the Defense

This section examines the factors of operational artillery during the defense of the Pusan Perimeter, the defense along Soyang River in May 1951, and along the 38th Parallel during the negotiations up to the armistice.[13] The lessons from the Second World War validated the importance of artillery in modern conflict and presented a number of recommendations for improving its effects on the battlefield. The structure of the force and doctrine after World War II centered on the concept of unlimited warfare using overwhelming firepower of nuclear weapons.[14] Artillery officers recommended increasing the number of artillery pieces in the organic division artillery formations, reestablishing the corps artillery headquarters as the command and control element for synchronizing fires, and pushing for more self-propelled artillery.[15] However, the drawdown of the US Army, the lack of training associated with the drain of experienced leaders, and overreliance on atomic weapons during the period before the Korean War hampered the implementation of these lessons.[16] Additionally, equipment and ammunition shortages compounded the problem. American military forces became accustomed with trading firepower for maneuver, preferring to remain static in the defense.[17] In some cases, the US Army would have to relearn the lessons of World War II to take advantage of the Army at hand. Operational leaders utilized artillery most effectively by massing divisional and non-divisional artillery forces to support the maneuver battalions, establishing unity of command to facilitate massed fires and ensuring artillery survivability. The fundamental principles of defensive artillery fire support as employed by large unit commanders in the Korean War were mass, unity of command, and security.

Using Artillery in the Defense: Mass

On 16 May 1951, amidst the North Korean and Chinese Second Spring Offensive, the US X Corps along with two Republic of Korea (ROK) Corps found themselves nose-to-nose along the Soyang River with a numerically superior force consisting of two Chinese Army Groups and two North Korean Corps.[18] The UN forces had just regained Seoul in March and repelled a communist attack against the South Korean capital in April. The X Corps occupied defensive positions along No Name Line and communist forces focused their attacks against them with over 15 divisions. General James Van Fleet, then commander of the Eighth Army, allocated an additional three battalions of corps artillery to General Ned Almond's X Corps giving him ten divisional artillery battalions, six battalions of corps artillery, and five additional reinforcing artillery battalions. Van Fleet increased the daily rate of fire enabling some of the battalions to fire in excess of 10,000 rounds during a single engagement. An excess of 1,000 sorties of close air support complemented these fires, all coordinated to maximize effects.[19] As thousands of Chinese troops flooded the X Corps' sector, a barrage of massed artillery fires and close air support stopped the offensive cold in its tracks.

During the Battle of the Soyang River, heavy concentrations of massed fires stopped a numerically superior enemy on the offensive. Commanders were no longer limited to directed ammunition restrictions and could finally maximize the number of rounds that the artillery fired.[20] The combination of more rounds to fire and accurately concentrated artillery proved extremely lethal. At the time of the Korean War, the 1949 Army *Field Manual 100-5, Operations* codified the concept of mass as a recognized principle of war. It defined mass as "the concentration of superior forces, on the ground, at sea, and in the air, at the decisive place and time, and their employment in a decisive direction" to create the conditions essential to victory.[21]

Applied to artillery, the concentration of effects from multiple artillery battalions as well as air support assets at the decisive place and time to provide an advantage over the enemy equaled massed fires. In order to concentrate and synchronize the effects of artillery and air support required detailed integrated fire planning, overlapping observation platforms and artillery mobility facilitated the defense. Behind the scenes of the UN's response was a honed artillery machine forged from their experiences from the past year's conflict and grounded in tested World War II doctrine.

At the time of the Korean War, there was no doctrinal definition of massed fires, but the clarification of the term emerged throughout the doctrine of the period.[22] The 1953 War Department Field Manual (FM) 6-20, *Artillery Tactics and Technics* described the use of artillery with respect to mass as a principle of employment: "The proper tactical and technical employment of artillery fire power exploits the principles of mass and maneuver. Artillery weapons and units are not physically massed in the manner implied for ground gaining arms; rather artillery is so employed as to provide the maximum capability for massing its *fires* when and where required to support the action of the ground gaining arms."[23] Essentially, the artillery should concentrate as many artillery weapons as possible on targets that are decisive to the maneuver element.

The relative lack of artillery in comparison to World War II led Army leaders to increase the amount of artillery rounds fired from each system. Comparatively, hardly any other modern war had higher rates of fire to compensate for this shortfall.[24] These two elements of concentrated effects and increased firing rates directly led to the successes of the defensive battles of August and September 1950 of the Pusan Perimeter and later at the Soyang River.[25]

Fire planning in the Korean War was not much different from that used in World War II. A fire plan was "the tactical plan for using the weapons of a unit so that their fire missions will be coordinated."[26] Doctrinally, coordinating fire missions were essential to concentrated fires because it synthesized the current targeting intelligence, prioritized the engagement of these targets, forecasted the logistical requirements, and synchronized the available artillery formations.[27] This process involved every member of the artillery team. The observers within the maneuver battalions nominated and refined targets synchronized with maneuver for execution while the unit artillery headquarters took these targets and determined the best way to support their execution through positioning of unit formations, type of missions required to achieve the desired effects, and the logistical support plan. These plans occurred at all levels with the subordinate plans feeding the higher operational picture.

One of the essential elements of fire planning was prearranged fires, "planned fire which is to be delivered at a specified time or for which a need for rapid delivery can be anticipated and for which firing data are prepared in advance and kept current."[28] Essentially, these fires were pre-determined targets that were on call from the supported unit. To develop these targets, artilleryman analyzed aerial photos or actually observed the terrain, determined the most likely enemy avenue of approach, and pre-coordinated the targets with maneuver.[29] This pre- coordination allowed for faster responsiveness and clearance of fires. In the defense, especially in Korea, prearranged fires on likely enemy avenues of approach delayed and reduced the effectiveness of enemy offensive operations against an established perimeter.[30]

Ultimately, pre-planned artillery could not completely account for every place that the artillery units planned to engage the enemy. Often artillery targets emerged that were absent from the initial fire plan and required a certain amount of flexibility to engage. Artillery planners attempted to build this type of flexibility into the fire plan. Planners would designate supporting artillery units to provide fires specifically for targets of opportunity while others would provide prearranged fires.[31] Engaging targets of opportunity required an extensive communication network that linked the observers with the firing unit.[32] While these fires were more difficult to coordinate and less responsive, they provided the much needed flexibility to engage an ever-elusive target set.

Underpinning the execution of fire planning was the ability to acquire targets for both prearranged fires and targets of opportunity. The integration of forward observers at the tactical level and the observation battalions and observation aircraft at higher levels was essential to providing integrated targeting and accurate target locations for execution. Each of these elements played a unique role in synchronizing effective massed fire and providing accurate target data throughout the defenses in Korea. During the Korean conflict, forward observers were resident to the artillery formations with a section in the divisional artillery for each maneuver battalion.[33] Representing their maneuver elements, they refined and nominated targets for preplanned artillery fires and effectively integrated them into the defensive plans. These observers were skilled in calling fires for targets of opportunity as well as directing close air support. They served as a direct link between the maneuver battalions and the direct support artillery headquarters. Whereas the observers were the link with direct support artillery headquarters, the Observation Battalion was the link with non-divisional and corps artillery headquarters.

Observation battalions provided additional observation capabilities beyond what the forward observers provided. During World War II, the corps observation battalions provided limited coverage due to the wide frontages and robust corps zones. Post-war organization increased the number of observation batteries in the battalions from two to three as well as provided a counter-mortar radar platoon to each battery to better meet the requirements for wide front.[34] Observation battalions were responsible for six principle missions: Location of hostile artillery, registration and adjustment of friendly artillery, collection of information, conduct and coordination of corps artillery survey operations, comparative calibration of friendly artillery, and provision of ballistic meteorological data for friendly artillery and for sound ranging.[35] Unfortunately, the First Field Artillery Observation Battalion would be the only one available in theater until 1953.[36] This left the forward observers and observation aircraft to do most of the observation.

The Korean topography was not ideal for quickly moving artillery units and supplies throughout the battlefield. The harsh landscape, inadequate improved roads, and extreme weather conditions restricted maneuver and limited logistical support.[37] The ability to quickly mass fires and protect the artillery laid in the flexibility of the artillery formations to meet the challenges posed by the terrain. Tactical mobility was the ability of the artillery formations to keep up with maneuver and traverse the terrain to maintain direct support artillery fires for maneuver.[38] Strategic mobility was the ability to quickly reposition artillery formations throughout the theater of operations to support the decisive operation, as well as providing the logistical train associated with drastically repositioning forces.[39] Strategic and tactical mobility in the Korean War required a mix of self-propelled and towed systems. Self-propelled artillery was a huge advantage for tactical mobility in the Korean War because of its ability to traverse rough terrain over the large fronts.[40] However, towed systems were lighter, easier to emplace and conceal, and were generally perceived as more strategically mobile.[41] The static nature of the defense in Korea coupled with the rugged terrain led to relying on the tactical mobility of the self-propelled systems that only existed in the non-divisional artillery formations. This allowed the corps the flexibility and mobility to quickly reinforce and augment divisional massed fires throughout the conflict. The mobility and range of self-propelled artillery made it possible to engage targets from greater distances and then quickly withdraw before coming into direct contact with the enemy.[42] Unfortunately, these systems were in short supply during the Korean War.

Up to April 1951, ammunition shortages restricted the number of rounds that artillery units could fire daily. The Army lifted this restriction just prior to the Battle of the Soyang River in May 1951 which enabled the artillery to finally operate at full capacity. Artillery Fire Support Officers planned prearranged fires for known concentrations of enemy forces, likely avenues of approach, and bridges across the Soyang. Artillery headquarters selected artillery units for execution of these fires in accordance with the plan. When the Chinese attacked on 12 May, the artillery units targeted enemy groups of 200 to 500 men with concentrated fires and achieved tremendous effects.

During the preparation of the defense of the Soyang River, the vast area between the main defensive line and the concentration of Chinese forces during the defense required combat patrols to operate well ahead of the defensive line to maintain contact with the enemy. The artillery battalions established advanced positions outside of the defensive lines in order to support these patrols. These positions necessitated the tactical mobility of the battalions to occupy and withdraw quickly in support of the maneuver formations. Ultimately, these conditions led to many lessons learned in the employment of massed fire.[43]

The Battle of Soyang River reinforced the lessons of massed fires learned throughout the Korean War. One of the keys to the success of UN forces in Korea was their ability to mass fires on targets of opportunity. The flexibility of massing fires on targets of opportunity provided the UN forces with a marked advantage in this respect. While neither MacArthur nor Ridgeway would ever receive all the artillery that they requested for the theater, they would make the best use of what they had.[44] Artillery leaders accomplished the effects of massed fires through preplanned and synchronized targeting at the divisional and non-divisional levels; the flexibility to mass fires on targets of opportunity through accurate target locating and mobility to position artillery forces to achieve those devastating effects.

Using Artillery in the Defense: Unity of Command

Non-divisional artillery battalions were in high demand throughout the duration of the Korean conflict because of the need to reinforce existing divisional artillery battalions and provide flexibility for the corps.[45] As the Army scrambled to fulfill this need, what became noticeable was the lack of continuity in the command and control of the non-divisional elements. In July 1950, the 92nd Armored Field Artillery Battalion left its parent unit, the 2nd Armored Division, to deploy as a separate battalion of the 5th Field Artillery Group, the only acting corps artillery headquarters in Korea at the time. For the remainer of the year, the 92nd Field Artillery Battalion participated in the Inchon amphibious assault, the Iwon amphibious landing, and the X Corps' defense in the northeastern sector of the peninsula after the Chinese intervention. The battalion's missions ranged from serving under direct centralized control by the 5th Field Artillery Group to an artillery reinforcement for the divisions under decentralized control. The battalion never maintained a habitual relationship with one command for longer than a month. This was the normal life of a non-divisional artillery battalion in Korea.[46]

During the Korean War, Field Manual 100-5 defined unity of command as "that unity of effort which is essential to the decisive application of the full combat power of the available forces."[47] Additionally, "unity of effort is furthered by full cooperation between the elements of command."[48] The first definition linked the ability to mass fires on the battlefield to the control of the artillery commander and the second with the ability of artillery and maneuver commanders to synchronize these effects. Artillery in Korea required an organizational command structure that allowed artillerymen to synchronize efforts and mass fires within their span of control while also meeting the needs of maneuver. To support the maneuver requirements, artillery commanders assigned specific roles or missions to the artillery units that explained the relationship of their support to the maneuver unit.[49] Another aspect of unity of command was the command relationships between artillery commanders and their supported unit commanders.[50] Organizationally, the Army classified artillery battalions as divisional battalions and non-divisional battalions. Divisional artillery battalions were "organic, assigned, or attached to the division."[51] Non-divisional artillery units formed a pool of battalions that the Army combined and centrally controlled by a group or corps headquarters or decentrally controlled by assigning them supporting roles within a division. This required non-divisional artillery battalions to move throughout the Korean theater, being assigned to different corps or groups in direct support, general support and reinforcing roles for all echelons from corps to battalion. These roles helped ensure a mutual understanding of responsibility of artillery commanders and their supporting relationship with the maneuver commanders. While this provided flexibility for allocating artillery resources, what was missing was a lasting relationship between non-divisional artillery battalions and their higher headquarters as well as their supported maneuver headquarters.[52]

Prior to the Korean War, artillery officers recommended creating an artillery division to organize non-divisional battalions that had their own organic artillery divided into groups and regiments that allowed the corps the flexibility to reallocate groups without losing continuity. However, when the Army implemented the reforms, they assigned organic artillery battalions to the group, but only semi-permanently attached the group to corps. The corps could then attach the group to a division in a supporting role. Ultimately, the Army assigned non-divisional battalions permanently for continuity and decreased fluctuation, while retaining flexibility within the corps. This was the only change to the organization of non-divisional artillery; the group remained the primary organizational method of employing non-divisional artillery.[53]

Aside from organizational changes, a key part of unity of command in the Korean War was the command responsibilities of the artillery commanders. Generally, in armies, corps, divisions, and task forces, the senior artilleryman was the commander of the organically assigned artillery units as well as the artillery officer on the special staff of the supported unit to advise the commander and staff on artillery matters and fire support coordination.[54] Doctrinally, artillery commanders only had command authority over the battalions that were organic to their headquarters. With the new group concept, this meant that corps artillery commanders did not have direct command over the group artillery and the groups did not have direct command over the divisional artillery.[55] This did not alleviate the artillery commander's responsibility to synchronize the effects of artillery within their maneuver headquarters, regardless of the echelon. One of the major developments during the interwar period to assist in this synchronization was the fire support coordination center.

Doctrine required army, corps, and division and task force artillery commanders at each level to "establish and supervise the fire support coordination center as fire support coordinator for the command."[56] Therefore, during the Korean War, artilleryman established formal fire support coordination centers at all corps and division fire direction centers, and subordinate artilleryman carried the concept to the infantry regimental and battalion levels.[57] In the fire support coordination center, artilleryman planned and synchronized air support, naval gunfire and artillery, and responded to targets of opportunity with the available means. This allowed units to de-conflict close air support and artillery fires and integrated the artillery observer into the process of determining the best asset to engage a given target.[58]

During the "Pusan Perimeter" defense, the only available artillery units were divisional artillery units.[59] Even as non-divisional artillery battalions entered the theater, they were attached as general support or reinforcing units for the divisions, only adding to the span of control for the division artillery commander. Artillerymen could only mass fires at the division level due to the absence of a corps artillery headquarters and the lack of non-divisional artillery battalions and often, due to the wide dispersion of units, this was difficult to accomplish. Each corps was authorized an artillery officer and small staff, but they had no command authority or capability to adequately synchronize fires across the corps.[60]

Initially, the X Corps utilized the 5th Field Artillery Group as its corps artillery headquarters due to the lack of a corps artillery staff. During the initial phases of the Korean War, the 5th Field Artillery Group served as the best example of employing and controlling non-divisional battalions. They controlled their two organic battalions directly as well as synchronized the artillery efforts within X Corps. During the push to the Chinese border in October and November 1950, they decentralized artillery employment to the divisions in order to keep up with the offense. As the Chinese launched offenses to push the X Corps back to the 38th Parallel, the 5th Field Artillery Group centralized the control of artillery to maximize the effectiveness of the withdrawal.[61] I Corps Artillery was the first official corps artillery headquarters to arrive in theater in February 1951 and by March, IX Corps Artillery arrived.[62] As more non-divisional battalions entered the theater, corps artillery commanders and their staffs could better reallocate and control how the attached units would support the overall corps fire plans. As the nature of the war transitioned to more of a static defense, artillery commanders placed even more emphasis on centrally coordinating and allocating non-divisional artillery to best disrupt the communist attacks.[63]

Unity of command of artillery forces in Korea centered on the flexible organizational structure of the groups, the command authorities and responsibilities of the artillery commanders, and the mission roles of the individual artillery battalions. Organizationally, the artillery group concept worked because it provided some continuity in command to the non-divisional artillery battalions while retaining the flexibility to move non-divisional units between corps and divisions. The concept still required a corps artillery headquarters to nest the non-divisional and divisional fire plans within the maneuver fire planning. Synchronization of artillery forces across the theater of operations required fire support coordination centers at all levels to coordinate artillery and integrate air support across a wide front. These centers served as the medium for more effective command and control.

Using Artillery in the Defense: Security

By September 1950, the North Koreans had confined the UN forces to the Pusan Perimeter and were pressing to disrupt the defense along the Naktong River. The 35th Infantry Regiment of the 25th Infantry Division was the division's right flank and the division was responsible for the southwestern portion of the Pusan Perimeter. On 3 September 1950, North Korean Forces launched an attack against the 35th Infantry line. The 64th Field Artillery Battalion was in direct support of the 35th Infantry and had established localized defenses around each of the battery position areas because they were keenly aware that they were responsible for their own defenses given the likelihood of enemy infiltration. Early that morning, the first sergeant of A Battery, 64th Field Artillery noticed a small element of men moving toward their position.

Before he could identify the element, they opened machine gun fire on the American position. Additional fires from all directions accompanied the initial attack. Before the men of A Battery could respond, the enemy killed five men, wounded one and destroyed the battery communications switchboard. At this point, A Battery's howitzers stopped all fire missions as the machine gun fire turned on their positions. By the time that A Battery returned machine gun fire, they realized that it was too late; the North Koreans had completely infiltrated its position. Some of the howitzers responded with direct fire against the infiltrators, but to no avail. The howitzers were lost until recovered later that morning.[64]

Figure 7.3. US Army 105-mm howitzer in action west of Yongsan, Korea, on 1 September 1950. Photo courtesy of US Army Center of Military History.

This example was not the first time that the enemy overran an American artillery formation in the war. The 63rd Field Artillery Battalion experienced the same type of event in July 1950, south of the Kum River.[65] In fact, artillery units were overrun close to a dozen times during the first nine months of the war.[66] With the limited amount of artillery deployed to theater, this became an operational level problem. The impact of the linear nature of World War II conditioned artillery units to rely on the safety of the contiguous front. This left artillery units unprepared to defend against the threat of North Koreans and Chinese infiltration that required mutually supporting defensive positions.[67] By the end of the Korean War, the US Army artillery units learned valuable lessons in protecting their vulnerable formations.

At the beginning of the Korean War, doctrine developed during World War II favored the offensive nature of warfare to annihilate the enemy. This did not fit well within the defensive nature of the limited war in Korea.[68] By 1953, artillery doctrine described the defense of an artillery position in terms of the batteries responsibility to protect their position. "All units prepare their positions for defense against enemy ground attack with particular attention to antitank defense. Units must be prepared to counter airborne attacks, guerrilla action, and infiltration." Additionally, the manual advocated training artillery units in infantry tactics and delivery of artillery direct fire in support of the battery defense, though it was only specific to airborne operations.[69] Ultimately, the defense of the battery position was the responsibility of the artillerymen. Artillery commanders understood the need to develop mutually supporting battery positions and integrating them with maneuver, but the lack of training in this respect during the interwar period made this difficult to accomplish.[70]

As the war progressed, North Korean and Chinese infiltration tactics exploited the weakness of artillery defenses and the breadth of the American's defense.[71] "Infiltrating enemy units frequently occupied positions to the Americans' rear, striking command posts, support units or artillery positions."[72] Later, the United States built more depth into their defenses and integrated the artillery position defense with maneuver forces. By the end of the conflict, the vulnerability of artillery formations was much improved. The Army learned two major lessons: batteries must be able to defend themselves, and the battalion must integrate a mutually supporting defense plan with maneuver. General Almond expanded on these areas adding, "Automatic weapons within artillery units must be ready at all times to defend their positions whether on the move or in position. Destruction of artillery units is a primary enemy objective. All units must stress defense against infiltration tactics, train for anti-guerrilla measures and be prepared for all-around defense."[73]

Conclusion

The elements of mass, unity of effort and security characterized effective defensive operational artillery employment during the Korean War. The ability to synchronize the effects of multiple divisional and non-divisional artillery battalions within the corps, groups, and divisions required a command and control relationship structure that facilitated a coordinated artillery defense. Faced with an enemy that favored infiltration tactics and the overall nature of defensive operations, the American and UN commanders recognized the importance of adequately securing artillery positions. Today, applying these same characteristics to the Army's current ability to provide adequate fire support in large-scale combat operations provides key insight into its preparation for future wars.

The concept of massed fires was not new to the Korean conflict. However, technological advances in the interwar period contributed to improved methods of target acquisition and communication between observers and the guns. The necessity to compensate for the lack of artillery units with concentrated fires honed the artillery system to prioritize prearrangement of targets in the defense. Target acquisition improvements allowed UN forces to engage targets of opportunity more readily. Additionally, the need to reallocate and redistribute non-divisional artillery battalions required strategic and tactical mobility to respond to the Communist threat. Ultimately, the UN's advantage over North Korean and Chinese forces was their ability to mass fires on targets of opportunity.

Unity of command for artillery units during the Korean War reflected the desire to combine the flexibility of the group concept of World War II while providing continuity for non-divisional battalions within the groups. The corps centralized control during static defensive operations and decentralized control to the divisions during offensive maneuver. During the defensive, centralized control allowed commanders to better synchronize the effects of massed fires and allowed the corps flexibility to respond to the largest threats. These concepts will be essential to coordinating artillery units in the future especially without an artillery headquarters above the brigade level.

Security of artillery units in the beginning of the Korean War was woefully inadequate. In the beginning of the conflict, artillerymen expected conflict to be similar to the linear battle during World War II. However, due to the enemy tactics of infiltration, they quickly realized that the artillery battalions had to defend themselves. Integrated battery defense plans nested within the maneuver defense improved throughout the conflict. Ultimately, by the end of the conflict, artillery battalions adjusted their methods to respond to security challenges.

Today, artillery doctrine still addresses each of these critical areas. The characterizations of mass are increased lethality, longer ranges, better target acquisition technology, and precision munitions. It could be said that advent of precision guiding munitions has somewhat changed the concept of massed fires by reducing the reliance on multiple artillery units to achieve desired effects. Regardless, the army's current artillery organization lacks the ability to integrate multiple battalions at the division level and higher.

The fact that contemporary doctrine addresses the aspects of mass, unity of command and security does not mean that the artillery units can actually perform the concepts well. Much like during the start of the Korean War, the current US Army's ability to execute all doctrinal artillery tasks such as massed fires is lacking. This is not necessarily for the same reasons as during the Korean War. Sound written doctrine does not necessarily mean that the army's artillery units can actually execute it. The last decade of counterinsurgency operations have certainly influenced the artillery's ability to mass fires above the battalion level. Today, an argument can be made that the artillery is unprepared to mass fires against a near peer army during large-scale combat operations. The degradation in the artillery's ability to mass fires and secure itself is due to the last ten years of conflict but adequate training can fix it. The aspect of unity of command, however, is a completely different problem.

Effective unity of command for artillery units must be able to accomplish a number of functions. Commanders must be able to control subordinate artillery elements and the artillery must be organized to effectively integrate with maneuver and synchronize the concentration of artillery throughout the entire theater of operations. The major change in unity of command since the Korean War for divisional artillery is the elimination of the division artillery headquarters from the current army structure. In fact, there is no command headquarters for artillery units above the brigade level. The Army eliminated the division artillery and transferred the role of synchronizing divisional artillery fires to the Chief of Field Artillery in the division headquarters and above. However, the Chief of Field Artillery has no command authority over any artillery battalions.

The US Army Field Artillery made great contributions to the overall success achieved by UN forces in the Korean War. The doctrinal concepts of mass, unity of command, and security evolved during the three years of conflict, and these concepts will continue to evolve as the Army shifts its focus to the conduct of large-scale combat operations against a near-peer threat. Artillerymen must ask themselves if they are prepared to execute these functions in a similar situation such as Korea. Has the artillery trained enough at massing fires above the battalion level? Is the Army's current unity of command adequate to synchronize the artillery of multiple divisions? And, do artillery battalions know how to adequately secure their formations during the conduct of large-scale combat operations?

Notes

1. Bevin Alexander, *Korea: The First War We Lost* (New York: Hippocrene Books, 1993), 135–36, 140–42; Roy E. Appleman, *South to the Naktong, North to the Yalu* (Washington, DC: US Government Printing, 1961), 248, 282–83, 343.

2. Janice E. McKenney, *Organizational History of Field Artillery 1775–2003* (Washington, DC: United States Army Center of Military History, 2007), 201.

3. US Department of the Army, Field Manual (FM) 6-20, *Artillery Tactics and Techniques* (Washington, DC: 1953), 35.

4. US Army, *Conference on Battle Employment of Artillery in Korea* (Fort Sill, OK: Artillery Center, 11 February 1952), 9.

5. US Army, *Conference on Battle Employment of Artillery in Korea,* 9.

6. Stanford Research Institute, *Operational Data for Selected Field Artillery Units During World War II and The Korean War* (Stanford, CA: Stanford Research Institute, 1954), 1.

7.Peter J. Lane, "Steel for Bodies: Ammunition Readiness during the Korean War" (Master's thesis, Command and General Staff College, 2003), 27.

8. William Glenn Robertson, "The Korean War: The United Nations' Response to Heavy Bombardment," in *CSI Report No. 13: Tactical Responses to Concentrated Artillery*, by Combat Studies Institute (Fort Leavenworth, KS: US Army Command and General Staff College, n.d.), 109–11.

9. Appleman, *South to the Naktong,* 241–249; George C. Herring, *From Colony to Superpower: US Foreign Relations since 1776* (New York, NY: Oxford University Press, 2008), 639–641.

10. Allan R. Millett, *The War for Korea, 1950–1951: They Came From the North* (Lawrence, KS: University Press of Kansas, 2010), 240; Walter G. Hermes, *Truce Tent and Fighting Front* (Washington, DC: Office of the Chief of Military History, United States Army, 1966), 10–14.

11. Millett, 384–387, 390–403, 411–16; Herring, *From Colony to Superpower,* 642.

12. Millett, 384–387, 390–403, 411–16; Herring, 642.

13. Operational artillery is the employment of non-divisional artillery assets to support the arrangement of tactical actions in time, space and purpose to achieve the operational or strategic objective.

14. Walter E. Kretchik, *US Army Doctrine: From the American Revolution to the War on Terror* (Lawrence, KS: University of Kansas Press, 2011), 164.

15. Boyd L. Dastrup, *The Field Artillery: History and Sourcebook* (Westport, CT: Greenwood Press, 1994), 243.

16. John D. Dill, *Fire Support in the Pusan Perimeter* (Fort Leavenworth, KS: US Army Command and General Staff College, 2000), 3.

17. Robert A. Doughty, *The Evolution of US Army Tactical Doctrine, 1946–76* (Fort Leavenworth, KS: Combat Studies Institute, US Army Command and General Staff College, 1979), 7–12.

18. A Chinese Army Group consisted of three divisions and approximately 30,000 soldiers. A North Korean Corps consisted of three to four understrength divisions and approximately 17,000 soldiers.

19. Millett, *The War for Korea,* 443–445; Russell A. Gugeler, *Army Historical Series: Combat Actions in Korea*, (Washington DC: US Army Center of Military History, 1987), 167; X Corps Artillery Report, "Battle of the Soyang River: An Analysis of Artillery Support, X Corps Sector, 1 May–29 May 1951."

20. Early ammunition restrictions were based on World War II expenditure rates and modified to compensate for the lack of available ammunition in theater. As more ammunition became available, UN forces were able to increase these rates.

21. Department of the Army, Field Manual (FM) 100-5, *Operations* (Washington, DC: 1949), 22.

22. A doctrinal definition is a commonly understood and agreed upon description of a term or concept that appears in a military manual.

23. Although published in 1953 as doctrine, the technique of massed fires was in use throughout the Korean War; Department of the Army, Field Manual (FM) 6-20, *Artillery Tactics and Techniques* (Washington, DC: 1953), 33.

24. Thomas S. Grodecki, "From Powder River to Soyang: The 300th Armored Field Artillery in Korea," (Washington, DC: Center of Military History), 71.

25. D.M. Giangreco, *Korean War Anthology: Artillery in Korea: Massing Fires and Reinventing the Wheel* (Fort Leavenworth, KS: US Government Printing Office, 2003), 7.

26. Department of the Army, FM 6-20, 136.

27. FM 6-20, 136.

28. FM 6-20, 138.

29. McKenney, *Organizational History,* 206.

30. US Army, Conference on the Battle Employment of the Artillery 1950–1951 (1952), 4.

31. Department of the Army, FM 6-20, 140–41.

32. Dastrup, *The Field Artillery,* 253.

33. McKenney, *Organizational History,* 190.

34. McKenney, 194.

35. Department of the Army, Field Manual (FM) 6-120, *The Field Artillery Observation Battalion and Batteries* (Washington, DC: 1951), 1-3.

36. McKenney, *Organizational History,* 200.

37. James F. Schnabel, *Policy and Direction: The First Year* (Washington, DC: US Government Printing Office, 1973), 1.

38. A.C. Bole Jr., "Towed Versus Self-Propelled Artillery in the Period Prior to 1955: An Historical Investigation of the Argument in the United States Army," (Fort Leavenworth: Command and General Staff College, 1966), 14.

39. While A.C. Bole uses the terms tactical and strategic mobility to define the characteristics of artillery mobility at the time, strategic mobility can also be understood as operational maneuver today. A.C. Bole Jr., "Towed Versus

Self-Propelled Artillery in the Period Prior to 1955: An Historical Investigation of the Argument in the United States Army," 15.

40. Bole, "Towed Versus Self-Propelled," 54–55.

41. Bole, 49.

42. Grodecki, "From Powder River to Soyang," 67–68.

43. US Army, "Conference on the Battle Employment of the Artillery 1950–1951." 1952, 2–3.

44. Robertson, "The Korean War," 107–17.

45. Millett, *The War for Korea,* 153–54.

46. Millett, 153–154.

47. Department of the Army, FM 100-5, 22.

48. FM 100-5, 22.

49. "Direct support artillery has the mission of supporting a specific unit of a command . . . is not attached to the supported unit, it remains under the command of the higher artillery commander, but its fires are not taken away from the supported unit except by the authority of the division or force commander. . . . General support artillery has the mission of supporting the force as a whole. Units with such a mission are held under the command of the artillery commander thus making immediately available to the force commander a reserve of fire with which to influence the action… A reinforcing mission requires the reinforcing artillery unit to augment the fires of the reinforced artillery unit on call." Department of the Army, FM 6-20, 37.

50. "When the artillery is assigned or attached to the force (supported unit), the artillery officer is both a subordinate command and a special staff officer of the force (supported unit) commander. When artillery is neither assigned nor attached to the force but is supporting the force, the artillery commander's relationship to the force commander is both that of an advisor and that of an independent commander obliged to render continuous effective fire support in accordance with his assigned mission." Department of the Army, FM 6-20, 10.

51. Department of the Army, FM 6-20, 8.

52. Grodecki, "From Powder River to Soyang," 72–74, 90.

53. McKenney, *Organizational History,* 195.

54. Department of the Army, FM 6-20, 10.

55. FM 6-20, 10.

56. FM 6-20, 13.

57. McKenney, *Organizational History,* 205.

58. Dastrup, *The Field Artillery: History and Sourcebook,* 259; Russell Wallace Jr., "For Battlefield Teamwork: Fire Support Coordination Center," *Combat Forces Journal,* May 1953, 24–26; Carl W. Schaad, "Fire Support Coordination," *Combat Forces Journal,* September 1952, 39–41; Eighth Army, "A Study of the Employment and Effectiveness of the Artillery with the Eighth Army during the period, October 1951–July 1953," 1954, 7–8.

59. Russell A. Weathersby, "The Field Artillery Group in Support of the Corps and Field Army, 1942–1953," Thesis, US Army Command and General

Staff College, 1966, 126; McKenney, *Organizational History,* 196–97; Schnabel, *Policy and Direction*, 90–92.

60. Russell A. Weathersby, "The Field Artillery Group in Support of the Corps and Field Army, 1942–1953," 126–127; Department of the Army, The Artillery School, "Report of the Artillery School Representative, AFF Observer team No. 2 Concerning Korean Campaign, September to October 1950, Inclusive, "27 November 1950, 134–41.

61. Russell A. Weathersby, "The Field Artillery Group in Support of the Corps and Field Army, 1942–953," 130.

62. Weathersby, 133.

63. Weathersby, 133–35.

64. Gugeler, *Army Historical Series,* 31–38.

65. Appleman, *South to the Naktong,* 126–28; Giangreco, *Korean War Anthology,* 3–5.

66. Giangreco, *Korean War Anthology,* 1.

67. Giangreco, 1, 5; Dastrup, *The Field Artillery,* 228–29, 242–43, 247, 25; Edward T. Klett Jr., "Solving the 6400-mil Nemesis," *Combat Forces Journal,* July 1951, 34.

68. Walter E. Kretchik, *US Army Doctrine: From the American Revolution to the War on Terror*, (Lawrence, KS: University Press of Kansas, 2011), 158; Scott R. McMeen, "Field Artillery Doctrine Development 1917–1945," Command and General Staff College, 1991, 48.

69. Department of the Army, FM 6-20, 93.

70. Giangreco, *Korean War Anthology,* 5.

71. Dastrup, *The Field Artillery,* 255; Giangreco, *Korean War Anthology,* 3.

72. Doughty, *The Evolution of US Army Tactical Doctrine,* 7–8.

73. US Army, Conference on the Battle Employment of the Artillery 1950–1951, 1952, 9.

Chapter 8
US Army Artillery in the Vietnam War
Boyd L. Dastrup

After eight years of fighting to preserve its colonial empire, France finally suffered defeat at the hands of Ho Chi Minh, an ardent Vietnamese nationalist and communist, when Dien Bien Phu fell in March 1954. This along with communist rhetoric about picking up the banner of nationalism by supporting wars of liberation influenced the United States to consider sending troops. Provisional agreements reached at Geneva, Switzerland, prevented this, divided the country at the seventeenth parallel, and scheduled reunification to come through a general election in July 1956.[1]

Fearing that the communists would eventually gain power, the United States began pouring in economic and military aid to buttress South Vietnam against subversion by the Viet Cong, a contraction of Vietnamese Communists, and the threat of invasion by North Vietnam. Although the Army had been sending advisors to Vietnam since the early 1950s, President John F. Kennedy's decision in the spring of 1961 to increase the American commitment greatly expanded the Army's advisory effort. As quickly as the Army could train advisory teams, it dispatched them to South Vietnam. Each field artillery advisory team included an officer, generally a captain, and a senior noncommissioned officer that was assigned to an artillery battalion in South Vietnamese divisions and corps. While the officer provided guidance to improve overall unit effectiveness, the noncommissioned officer assisted the battalion operations officer and operations noncommissioned officer in training firing batteries and gun sections. In the meantime, an American artillery officer, normally a major, was assigned to each corps and division to counsel senior South Vietnamese commanders on artillery matters and coordinated the efforts of the advisory teams in subordinate battalions. Although the Americans faced soldiers with a different set of values, they produced a better led and trained South Vietnamese artillery by 1965 than the one encountered in 1961.[2]

In the meantime, North Vietnam built a military force to gain control of Vietnam. By the early 1960s North Vietnam had a formidable army that had been organized, equipped, and trained along Chinese lines and that relied upon stealth and foot mobility. North Vietnamese divisions had around ten thousand lightly armed and equipped men with a ready reserve of approximately 500,000 men. To compensate for the lack of firepower the North Vietnamese stressed rigorous discipline, tactical superiority, and careful preparation. The Viet Cong gave the North Vietnamese another tool to bring down the South Vietnamese government by infiltrating South Vietnam and conducting sabotage, terrorist, and propaganda campaigns.[3]

Encouraged by the deaths of Ngo Dinh Diem, the premier of South Vietnam, and President Kennedy, North Vietnam intensified its political and military offensive against South Vietnam in 1964.[4] To meet the external threat the Army abandoned its defensive strategy for aggressive offensive actions.[5] After a series of limited offensives, General William Westmoreland, Commander, US Military Assistance Command, Vietnam, opened a campaign to counter North Vietnamese moves to cut South Vietnam in half. After an attack on a Special Forces camp at Plei Me in October 1965, he sent the 1st Air Cavalry Division (Airmobile) under Major General Harry W.O. Kinnard to destroy the retreating North Vietnamese units responsible for the assault.[6]

The Battle of the Ia Drang Valley

Late in October 1965, the 1st Cavalry Division moved into the Ia Drang Valley. After several days of searching, the 1-9 Cavalry bumped into the enemy on 1 November. As the fighting grew hotter, the 1st Cavalry quickly concentrated by using the helicopter's mobility, defeated the North Vietnamese, and forced them to retreat. That same day, 1-9 Cavalry's airborne scouts spotted a battalion-size enemy force advancing towards the recent fight. The scouts fired on the North Vietnamese. Without any artillery support the 1-9 Cavalry along with reinforcements airlifted into the battle area repeatedly repulsed enemy assaults. The enemy's proximity to American troops precluded aerial artillery from being employed, while tube artillery was out of range. On 3 November the 1-9 Cavalry squadron began conducting a reconnaissance-in-force along the Cambodian border. After establishing a patrol base, it staked out ambushes to catch North Vietnamese units fleeing to safety. That night the North Vietnamese ferociously hit the 1-9 Cavalry. Aerial artillery and a dogged defense turned back many enemy attacks. Outside of aerial artillery, the 1st Cavalry's field artillery provided minimal support. The short, intense battles fought at distances beyond towed artillery's range simply precluded any help.[7]

During the second week of November, both sides opened offensives to gain control of the Ia Drang Valley. On 14 November, CH47 Chinook helicopter airlifts placed two batteries at Landing Zone Falcon to support the 1-7 Cavalry's offensive at Landing Zone X-Ray. Gun crews concentrated their fire around the landing zone. As tube artillery lifted its fire, aerial artillery blasted the area to allow the infantry to land. This action totally disrupted North Vietnamese plans to attack Plei Me and put them on the defensive. Even though they were surprised, the North Vietnamese slugged the Americans viciously with small arms, rocket, and mortar fire. To repel the assaults the Americans airlifted in reinforcements throughout the day under the cover of artillery fire from landing Zone Falcon. These bombardments along with small arms fire broke up several attacks during the day. Throughout the night the North Vietnamese continued their attempt to defeat the Americans, but intensive fire from the two batteries at Landing Zone Falcon and aggressive fighting by the cavalry repulsed the charges.[8]

The battle at X-Ray carried on over the next two days. On the fifteenth the North Vietnamese repeatedly assaulted the Americans, Small arms fire became so intense that the forward observer from the most hard-pressed American company was pinned down and could not call in artillery fire. Fortunately, the artillery officer located back at 1-7's command post could see the fighting, adjusted artillery fire, and directed aerial artillery attacks and tactical air strikes. Despite effective air

Figure 8.1. US Army CH-47 delivers ammunition to a combined 105-mm and 155-mm howitzer battery in Vietnam. Photo courtesy of The Center of Military History.

and artillery support, the enemy closed in on the perimeter and assailed it from all directions. Using colored smoke rounds to identify the precise outline of his perimeter, Lieutenant Colonel Harold G. Moore, the 1-7 Infantry battalion commander, called for additional artillery support. Heavily armed helicopter gunships entered the fray, while the two batteries at Landing Zone Falcon and two at Landing Zone Columbus laid down a devastating shield of iron. This combination broke the enemy's attacks for the day. The following day, the North Vietnamese renewed their assaults but ran into a curtain of artillery rounds. Using this as protection, the Americans then pushed towards the North Vietnamese, who retreated.[9]

On 17 November, the 2-7 Cavalry and the 2-5 Cavalry, which had joined Moore's command on the 15th at X-Ray, moved on a sweep north to cut off North Vietnamese elements moving towards Columbus and Falcon. The 2-5 Cavalry arrived at Columbus without contacting the enemy, but the 2-7 Cavalry were ambushed en-route to Landing Zone Albany by several North Vietnamese units. The engagement quickly deteriorated into a wild melee. Unable to distinguish between friend and foe, gun crews from Landing Zone Columbus and airmen waited patiently four hours before they could respond. In mid-afternoon aerial and tube artillery and tactical air support joined the fight. Although the enemy applied pressure into the evening, a continuous ring of artillery shells and tactical air strikes prevented the Vietnamese from further penetrations of the perimeters. Unable to take such punishment, the North Vietnamese finally abandoned their drive to destroy the artillery that had been so destructive at X-Ray. The North Vietnamese hit Columbus with mortar and machine gun fire on 18 November and battled the Americans at several other locations, but the fighting at Albany marked the last of major combat in the Ia Drang.[10]

Lessons Learned from the Ia Drang

After the Battle of Ia Drang, General Kinnard had nothing but praise for his field artillery. "Using Chinooks, we had been able to position tube artillery in the midst of a literally trackless jungle where it provided close support to our infantry and gave them a vital measure of superiority," Kinnard wrote in *Army* in 1967.[11] Besides lauding tube artillery, he boasted that aerial artillery had matured in the Ia Drang by supplementing tube artillery and in some cases providing the only firepower. Taking his argument even further, Kinnard insisted that the 1st Cavalry lured the enemy into battle by teasing it with a "seemingly unprotected airmobile infantry battalion."[12] Once the enemy struck, the 1st Cavalry hit it hard with "massive artillery support."[13] Simply stated, the battles of Ia Drang vindicated the airmobile concept and showed the field artillery's capacity to provide close support in difficult terrain.[14]

Lieutenant Colonel Lloyd J. Picou of the 1st Cavalry's artillery responded with the same enthusiasm. Writing in *Artillery Trends* in August 1967, Picou explained that airmobile artillery proved its versatility and mobility, its ability to displace quickly, and its mastery of airmobile artillery techniques.[15] The following year, Picou explained in *Military Review*, "From the division artillery viewpoint, the most significant outcome of this campaign [Ia Drang] was the use of aerial artillery."[16] Aerial artillery gunships flew to the scene and were able to locate and attack enemy forces. Pilots contacted ground units and then adjusted tube artillery on the fringes of the battlefield. As his article indicated, he believed that the field artillery had made a significant breakthrough with aerial artillery because it provided effective support to airmobile units.[17]

The Army and 1st Cavalry Division drew two more conclusions. Both pointed out that operations in the Ia Drang revealed the importance of having mutually supporting field artillery positions. Towed 105-mm howitzers could not be used in a direct fire role on a landing zone surrounded by dense vegetation without causing extensive casualties to the security force. To protect one landing zone and its batteries, the field artillery had to site at least two batteries within range of each other. Because of guerrilla warfare, commanders simply could not position their field artillery without adequate protection.[18]

In their efforts to justify airmobile operations, Kinnard and other officers overlooked an important weakness. During the short but intensive battles on 1–3 November between small forces, tube artillery failed to furnish any support because it was out of range of the fights whereas aerial artillery rushed quickly forward to hit enemy units. Even though it was transported by helicopter, tube artillery lacked sufficient mobility to respond to fast-moving situations. This meant that the infantry and cavalry would have to fight alone on the enemy's terms unless they were under a protective umbrella of fire support. Likewise, firepower succeeded only because the North Vietnamese stood and fought. Although firepower was a decisive factor, it had limitations. Late in 1965, it could not be applied at will.

Because the Ia Drang acquainted the enemy with American firepower and influenced it to avoid such encounters in the future, the Army had to inaugurate search-and-destroy operations in 1965-66 to ferret out the enemy.[19] For example, covered by 105-mm and 155-mm howitzer batteries positioned in the mountains bordering the Bong Son River, assaults by the 3rd Brigade, 1st Cavalry, landed south of the river on 28 January 1966 to deceive the enemy, attacked northward over the river with the Vietnamese Airborne Brigade, and destroyed two enemy battalions. On 6 February as a battalion of Marines sealed off the north end of the An Loa Valley to prevent the enemy from escaping, the division's 2nd Brigade air assaulted into An Lao Valley. As the 2nd Brigade opened a thrust south down the valley, the rest of the division pushed rapidly southwest of Bong Son.[20]

This rapid sweep taxed the 1st Cavalry's artillery's ability to support the maneuver elements. Even though field artillery officers tried to minimize displacements, the speed of the ground troops and the size of the area compelled them to make over 160 displacements, which strained the division's air resources. When the pieces were moved by helicopter, field artillerymen generally transported ammunition and guns separately. To economize and speed up displacements they devised a system of using one helicopter to carry both. They suspended the ammunition and the howitzer beneath the helicopter by means of a double-sling system to allow the transportation of a complete firing section. By doing this, field artillerymen reduced the time required to occupy a position and dispelled fears about the field artillery's inability to keep up with the other combat arms on a highly mobile battlefield.[21]

Even though 1st Cavalry field artillerymen could maneuver their 105-mm howitzers around, they wanted still more firepower. Without suitable roads 155-mm howitzers could not occupy positions within range of the objective. To resolve that shortcoming field artillerymen airlifted the howitzers. Using CH-54 Flying Cranes and CH-47 Chinook helicopters and reducing the weight of the 155-mm howitzer by eliminating unnecessary equipment, the 1st Cavalry flew a four-gun battery a distance of 15 miles in approximately two hours to provide fire support for the ground forces. This movement set an important precedent as it indicated that medium guns could be air lifted and therefore possess the same mobility as lighter pieces had.[22]

During those early days of 1966, field artillerymen in the 1st Cavalry also developed new tactics for aerial artillery. While tube artillery was adjusted on a target, aerial artillery orbited as near as possible. If any enemy tried to escape, aerial gunners fired on them. Whenever possible or appropriate, the pilots adjusted tube artillery to flush personnel into the open and then attacked. The ability to airlift towed 105-mm and 155-mm howitzers and the rapid response of aerial artillery signified important changes in tactics. The 1st Cavalry had the capability to maneuver their artillery aggressively on the battlefield to destroy the enemy and refused to allow difficult terrain to hinder delivering huge amounts of firepower upon enemy positions.[23]

The war concurrently forced the field artillery to refine certain gunnery techniques. In past wars field artillerymen could predict the enemy's moves because they were primarily confined to a sector and could be plotted on a map with some degree of accuracy. Vietnam changed this. Because of the North Vietnamese and Viet Cong practice of hitting from any direction at any time, gun crews had to respond quickly and deliver fire in a full circle.[24] Realizing that existing procedures were inadequate, gun crews improvised their own to furnish fire in a complete circle. This created varying ways. To eliminate confusion, The Artillery and Missile School devised a method to fire in a complete circle in 1966 and disseminated it throughout the Army.[25] Moreover, the school increased its instruction time on firing in a complete circle (6400-mils) to prepare graduates better for combat in Vietnam.[26]

As important as technique was, suitable field pieces facilitated firing in a complete circle. The M108, Ml09, and M102 howitzers had the capability of traversing 360 degrees with ease, offset the limited traverses of

Figure 8.2. M107 175-mm gun firing during the Vietnam War. Photo courtesy of The Center of Military History.

other field guns, such as the 8-inch howitzer and 175-mm gun, and complemented the revised 6400-mil firing chart.[27]

Although search-and-destroy operations of late 1965 and early 1966 were successful, the Army still had difficulties protecting the countryside. To ensure that the maximum area was defended by available troops, the Army assigned an area of operations to each unit from the highest to the lowest. This dispersed the Army throughout the countryside. Because of the size of the brigade's area and range limitation, the division artillery commander attached a battery to a particular battalion to provide the maximum coverage. Consequently, an artillery battalion no longer supported an entire brigade as it had done in previous wars. This habitual association decentralized fire direction from the battalion to the battery and frequently isolated the battery from the rest of its battalion. Addressing this development, Brigadier General James G. Kalergis, Commander, I Field Force Vietnam Artillery, explained in 1967 that field artillery batteries normally performed as if they were battalions and that battalions acted as if they were division artillery or group head quarters. This transferred the authority to make key decisions from the battalion commander or higher to the battery commander. For example, Operation Fitchburg of late 1966 and early 1967 in Tay Ninh Province gave the battery commander "an excellent opportunity to exercise command and control independent of the artillery battalion" because one 105-mm. howitzer battery was placed in direct support of each maneuver element.[28]

Commanders permitted batteries to operate independently because the war was basically a small unit conflict and was being fought over a large area. Although commanders preferred to keep fire direction under the battalion's control, batteries had to be able to direct their own fire since they were often employed piecemeal into battle. In some cases, batteries fragmented operations even more by assigning part of their guns for base camp defense and the other for tactical employment.[29]

Because of operations over vast areas, numerous displacements, short, violent actions, and an undefinable front and rear in 1965–66, the field artillery found the battery-battalion arrangement to be logical and to provide fast, accurate fire. As a result, the enemy feared American field artillery and made batteries prime targets for infiltration or full-scale attacks. Unable to perform their missions and protect themselves simultaneously, field artillerymen created fire support bases by positioning their pieces with the command post of a maneuver battalion. From these positions located so that any point in the area of operations could be reached by at least one battery and usually two or more, the maneuver commander conducted offensive operations, while field artillery, ranging from 105-mm howitzers to 175-mm guns, furnished fire support and helped defend other fire bases as required. This arrangement guaranteed a rapid response by the artillery when called upon, simplified furnishing fire support in guerrilla warfare, and saved lives. The base along with the availability of naval gunfire and tactical air gave the Army the capacity to rain deadly fire and reinforced the growing trend of relying upon firepower rather than maneuver for defeating the enemy.[30]

Most commanders concluded that the overriding lesson of 1965–66 was the importance of firepower. As the battles indicated, American ground forces were vulnerable when they lacked fire support. Because of that, many commanders reluctantly operated beyond their artillery or tactical air support and refused to fight on equal terms with the enemy.[31] Commenting on this, Brigadier General Willard Pearson, Commander, 1st Brigade, 101st Airborne Division, wrote in December 1966 that his unit's motto was "Save Lives, Not Ammunition."[32] Given this, he wrote in December 1966 that the ground forces' main task involved finding the enemy. Artillery and air power had the responsibility of defeating, routing, or destroying the enemy. In December 1966 he admitted, "Our airmobile operations and fire support then become the mainstay of our offensive."[33] Along with other commanders, Pearson insisted that massive artillery and air fire were the most effective ways to crumble enemy resistance. Although some officers opposed such a tactic, most commanders valued firepower because it preserved lives. A memorandum for General Kalergis pointed out "There is not [a] price tag in [on] the life of a US soldier; massive use of artillery, air and naval support will save US lives."[34]

The war in 1965–66, therefore, forced the field artillery to modify tactics and organization. Without a front line gun crews did not have the luxury of establishing positions in the rear areas, had to fire in a complete circle, had to defend themselves from infiltrators, had to airlift their pieces into remote areas, and had to decentralize their batteries through habitual association to provide support in many cases. Even though habitual association created fierce loyalties between the infantry and field artillery, it made massing battalion and division fire difficult and elevated the importance of the battery fire direction center. Despite these adaptations during the heat of combat, the field artillery gave prompt, reliable support. Along with the pressure from public opinion to preserve lives, by 1966 the Army made field artillery, naval, and air firepower more important than maneuver since infantry, armor, and cavalry units would not conduct operations unless they were under the protective umbrella of fire support.

Operations Cedar Falls and Junction City

Battles in 1967 and 1968 also reflected this preoccupation with fire-power. Despite the success of the search-and-destroy operations in 1966, hostile bastions still dotted South Vietnam. Carefully situated in hard-to-reach areas-jungles, mountains, and swamps and provided with escape routes, the bastions furnished the enemy excellent bases from which they assaulted South Vietnam. Since the Iron Triangle was a formidable arrow tip pointing straight at Saigon, the Army decided late in 1966 to destroy that preserve even though previous attempts had failed. Early in January 1967, the 1st Infantry Division, the 25th Infantry Division, the 173rd Airborne Brigade, the 11th Armored Cavalry Regiment, and separate battalions of the Army of the Republic of Vietnam opened Operation Cedar Falls. The units moved into pre-arranged positions around the Triangle to seal it off and attacked.[35] As expected, main force Viet Cong units dispersed as the Americans and South Vietnamese pushed into the bastion. Although enemy resistance was light, the field artillery fired missions from bases ringing the area of operations to seal off escape routes or reduce small points of resistance and fiercely shelled landing zones. Nevertheless, division artillery commanders had difficulty locating moving units and coordinating supporting fires. Because of this, the 1st Division's artillery commander delegated fire control to commanders of direct support battalions, who helped convert the Iron Triangle from a haven into a no man's land by the end of January.[36]

Shortly thereafter, the Army launched another multi-division operation called Junction City. For years the insurgents had a major stronghold along the Cambodian border from which they had hit the South Vietnamese. Late in February, the Americans surrounded the area with 18 battalions and 13 mutually supporting fire bases and conducted search-and-destroy operations over the next three weeks.[37]

Junction City culminated with the battles of Ap Bau Bang II, Suoi Tre, and Ap Gu. In each case Viet Cong forces attacked American fire bases with mortar rounds, rifle grenades, rockets, and recoilless rifle fire. To fight off the assaults the Americans employed small arms fire, field artillery, and air strikes. According to Brigadier General David E. Ott, Commander, 25th Division's artillery, the most significant artillery action occurred around Fire Support Base Gold during the Battle of Suoi Tre. As infantry patrols swept around the base on 21 March, they bumped into a Viet Cong force that was preparing to assail the base. The accidental confrontation prematurely triggered a violent enemy attack. To defend themselves American gun crews levelled their tubes and spewed beehive rounds (canister rounds filled with hundreds of metal darts) into the Viet Cong. At point-blank range round after round hit the assaulting force as batteries from other bases threw up a continuous wall of shells around the perimeter and as air strikes pounded the attackers. This demonstration of firepower along with small arms fire compelled the Viet Cong to withdraw.[38]

As Lieutenant General Bernard W. Rogers, who was the assistant division commander of the 1st Infantry Division in 1967, recalled in 1974, Cedar Falls/Junction City operations confirmed the importance of field artillery and air power. They verified the need to get as much firepower on the enemy as quickly as possible and to use artillery and air strikes simultaneously. Equally important, these operations reemphasized the value of 105-mm howitzers because of their rapidfire capabilities and strengthened the requirement for mutually supporting bases.[39]

In *Summons of the Trumpet: US-Vietnam Perspective* (1978), David R. Palmer, an advisor to the Vietnamese Military Academy and Vietnamese armor units during the Vietnam War, caught the essence of the transformation-of Army tactics caused by the drive for fire support. By 1967 only a foolhardy or a desperate commander would ever engage the enemy by any means other than firepower. Early drifts towards this mentality started in Ia Orang and culminated in 1967. Even though Army doctrine still called for fire and maneuver, practice in Vietnam differed considerably. Commanders located the enemy with infantry and then attacked with field artillery and air strikes. After leaving Vietnam, General Westmoreland criticized this routine vigorously when he admitted that artillery and air power had produced a firebase psychosis.[40]

The Tet Offensive and the Vietnamization of the War

In 1968, the North Vietnamese abandoned their strategy of a protracted war. Within 24 hours after the beginning of Tet, on 30 January 1968, Hanoi launched a series of attacks from the demilitarized zone to the southern tip of Vietnam. The Viet Cong and North Vietnamese struck six major cities, 64 district capitals, and 50 hamlets and caught the Americans and South Vietnamese off guard. In Saigon the Americans and South Vietnamese repulsed the initial assaults and cleared the city within several days. A similar pattern emerged in other places with the exception of Hue. After three weeks of heavy bombing and intensive artillery fire, the Americans and South Vietnamese finally liberated the city.[41]

Generally, post-Tet operations reflected past counter-guerrilla operations. Enemy tactics compelled the resumption of small unit actions, ranging from squad- to company-size. As the other combat arms scoured the countryside, gun crews supplied close support by shelling enemy positions. As a means to extend offensive operations, the Army conducted artillery raids from fire bases into remote areas by displacing artillery to supplementary positions and quickly withdrawing. Normally, a raid included one 105-mm howitzer battery, one understrength 155-mm howitzer battery (three howitzers), one rifle company for security, aerial observers from division artillery, and air cavalry for target acquisition and damage assessment when it was available. Equally important, American field artillerymen created a fourth firing battery in direct support battalions because of the clamor for more firepower and because of a surplus of guns and ammunition and increased the use of the Field Artillery Digital Automatic Computer (FADAC) that had been introduced in Vietnam in 1966–67. In fact, FADAC had become the primary means of computing firing data by 1969.[42]

Although FADAC did not eliminate the need for manual computation for backup capability, it greatly altered the field artillery's performance in Vietnam. It reduced fatigue and the resulting errors of fire direction center personnel. By doing this FADAC greatly increased accuracy, decreased response time, and allowed gun crews to fire longer missions and hit more targets with less ammunition. For the field artillery these capabilities were critical because the North Vietnamese and Viet Cong were elusive, used hit-and-run tactics, and engaged the Americans and their allies at close distance with the idea of negating their superiority in artillery, helicopter, and tactical air support.[43]

The war assumed a new dimension following Tet. Even though the North Vietnamese did not achieve their objective, their ability to initiate such an offensive stimulated a great debate in the United States. For many Americans the offensive symbolized the senseless destruction of the war. For the military Tet presented a golden opportunity to crush the Viet Cong and North Vietnamese because they were weakened by that great effort. Seeking to take advantage of the enemy's condition, Westmoreland proposed a two-fisted offensive, a ground attack against sanctuaries in Laos and Cambodia and an intensive bombing campaign. In contrast, Pentagon civilians urged shifting from search-and destroy operations to population security by deploying the bulk of the military forces along the demographic frontier, a line just north of the major population centers. From here the military would defend against a major North Vietnamese thrust and engage in limited offensive operations to keep the enemy off balance. Pentagon civilians also wanted the South Vietnamese to assume more responsibility for their own defense and hoped to end the war through negotiation rather than a resounding military victory. Even though the military bitterly denounced this position and warned that it would produce certain disaster, President Lyndon B. Johnson's administration accepted it in March 1968, an election year. Because of his opposition to expanding the war, President Johnson cut back bombing, informed the South Vietnamese that they had to shoulder more of the burden for defending themselves, and launched a peace initiative to create an independent, non-communist South Vietnam.[44]

Although the Army continued fighting into 1973, Vietnamization changed the field artillery's primary mission. Beginning early in 1969, the Americans upgraded assistance programs to improve South Vietnamese artillery operations, allowed the South Vietnamese to function independently, and launched equipment modernization and training programs. Despite these efforts and those that strengthened the South Vietnamese army as a whole, South Vietnam finally collapsed in 1975 in the face of a determined North Vietnamese onslaught.[45]

Even though the Vietnam War demonstrated the Army's flexibility to move from its preoccupation with nuclear war to unconventional war, it also revealed the Army's growing reliance upon firepower. Exploiting improved artillery systems coming off production lines, using FADAC to assist with automated gunnery procedures and dusting off forgotten tactics and techniques, field artillerymen delivered unprecedented accurate fire to shatter enemy attacks and seal off the battlefield and showed their ability to furnish huge quantities of fire. Ironically, the Army's past conditioned soldiers to see firepower-artillery, naval guns, and tactical air-as the preferable solution.

The Artillery Branch Study

Additionally, the Vietnam War highlighted the inherent shortcomings of consolidating the field and coast artillery. Following the closing of the Seacoast Artillery School in 1950 and disbanding coast artillery units or converting them to field or antiaircraft artillery that same year, only field and antiaircraft artillery (called air defense artillery after 1957) existed as part of the Army's artillery. Because of the growing divergence of techniques, tactics, doctrine, equipment, and materiel for the two artilleries, the Continental Army Command outlined a plan in 1955 to develop basic courses in field artillery and antiaircraft artillery for new officers. Integrated basic and advanced officer courses, which had been initiated in 1947, had failed to provide officers with adequate preparation to serve effectively in either artillery.[46] With support from the Army's Assistant Chief of

Staff for Training, the Continental Army Command created basic courses for the two artilleries in 1957 but reintegrated basic officer training in 1958 through 1961 because of the lack of officers and money.[47] In the meantime, the Continental Army Command retained the integrated artillery advanced course for officers with five to eight years of experience because of pressure to maintain flexibility in officer assignments.[48]

The pressure to end integrated training and form field artillery and air defense artillery as two distinct combat arms branches mounted. Based upon the report of the Army Officer Education and Review Board of 1958, the Continental Army Command reintroduced separate basic officer courses in 1962 because of the need for specialized training for new officers. Because the Army wanted flexibility to shift experienced artillery officers easily between field and air defense artillery units, the command retained the integrated advanced course. As a part of the advanced course, student officers received instruction at the Artillery and Guided Missile School and the Air Defense School at Fort Bliss, Texas. In a student thesis at the Army War College in 1963, Colonel William F. Brand pointed out that integrated training provided an inadequate amount of time for detailed instruction on all artillery weapons, which meant that officers left the advanced course without mastering any of the weapons. As a result, Colonel Brand urged separate training for field artillery and air defense artillery. At the direction of the Commanding General, Continental Army Command, the Artillery and Guided Missile School and the Air Defense School explored the desirability of dividing the artillery into two branches. In 1963 the schools recommended separation because of the difficulty of cross training and the growing difference between the two artilleries. In line with this, the authors of "The Artillery Branch Study" of 1966 wrote that integrated training 'spawned mediocrity.'"[49]

In 1965–1967 the demand for field artillery officers with highly professional skills in the Vietnam War finally caused the Army and the Continental Army Command to reorganize the artillery. Because of the one-year tour that left little time for on the-job training, combat in Vietnam required the officer to arrive as a proficient field artilleryman and not a hybrid field and air defense artilleryman. Army commanders in Vietnam simply did not have the time to train an air defense artilleryman to be competent in field artillery and upgrade the skills of a field artillery man, who had had insufficient training in the basic techniques.[50] Viewing the past years of integration and its detrimental impact on field and air defense artillery and the need for qualified officers in both artilleries, authors of "The Artillery

Branch Study' urged ceasing the practice of cross training and forming two separate branches of artillery.[51]

The Army concurred with the recommendations and split the field artillery and air defense artillery into two distinct combat arms with their own training programs in 1968. This freed field artillerymen to concentrate on field artillery subjects. Yet, separating the two artilleries had little impact upon the Artillery and Guided Missile School, which was renamed the Field Artillery School, because it was already focusing its energies on field artillery.

Conclusion

The Vietnam War had a profound impact on the field artillery. After years of debate over the validity of consolidating field and air defense artillery, the war prompted the Army to recognize the existence of two artilleries and to make them independent of each other. Also, the war compelled the field artillery to adapt to fight a small-unit war, but it never abandoned its faith in massing fire or being to fight large-scale combat operations against a near peer threat. The operational environment imposed many challenges on artilleryman that they had not trained for nor experienced since conducting operations during the Pacific campaign in the Second World War. In the end, US Army artillery proved once again that it could provide fire support to maneuver forces when and where it was needed. More importantly, artilleryman demonstrated flexibility, adaptability and ingenuity in accomplishing whatever mission was assigned them. Lessons learned from the Vietnam War would be put into practice 15 years later in the deserts of Kuwait and Iraq during the First Iraq War, 1990 to 1991. This time however, artilleryman found themselves operating in an operational environment they had trained for thanks in part to the many unit rotations conducted at the National Training Center (NTC) and elsewhere.

Though methods of the employment of fires, both lethal and non-lethal, have changed since the end of the Vietnam War, it is vitally important that Field Artillerymen today continue to focus on developing the necessary skills and abilities to provide "collective and coordinated use of Army indirect fires . . . in support of offensive and defensive tasks to create specific lethal and nonlethal effects" against a near-peer threat in large-scale combat operations.[52]

Notes

1. Report on the War in Vietnam. Admiral U.S.G. Sharp, Commander in Chief Pacific and General W.C. Westmoreland, Commander, US Military Assistance Command, Vietnam, 30 June 1968 (Morris Swett Library hereafter MSL), 98.

2. David E. Ott, *Field Artillery: 1954–1973* (Washington DC: Department of the Army, 1975), 22–37.

3. George C. Herring. "The 1st Cavalry and the Ia Drang Valley, 18 October–24 November 1965," in Charles E. Heller and William A. Stofft, eds., *America's First Battles, 1776–1965* (Lawrence, KS: University Press of Kansas, 1986), 300–01; Allan R. Millet and Peter Maslowski, *For the Common Defense,* (New York: The Free Press, 1984), 547.

4. Report on the War in Vietnam. Admiral U.S.G. Sharp, Commander in Chief Pacific: and General W.C. Westmoreland, Commander, US Military Assistance Command, Vietnam, 30 June 1968 (MSL), 98.

5. *Artillery Trends,* January 1967, 1; I.etter, HQ 2nd Battalion, 32nd Artillery, to CG, US Army Artillery and Missile School, "Heavy Artillery in the Guerrilla Warfare Environment," 24 January 1966, in Correspondence Received from Vietnam File, MSL; Herring, "The 1st Cavalry and the Ia Drang Valley," 306.

6. George C. Herring, *America's Longest War: The United States in Vietnam, 1950–1975* (New York: John Wiley and Sons, 1979), 151; George C. Herring. "The 1st Cavalry and the Ia Drang Valley, 303–304; Robert H. Scales, "Firepower and Maneuver in the Second Indochina War," *Field Artillery Journal*, September–October, 1986, 48; Harry W.O. Kinnard, "A Victory in the Ia Drang: Triumph of a Concept," *Army*, September 1967, 77.

7. Kinnard, "A Victory in the Ia Drang," 78–83; After Action Report, 1st Cavalry Division, 23 October–26 November 1965, 45, 51, 54, MSL.

8. Kinnard, "A Victory in the Ia Drang," 84–86; Scales, "Firepower and Maneuver in the Second Indochina War," 49–50; After Action Report. 1st Cavalry Division, 23 October–26 November 1965, 84; Report, CG, 1-7th Cavalry, 1st Cavalry Division (Airmobile), "After Action Report, Ia Drang Valley Operation, 1st Battalion, 7th Cavalry," 14–16 November 1965, 3–11.

9. After Action Report, 1st Cavalry Division, 23 October–26 November 1965, 87; Herring, "The 1st Cavalry and the Ia Drang Valley," 319; Kinnard, " A Victory in the Ia Drang," 86–87; Scales, "Firepower and Maneuver in the Second Indochina War," 50; Report, CO, 1-7th Cavalry, lst Cavalry Division (Airmobile), "After Action Report, Ia Drang Valley Operation, 1st Battalion, 7th Cavalry," 14–16 November 1965, 13–15.

10. After Action Report, 1st Cavalry, 23 October–26 November 1965, 93–94, MSL; Herring. "The 1st Cavalry and the Ia Drang Valley, 18 October–24 November 1965," 320; Kinnard, "A Victory in the Ia Drang," 88–89; Ott, *Field Artillery*, 94–95.

11. Kinnard, "A Victory in the Ia Drang," 85.

12. Kinnard, 85.

13. After Action Report, 1st Cavalry, 23 October–26 November 1965, Forward, MSL.

14. After Action Report, 1st Cavalry, 23 October–26 November 1965, Forward, MSL.

15. Lloyd J. Picou, "Airmobile Artillery in Combat," *Artillery Trends,* August 1967, 20. *Artillery Trends* was a small journal published by the Artillery and Guided Missile School during the late 1950s through early 1970s. During those years the journal went by several different names: The *Artillery Quarterly, Trends in Artillery for Instruction,* and The *Field Artilleryman.* Basically, the journal was designed for in-house use by instructors at Fort Sill and for wide distribution.

16. Lloyd J. Picou, "Artillery Support for the Airmobile Division," *Artillery Trends*, October 1968, 7.

17. Picou, 7.

18. After Action Report, 1st Cavalry, 23 October–26 November 1965, 127; Report, US Army Vietnam, "Battlefield Report: A Summary of Lessons Learned," n.d., 52–55, MSL.

19. Report on the War in Vietnam, 30 June 1968, 114, MSL.

20. Lloyd J. Picou, "The Day the Artillery Sprouted Wings," Army Information Digest, November 1966, 24–25; Ott, *Field Artillery*, 100–101; Report, 1st Air Cavalry Artillery, "Operation Masher and White Wing (Eagle Claw)," 14 March 1966, 49; *1st Air Cavalry: Memoirs of the First team, Vietnam, August 1965–December 1966* (Tokyo: Dia Nippon Printing Company, Ltd, n.d.), 30–32.

21. Ott, *Field Artillery*, 105–106. After Action Report, 1st Air Cavalry Division Artillery, 16 May 1966, 10, MSL.

22. Lloyd J. Picou, "Artillery Support for the Airmobile Division," *Military Review,* (October, 1968), 9–10.

23. Picou, "Artillery Support for the Airmobile Division," 11; Report, 1st Air Cavalry Artillery, "Operation Masher/White Wing (Eagle Claw)," 14 March 1966, 5.

24. Picou, "Artillery Support for the Airmobile Division," 11; Report, 1st Air Cavalry Artillery, "Operation Masher/White Wing (Eagle Claw)," 14 March 1966, 5, MSL.

25. Letter, 3rd Battalion, 18th Field Artillery to US Army Artillery and Missile School, "Artillery Employment," 8 August 1966, in Lessons Learned, 18th Field Artillery File, Morris Swett Library; Report US Army, Vietnam, "A Summary of Lessons Learned," 30 August 1965, II-I, MSL; report, US Army, Vietnam, "A Summary of Lessons Learned," n.d., 55, MSL.

26. "Simple Solutions to 6400-mil Charts, *Artillery Trends*, January 1967, 11.

27. Report , Major General Charles P. Brown, Commandant, The Artillery and Missile School, 11–24 September 1967, MSL; "Field Artillery Equipment," *Artillery Trends*, July 1966, 3–11

28. After Action Report, 196th Light Infantry Brigade, 25 November 1966–68, April 1967, 3; Picou, "Airmobile Artillery in Combat," 12–14; Memorandum for Commanding General, I Field Force V Artillery, 5 December 1967, in letter,

HQ I Field Force V, to Brigadier General John J. Kenney, Assistant Commandant, Artillery and Missile School, 4 January 1968, MSL.

29. Memorandum for Commanding General, I Field Force V Artillery, 5 December 1967; DF, "Observations of Artillery Operations in Vietnam," 14 May 1968, TAB A, MSL.

30. Bruce R. Palmer, Jr., *The 25 Year War: America's Military Role in Vietnam* (Lexington, KY: The University Press of Kentucky, 1984), 158; Report on the War in Vietnam, 30 June 1968, 120; Letter, Headquarters 3rd Battalion, 319th Field Artillery to Commandant, US Army Artillery and Missile School, 15 January 1966, in Correspondence Received from Vietnam File, MSL; Ott, *Field Artillery*, 42–45; Piccou, "Airmobile Artillery in Combat," 12–18; Captain F.H. Hemphill Jr., "Defence of the Artillery Battery." *Artillery Trends*, January 1967, 27–32; Colonel R.E. Cavazos, et al., *Analysis of Fire and Maneuver in Vietnam*, June 1966–June 1968 (Carlisle Barracks, PA: US Army War College, 1969), II-16–25; Captain Gary J. Pieringer, "Counting the Sappers," *Field Artillery*, August 1988, 6; Ott, *Field Artillery*, 55–58, 238.

31. Robert A. Doughty, *The Evolution of US Army Tactical Doctrine, 1946–1976* (Fort Leavenworth, KS: Combat Studies Institute, US Army Command and General Staff College, 1976), 36–38.

32. Willard Pearson, "Find 'em, Fix 'em, Finish 'em," *Army Information Digest*, December 1966, 19.

33. Pearson, "Find 'em, Fix 'em, Finish 'em," 19.

34. Memorandum for Commanding General, I Field Force V, 5 December 1967, MSL; Scales, "Firepower and Maneuver in the Second Indochina War," 53.

35. Ott, *Field Artillery*, 110; David R. Palmer, *Summons of the Trumpet: US-Vietnam in Perspective* (San Francisco, CA: Presidio Press, 1978), 134–137; Bernard W. Rogers, *Cedar Falls-Junction City: A Turning Point* (Washington DC: Department of the Army, 1974), 16–217.

36. After Action Report, 173rd Airborne Brigade, 25 February 1967, 3–4, MSL; After Action Report, 1st Division, 13 March 1967, Annex F, MSL; Rogers, 24–43, 75–76.

37. Rogers, *Cedar Falls-Junction City*, 83, 103, 107, 110.

38. Rogers, 129–140; Ott, *Field Artillery,* 113–118.

39. Rogers, 156.

40. Palmer, *Summons of the Trumpet*, 140–146.

41. Herring, *America's Longest War,* 185–187.

42. Ott, *Field Artillery*, 157–169, 184–185; Major Robert E. Gilbert, "FADAC," *Artillery Trends*, May, 1968, 45; Major Martell D. Fritz, "Revised Programs for FADAC, *Artillery Trends*, April 1969, 36; Lieutenant General Richard G. Stilwell, "Evolution in Tactics: The Vietnam Experience," *Army*, February 1970, 21; Lieutenant General Frank T. Mildren, "From Mekong to DMZ: A Fighting Year for the US Army's Best," *Army*, November 1968, 88.

43. Lieutenant Colonel Matthew J. Ringer and Major Martell D. Fritz, "FADAC Computations versus Manual Computations," *Artillery Trends*, April 1969, 40; Mildren, "From Mekong to DMZ," 88.

44. Herring, *America's Longest War,* 189–197, 204–205.

45. Herring, 189–197, 227–252.

46. Letter, Headquarters, Continental Army Command to Assistant Chief of Staff, G3, 9 February 1955, The Artillery Center, Integration of the Artillery Schools, MSL; "The Artillery Branch Study," 35, 36, 41 MSL; Disposition of Enclosures, "Integration of the Artillery," n.d., The Artillery Center, "Consolidation of the Artillery School;" "Army Reorganization," *Antiaircraft Journal*, July–August 1950, 27.

47. "The Artillery Branch Study," 61.

48. "The Artillery Branch Study," 41; Acting Assistant Chief of Staff, G3, to Commanding General, Continental Army Command, "Training and Assignment of Artillery Officers," 11 June 1955, The Artillery Center, Integration of the Artillery School; Letter, de Shazo to Commanding General, Continental Army Command, "Integration of the Artillery," 16 May 1956, US Army Artillery Center, Integration of the Artillery Schools, MSL.

49. "The Artillery Branch Study," 45, 46, 93; William F. Brand, "A Re-examination of the Integration of the Artillerists," Thesis, US Army War College, 1963, 31–32.

50. William F. Brand, "A Re-examination of the Integration of the Artillerists," Thesis, US Army War College, 1963, 118–119.

51. "Two Career Fields Formed for Artillery," *The Journal of the Armed Forces*, 15 June 1968, 29; "Air, Ground Artillery Split," *Army Times*, 19 June 1968, 1; William F. Brand, "A Re-examination of the Integration of the Artillerists," 24; "The Artillery Branch Study," 52–53.

52. Department of the Army, Army Doctrine Reference Publication (ADRP 3-0), *Operations* (Washington, DC: 16 August 2017), 5-4.

Chapter 9

Close Air Support and Bombardment Theory: Operation Cobra

Mark T. Calhoun

After more than two decades of US Army involvement in counterinsurgency, counterterrorism, and stability operations, today's senior leaders have expressed concern about the Army's preparedness to engage in large-scale combat operations (LSCO) against peer and near-peer threats.[1] While most of today's Army personnel have participated in limited wars, few have experienced LSCO. This begs the question how the Army should prepare for multi-domain battle (MDB) in the anticipated future operational environment.[2]

In *On War*, Carl von Clausewitz described practice through maneuvers that include elements of friction and physical exertion, like those experienced in combat, as the next-best thing to actual combat experience.[3] In addition to realistic maneuvers, Clausewitz advocated critical thinking, a means of testing military theory through objective analysis of history, as another way to prepare for war, arguing that "The influence of theoretical truths on practical life is always exerted more through critical analysis than through doctrine."[4]

Operation Cobra, the American breakout from Normandy in late July, 1944 illustrates the validity of Clausewitz's assertions. Cobra serves today as a testament not only to the US Army's maturation through the interwar years, but also to the harmful effects of branch parochialism. This resulted in both the most effective and the most tragic use of strategic bombers in close support of US ground troops during World War II (WWII).

Theoretical debates plagued air-ground cooperation before and during WWII, and have continued to do so ever since. In his study of Close Air Support (CAS) doctrine and capability, US Air Force Major Russell Fette described this pattern as an "ebb and flow" of American air-ground cooperation.[5] Fette argued that CAS competency requires good relationships between the air and ground arms, which enables the cooperation needed to develop sound doctrine, tactics, and training. He found that over the past century, the US military's air-ground relationship has atrophied during peacetime as services competed for higher budgets and new equipment. The relationship tends to recover in combat, when a common enemy motivates land and air forces to rebuild relationships that enable development of effective CAS tactics, techniques, and procedures (TTP), but this takes place slowly, resulting in poor CAS in the early phases of conflict that gradually improves over time.[6] In the interwar years, branch parochialism outweighed critical analysis as strategic bombardment theory came to dominate Army Air Corps (AAC) doctrine, education, training, and aircraft development.

The Development of a Strategic Bombing Theory

The airpower debate began in earnest soon after World War I (WWI), when AAC leaders embraced independent strategic bombing theory, advocated by Italian theorist Giulio Douhet and later by American pilots like William "Billy" Mitchell.[7] Rapid advances in bomber range, payload, and self-defense capability seemed to promise victory in future wars without the need for ground combat. Further, many pilots saw bombardment theory as the means to achieve their longstanding goal of independence from ground forces' control, given the theory's central premise that airpower had a unique, strategic mission.[8] By contrast, non-flying Army leaders argued that airpower could not win wars alone, emphasizing combined arms fighting and the need for close air-ground cooperation. Still, strategic bombing, while purely theoretical, took an increasingly central role in US Army Air Corps (AAC) doctrine.

Bombardment theory soon dominated the curriculum at the Air Corps Tactical School (ACTS), the AAC's highest educational institution and doctrinal center during the interwar period. Major Harold George, a senior instructor at the ACTS, emerged after Billy Mitchell's court martial and dismissal from the Army as one of the AAC's most influential proponents of the bombardment theory. As noted by historian Thomas Hughes, "Harold George, more than anyone else, provided the intellectual groundwork for what became a fully-articulated independent-strategic-air theory." [9] Most of the other instructors soon shared George's views on the future of airpower, and together they emphasized bombardment theory at the expense of instruction on the use of tactical airpower.

Rapidly increasing bomber technology led to the appearance in 1936 of the B-17 "Flying Fortress," the first heavy bomber designed to provide its own self-defense, thereby making fighter escorts obsolete. With President Franklin Delano Roosevelt's support, the AAC budget grew rapidly, with most of the additional funding spent on bomber development and production. In the 1930s alone, three new bombers left American assembly lines, including the B-10 in 1931, the B-12 in 1932, and the B-17 in 1936. By contrast, the US Army did not begin production of the P-40 Mustang—the first significant development in American fighter technology in ten years—until 1940.[10]

Most Army pilots embraced bombardment theory, including AAC war planners who, under the direction of General Henry "Hap" Arnold, based their concept of airpower employment on the theory's central tenets. An absence of critical thinking took hold as bombardment theory increasingly dominated AAC doctrine. With a major war brewing on the horizon, not only pilots in the AAC and the Royal Air Force (RAF), but also many American and British senior military and national leaders accepted the theory as dogma. Some of the interwar period's most influential bombardment theory advocates later acknowledged the imbalance its adoption created in the air arm's combined arms capability. Haywood Hansell, another ACTS instructor and bombardment theory proponent during the interwar years, reflected after the war, "I think we got carried away so far on this strategic thing . . . that we have decimated, we've emasculated our own force."[11]

Despite these challenges, some Army pilots before WWII remained open to the idea of tactical air-to-ground support. In this contentious environment, a young pilot named Pete Quesada emerged as an agent of change, retaining his enthusiasm for CAS despite the AAC's focus on strategic bombing theory. Quesada attended the Command and General Staff College (CGSC) after the ACTS, where he developed close relationships with many non-flying Army officers and often discussed with them the value of tactical air support to ground combat troops. The perspective Quesada gained at CGSC deepened his conviction that the AAC needed a powerful tactical air capability to complement the strategic bombing mission.[12]

Still, this remained a minority view, and Quesada lacked the rank or influence to change minds already fixed on bombardment theory. He did, however, have an excellent reputation among both flying and non-flying officers. He served throughout the interwar period as an aide to many senior leaders, including three months working for Colonel George C. Marshall during his tenure as commandant of the Infantry School at Fort Benning, Georgia. Marshall liked to fly and spent many hours with Quesada in a small observation aircraft, developing a very favorable opinion of him.[13]

He also made a good impression on Hap Arnold, who brought Quesada to the War Department in 1942 to serve on Arnold's newly-designated, independent Army Air Forces (AAF) staff. A few months later Arnold, with Quesada in tow, traveled to London in the aftermath of the Battle of Britain. Both Arnold and the leaders of Britain's Royal Air Force (RAF) saw the devastation of London as validation of bombardment theory. Ironically, even though it was RAF fighter pilots who finally drove the Germans out of British skies, the Battle of Britain seemingly ushered in the age of the strategic bomber. Men like Hap Arnold believed that the

Germans would have won the Battle of Britain if only they had possessed advanced bombers like the B-17.[14]

When Arnold returned to the War Department he created the Air War Planning Division (AWPD). Manned exclusively by AAF pilots committed to the independent strategic bombing concept, the AWPD developed war plans that reflected this view. As Quesada put it in a post-war interview, "they allowed their doctrine to become their strategy."[15] This strategy would soon be put to the test. As Hughes wrote, "Now these men had to justify spending billions of dollars, and the use of almost a third of the Army's manpower on independent air power. To do so, they created a war plan that mirrored their beliefs and hopes."[16]

Quesada emerged from this period with his views on tactical airpower intact, but he lacked the ability to influence war planning. Still, the young major possessed the talent and drive that Army Chief of Staff General George C. Marshall valued when selecting young officers to replace the Army's aging senior leaders and mobilize newly formed units for combat. By the fall of 1942, Marshall had arranged for Quesada's rapid promotion from major to brigadier general, and Arnold selected him to command the First Air Defense Wing. Quesada soon received orders to join the Allied task force in Tunisia, only two months after Operation Torch, the amphibious assault of North Africa.[17]

The Air War in North Africa

Quesada arrived in Tunisia on 27 January 1943, where he soon learned of British military leaders' disappointment in the Americans' combat performance. If the Western Desert Forces, commanded by Lieutenant General Dwight D. Eisenhower, had secured Tunis before weather forced the Allies to cease operations, they would have trapped Field Marshal Erwin Rommel's *Afrika Korps* between the British Eighth Army to the south and Eisenhower's forces to the north and northwest. Instead, the Germans won the "race for Tunis" and still controlled this vital communications node, enabling arrival by sea of supplies and reinforcements.[18]

During the weather-induced pause in combat, Eisenhower reflected on the performance of his Western Desert Forces during their first two months in combat. Many participants and observers saw the Allies' failure to seize the port city of Tunis before the rainy season in December 1942 as a failure of American leadership and evidence of the US Army's poor state of readiness. This led to angst among the British and American Allies that exacerbated an already bad situation.[19]

Concerned about the AAF's poor performance in November and December of 1942, Eisenhower concluded that much of the problem resulted from the air planners' focus on bombardment strategy, and their neglect of basic and predictable factors like weather, terrain, and disease. Challenges created by poor planning and difficulties coordinating air support between the British Eastern Air Command and the US Twelfth Air Force—separated both by distance and nationality—convinced Eisenhower that he must consolidate all airpower in the theater under a single command. On 5 January 1943, the Combined Chiefs of Staff approved creation of the Allied Air Force. While this umbrella organization centralized control over all air forces in the Mediterranean, it lacked the integration needed at lower levels to improve air-ground coordination.[20]

In February, Eisenhower again reorganized his air forces, creating the Mediterranean Air Command. This headquarters commanded the newly-designated Northwest African Air Forces, which further subdivided into five organizations, consolidating American and British air forces by function—an unprecedented move, but one that most air and ground commanders supported in hopes of improving airpower's effectiveness.[21]

Significantly, the primary air effort throughout the Tunisian campaign remained interdiction of enemy shipping. While this mission provided no visible benefit to ground combat units, it significantly hindered delivery by sea of logistics materiel and reinforcements to Axis forces. By contrast, tactical air support, although it often provided a morale boost to the ground forces, remained in a rudimentary stage of development. Fighter pilots slowly worked out basic air-to-ground procedures while facing many challenges, including faulty radar and communication systems, difficulty distinguishing friend from foe, lack of established air-to-ground coordination procedures, and slow response to air support requests.[22]

Still, German air superiority remained the most significant problem for Allied airpower in North Africa. High-altitude bombers rarely experienced attacks by the Luftwaffe, but many dogfights took place between Allied and German fighters. While AAF pilots generally performed well in these air-to-air engagements, German control of the air often diverted scarce tactical aircraft from assigned CAS missions, leaving ground forces vulnerable to Stuka dive bombers. The Allies finally achieved air superiority in North Africa in April 1943—just one month before the last German units evacuated Tunis by sea. Hap Arnold, commanding the independent Army Air Forces (AAF), sent an observer to the Mediterranean in the summer of 1943 "to capitalize on the practical field experience . . . which may be at variance to more established theories of air warfare."[23]

Eisenhower remained in Tunisia after the Allied victory to oversee planning for upcoming operations in the Mediterranean Theater. At three conferences held in November and December 1943, Allied military and national leaders met to forge agreements related to matters of coalition strategy. During the first Cairo Conference, from 22–26 November, Roosevelt and Churchill met with Chiang Kai-Shek and his wife to discuss China's role in the Far Eastern Theater. Roosevelt and Churchill then traveled to Tehran where, from 27 November to 2 December, they met with Joseph Stalin to discuss the Allied invasion of Western Europe. Stalin insisted that the invasion take place no later than May 1944, to take pressure off the Red Army on the Eastern Front. Churchill and Roosevelt traveled directly back to Cairo from Tehran, meeting with the Combined Chiefs of Staff from 2 to 7 December, 1943 to discuss final plans for the invasion of Normandy. One important decision remained in flux until 6 December, when Roosevelt finally announced that he had selected Eisenhower to serve as the Supreme Commander, Allied Expeditionary Forces for Operation Overlord.[24]

The Role of Air Support in Operation Overlord

Eisenhower and his staff had much to do, with D-Day of Operation Overlord only five months away. Reflecting on his experience in North Africa, Eisenhower knew that he must once again consolidate all ground forces and airpower in theater under a single command structure. In this case, however, planning for command arrangements began well before execution of the amphibious assault in Normandy, giving senior leaders time to prepare for their new roles in Western Europe.[25]

Eisenhower expressed his concept of ground command arrangements in a cable to Marshall on 23 December 1943.[26] While this concept worked effectively throughout the campaign in Western Europe, the air organization still suffered from the divisive effects of bombardment theory. Significant differences in air leaders' views on strategic versus tactical employment of airpower created friction both among air leaders and between air and ground commanders. Despite several changes of command before D-Day, this friction remained problematic throughout the war.[27]

Eisenhower found these disputes and leadership changes especially frustrating during the final planning for Operation Overlord, when they disrupted efforts to develop a detailed air support plan for the operation. One of the main disputes involved the use of heavy bombers in a ground support role. Eisenhower intended to use this method in support of Overlord even though many senior pilots remained opposed to it. On 22 March, Eisenhower expressed his frustration in a memorandum for record, which he instructed his aide to handle personally to keep his remarks secret: "The actual air preparatory plan is to be the subject of a formal meeting on this coming Saturday, March 25. . . . If a satisfactory answer is not reached I am going to . . . request relief from this Command."[28] Fortunately, one critical position remained unchanged throughout operations in Western Europe. While his peers bickered over appropriate use of strategic bombers, Pete Quesada, Promoted to Major General in April 1944, commanded the IX Fighter Command, composed of the IX and XIX Tactical Air Commands. In this role, Quesada finally had both the opportunity and the authority to develop CAS TTPs in preparation for the Normandy invasion and follow-on operations in Western Europe.[29]

In Quesada, Eisenhower had exactly what he wanted—an experienced and respected combat air leader who remained a staunch advocate of CAS. Quesada's experience gave him a clear view of the halting advances in the use of tactical airpower in Tunisia and the Mediterranean, and the remaining challenges that needed solutions. In dealing with these challenges, Quesada—now an empowered agent of change—worked closely with ground commanders to improve mission coordination and develop CAS TTPs that proved essential in the coming campaigns.[30]

Quesada worked relentlessly preparing his pilots for their tactical support mission. He sent newly arrived pilots to the Mediterranean to learn from tactical air units operating there and share their new knowledge with their peers. He led training events in which his

Figure 9.1. Major General Elwood R. "Pete" Quesada, Commander, IX Fighter Command. Photo courtesy of US Army Center of Military History.

pilots practiced bombing and strafing techniques, essentially creating optimal procedures from scratch. In the weeks before Operation Cobra, Quesada's pilots roamed the skies over France daily, attacking troop concentrations, strong points, and troop transports. By co-locating his advance Command Post (CP) with Bradley's, Quesada worked with supported units to develop new procedures for CAS. To resolve communication problems with ground units, he had VHF radios installed in tanks, operated by a pilot serving in the tank crew. These tanks led columns in the advance, with the air liaison providing target information to fighter-bomber escorts. Referred to as armored column cover, this method greatly enhanced the speed and effectiveness of armored advances. Similarly, he provided VHF radios to ground unit CPs, enabling tactical aircraft to provide area cover for advancing units, directed by a reconnaissance aircraft in communication with ground forces. These methods, employed by the IX Tactical Air Command throughout the campaigns in Western Europe, enabled the most effective CAS US Army ground units had ever received, greatly enhancing their offensive power.[31]

By June 1944 Operation Pointblank, the strategic bombing campaign against Germany's industrial centers, had damaged German morale and production capacity—but not to the degree anticipated by Arnold's AWPD. However, in defending Germany from air attacks, the Luftwaffe lost aircraft and crews at an unsustainable rate. Tactical air support both before and after D-Day focused on the destruction of airfields, supply depots, and transportation infrastructure, while high-altitude heavy bombers and fighter-bombers crippled the road, railroad, and communication networks, effectively isolating Normandy and preventing much-needed reinforcements and materiel arriving from Germany.[32]

These preparatory operations also compelled the Luftwaffe to fight, enabling the Allies to establish control of the skies over France before D-Day. The Western Allies enjoyed air superiority for the rest of the war in Europe (although anti-aircraft artillery remained a threat, particularly to low-flying aircraft). Eisenhower later wrote that the Western Allies' success in the critical early stages of the Normandy invasion depended in large measure on Allied dominance of the air.[33]

The Anglo-American Allies advanced slowly after the initial invasion and establishment of beachheads in Normandy. To the east, Lieutenant General Miles C. Dempsey's British Second Army had not yet secured the city of Caen, an objective that Field Marshal Sir Bernard L. Montgomery, 21st Army Group and overall land forces commander, had planned to capture on D-Day. German control of Caen left a vital crossroads in enemy

hands and offered a route for a German counterattack that could potentially endanger the Allied beachheads. Further, Caen's road network controlled movement to the open terrain east and southeast of the city. Most
significantly, the protracted battle to secure Caen served as a daily remind-
er of the Allies' slow progress, damaging morale up and down the chain
of command. Historian Martin Blumenson described the failure to capture
Caen by 1 July as "the greatest single disappointment of the invasion."[34]

To the west, Lieutenant General Omar Bradley's American First Army
remained bogged down in the *bocage*, terrain that Eisenhower described
in a letter to Army Chief of Staff General George C. Marshall on 5 July
1944: "Our whole attack has to fight its way out of very narrow bottlenecks

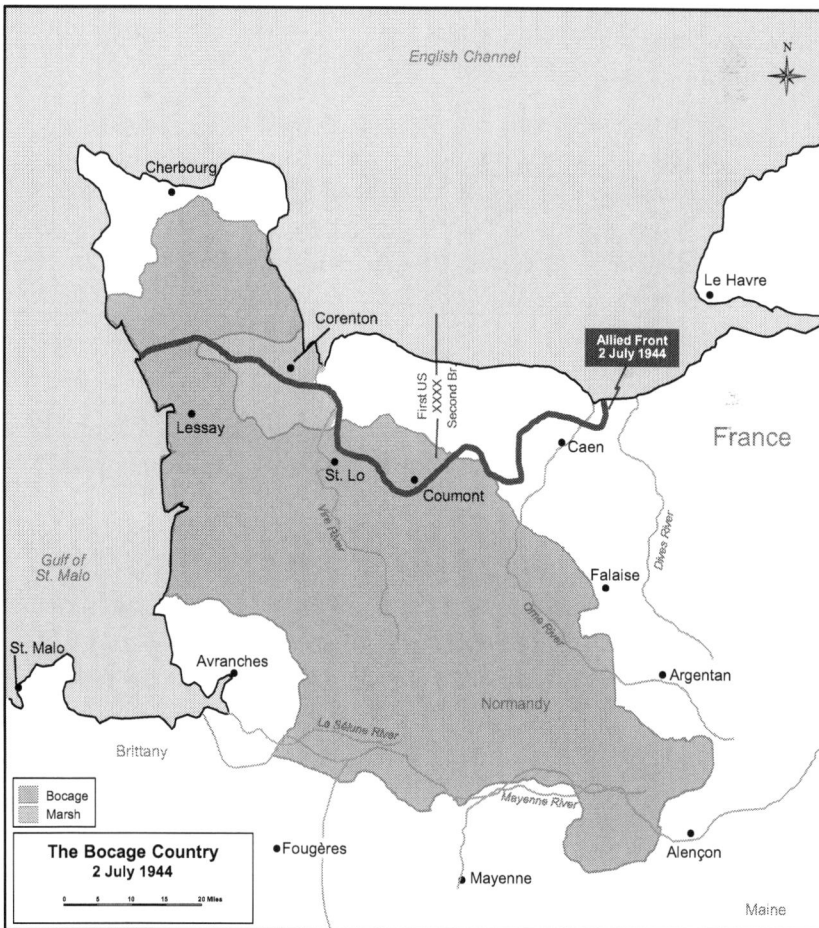

Figure 9.2. "The Bocage Country" in Normandy, France, June 1944. Map created
by Army University Press, courtesy of the US Army Center of Military History.

flanked by marshes and against an enemy who has a double hedgerow and an intervening ditch almost every fifty yards as ready-made strong points."[35] This network of sunken ditches covered by dense hedgerows made a checkerboard of the Norman countryside, providing excellent cover and concealment for German defenses in depth. While fighting in the *bocage*, the First Army measured its daily progress in yards, at the cost of 28,346 casualties through 22 June.[36]

A lack of port facilities further delayed the Allied advance as the front moved away from the beachhead, lengthening supply lines. The original invasion plan called for the liberation of Cherbourg, the port nearest to the invasion beaches, as quickly as possible after securing the beachhead. This would clear the way for Lieutenant General George S. Patton's Third Army to occupy the American right flank and clear Brittany of German forces before turning east toward Germany.[37]

By mid-June 1944, both Bradley and Montgomery, worried that the front might devolve into a WWI-style stalemate, began planning breakthrough operations. After nearly three weeks of struggling through the *bocage*, the Allies needed to reach open terrain where their armored and mechanized divisions could take advantage of their mobility and force the determined German defenders to retreat.[38]

Eisenhower's chief of staff, Brigadier General Walter "Beetle" Smith assessed the situation:

On June 24th, when the Supreme Commander visited Bradley, it was plain that we would soon have Cherbourg, and the need for elbow room was becoming very important. The Supreme Commander had already made up his mind that the full weight of US strength should be used to break out into the open on our right. By June 30th the British Army had *not* captured Caen, and now Montgomery issued his first directive that showed *an intention of holding on the left and breaking through on the right*. He directed the British to contain the greatest possible part of the enemy forces [in support of American breakthrough operations]. . . . However, as late as July 7th, Montgomery, in a letter to the Supreme Commander, was uncertain at which point our main effort would have to be made.[39]

This uncertainty did not bode well for the success of a future breakthrough attempt. With combined operations about to commence on both sides of a boundary between Allied armies, Montgomery, as overall commander of Allied land forces, should have made his intent clear both up and down the chain of command. Instead, planning continued in the British Second Army and the American First Army headquarters in parallel, with minimal integration of effort or information sharing.[40]

In early July, Dempsey's Second Army gained Montgomery's approval to conduct Operation Goodwood, intended to finally secure Caen and occupy the open terrain southeast of the city. Having seemingly developed high hopes for a British breakout, Montgomery assured Eisenhower that his "whole eastern flank" would "burst into flames," although the details of his plan remained unclear to both Eisenhower and First US Army.[41]

To open the way for a penetration by British armored columns, Montgomery requested (and received) maximum air support to conduct preparatory bombing throughout the attack corridor. To avoid cratering along the maneuver corridor, heavy bombers carpeted the area in and around Cain that remained in German control while medium- and fighter-bombers engaged enemy positions with 100-pound bombs and strafing attacks. Still, as the bombing ended and Dempsey's troops crossed the line of departure, many of the German troops emerged from foxholes and trenches to occupy well-constructed strongpoints, forming a powerful defense in depth. Dempsey's attack stalled after several hours, at which point Montgomery reverted to a defensive posture. Despite its failed attempt at a breakthrough, Goodwood accomplished its secondary objective of tying down most German panzer units in the area. This left the line in front of Bradley's First Army relatively strong, but lacking in depth and still short on armored support.[42]

Operation Cobra

Meanwhile, Bradley and his subordinate air and ground commanders made final preparations for Operation Cobra as the fighting in the Cherbourg Peninsula continued. With Cherbourg finally captured in late June, Bradley ordered his forces on the peninsula to leave behind just enough troops to retain control of the city and redeploy the rest to the south to rejoin the First Army's front line. In early July, Bradley ordered VII Corps to continue the offensive in the south, in hopes of reaching the eastern edge of *bocage* country in preparation for a breakthrough attempt. After several days of fighting, elements of VII Corps captured the city of St. Lô on 18 July, weakening the German line on both sides of the city. Bradley's forces—now in control of key terrain that served as a gateway to the open ground east of the hedgerows—consolidated and awaited the breakthrough operation scheduled for 21 July (bad weather forced Bradley to postpone Cobra until 24 July).[43]

Bradley planned to conduct the breakthrough at a weakly defended point just west of St. Lô, where Major General Joe Collins' reinforced VII Corps would penetrate the German lines after an intense preparatory bombardment. Upon achieving a breakthrough, Collins would expand and hold the gap open with infantry divisions while armored and mechanized divisions poured through the opening, bypassing strong points and enveloping or pursuing retreating units. The plan for Operation Cobra included a massive preparatory bombing that American medium and heavy strategic bombers, along with fighter-bombers of the American IX Tactical Air Force, would carry out.[44]

During the planning for Cobra, Bradley and Collins—whose VII Corps would lead the breakthrough attempt—met with the senior leaders of the American air organizations scheduled to support the attack. Historian Steve Ossad has described this fateful meeting in detail. The exact origins of the preparatory bombing plan remain unclear, although Major General Quesada recommended to Bradley as early as 18 June that any breakthrough attempt should begin with a massive bombardment using heavy, medium, and fighter bombers. Whatever the original source of the idea, Bradley maintained throughout the planning for Cobra that success would rely on a massive preparatory bombardment.[45]

Bradley met with the senior air commanders who would support this operation on 19 July, hoping to ensure complete understanding of the plan and gain their support. At this meeting, Bradley described the air support plan developed by his planners and air liaison officers from Quesada's IX and XIX Tactical Air Forces. Bradley intended to exploit the effects of a massive preparatory air bombardment of a 7,000-yard-wide by 2,500-yard-deep rectangular area directly in front of First Army's position, just south of a straight road running northwest to southeast towards St. Lô. Bradley noted that this road would serve as a useful navigation aid for pilots, who could simply follow the road to the target area, flying parallel to the long northern edge of the rectangular objective.[46]

Although Bradley left the meeting believing that he had gained concurrence on the use of a parallel flight path, leaders from bomber command believed that they had argued successfully against a parallel approach. Ultimately, air planners adjusted the approach to run perpendicular, not parallel to the northern long edge of the target area, since only a perpendicular approach would enable more than 2,000 bombers to strike the target area in the one hour allotted. Still, the air planners never communicated this change to First Army.[47]

Another topic of debate involved how far away from the target area front line troops would wait during the preparatory bombing. If units did not withdraw far enough they risked casualties caused by errant bombs; if they withdrew too far, they risked giving the enemy too much time to recover from the bombing's effects before engagement by ground maneuver units. While a Ninth Air Force report on CAS during operations to clear Cherbourg noted the importance of "Immediate Follow-Up," its claim that careful planning could allow ground troops to remain within 500 yards of the bomb line seems overly optimistic.[48] Bradley initially proposed withdrawing front line units only 800 yards, while a senior liaison officer representing the US Eighth Air Force argued for a minimum distance of 3,000 yards. After some debate, Bradley and the air commanders agreed to 1,500 yards, although this distance had proven inadequate in previous missions.[49]

After days of waiting for the weather to clear, 24 July looked promising; but after more than 2,000 bombers departed air bases in England, low clouds over the objective led to a weather recall. About half the bombers received the recall order and complied, but the rest, already beyond radio range, continued to the target area. As Collins' reinforced VII Corps waited to attack, waves of medium and fighter-bombers arrived over the target area as Bradley and his personal staff watched from an advance CP a few thousand yards away. Everything seemed to be going well until the heavy bombers began to arrive over the objective via a perpendicular approach, dropping thousands of tons of bombs—some in the target area, and many others south of it, on top of US troops. Confusion and chaos set in as the "short drops" caused 156 casualties, including 25 killed. Bradley cancelled the operation as his staff tried to sort out the extent of the damage.[50]

Despite frustration over the perpendicular bomb line and the friendly casualties, Bradley approved another attempt for the next day, 25 July. This time weather did not interfere, so the full complement of bombers—the largest tactical ground support bombardment to date—approached the target area with the heavy bombers once again making a perpendicular approach. Massive clouds of dust quickly obscured the road and dispersed smoke intended to mark the objective, and once again bombs began to fall on American troops, this time resulting in 601 casualties, including 111 killed.[51]

General Lesley J. McNair, selected by Eisenhower to replace Patton as the commander of the fictional First US Army Group (FUSAG), visited the front in Normandy enroute to his new assignment in England, where the highly successful Operation Fortitude continued to tie up German forces awaiting another amphibious assault in the Pas de Calais region. While his presence at the front was intended to make his replacement of Pat-

Figure 9.3. General Lesley J. McNair, Commander, Army Forces Command. Photo courtesy of the US Army Center of Military History.

ton more plausible, it also led to his death. After experiencing a close call on the morning of the 24th, McNair promised not to observe the next day's barrage from the front lines. However, after Soldiers told him how much they appreciated his presence at the front, McNair once again occupied a slit trench dangerously close to the objective area on the 25th, where an errant bomb struck a direct hit, throwing McNair's body many yards. Hearing rumors of the death of a three-star general at the front, McNair's aides rushed forward after the bombing ended. They managed only to find his West Point class ring and the three-star insignia from his uniform. The loss of the highly respected and capable McNair added to the grief of the American forces—particularly the senior leaders.[52]

Several factors coalesced to create the conditions that led to the tragic events of 24 and 25 July 1944—events that nearly ended Operation Cobra before the ground forces could strike. Only the initiative of perceptive corps and division commanders—who shook off the effects of the second morning in a row of casualties caused by errant bombs—enabled the Americans to finally break through the German line west of St. Lô on the night of 25 July. Despite the determined enemy resistance, Collins observed signs that indicated serious trouble in the German defenses. "Noting a lack of coordination in the German reaction, particularly in their failure to launch prompt counterattacks, I sensed that their communications and command structure had been damaged more than our front-line troops realized." [53] Collins and his division commanders planned to exploit their success.

Bradley approved Collins' request to continue the attack the next day, when his mechanized forces pushed even farther behind the shattered enemy lines, converting a planned breakthrough into a highly successful breakout operation. Benefiting greatly from the vast improvements in

American tactical air support since the campaign in Tunisia, VII Corps penetrated enemy lines on 26 July, routing the shaken German defenders and setting conditions for exploitation over the coming days. Indicating the extent of the German collapse, the commander of the *Panzer Lehr* division reported his unit "finally annihilated" on 27 July.[54]

Perhaps most significantly, the air-tank team concept worked brilliantly, as air liaisons operating from tanks directed fighter-bombers over enemy strong points and armored columns, clearing the way for the ground troops' rapid advance. Months of practice perfecting new TTPs before Operation Cobra resulted in the most effective tactical CAS the US Army had received to date.[55]

While the preparatory bombing for Operation Cobra enabled the conversion of Bradley's breakthrough operation into a true breakout, the high cost in friendly casualties left many senior leaders disheartened. Eisenhower declared that he would never again use heavy bombers for CAS, although time would ease his frustration. As the Anglo-American Allies continued the advance toward Germany, strategic bombers remained a source of cross-domain firepower during major operations. Never again, however, did they achieve the level of success enjoyed during Operation Cobra.

By contrast, the development of new TTPs for tactical CAS—largely a result of Quesada's tireless efforts—helped make Eisenhower's goal of effective CAS a reality. Throughout the remaining operations in Western Europe, Quesada's IX Tactical Air Force continued to provide highly responsive and effective CAS to American troops, while bombardment theory advocates stubbornly continued to pursue strategic victory from the air.

Conclusion

The post-war Air Force drew surprising conclusions from the employment of airpower during WWII. The use of atomic bombs over Hiroshima and Nagasaki in 1945 gave airpower theorists a new weapon around which they could justify a resurgence of strategic bombing theory as an independent, war-winning option. Air-ground relationships ebbed once again, hindering critical thinking about the future of combined arms and relegating development of cross-domain tactical fires once again to a low-priority mission. In later wars, CAS improved slowly as the threat of a common enemy led to improved air-ground relationships and, eventually, well-established CAS procedures.[56]

Today's US military can learn much from Operation Cobra that would ensure better preparation for America's next war against a peer- or near-peer enemy. The AAC's strong embrace of strategic bombardment theory during the interwar years impeded critical thinking about the future role of aircraft as part of the combined arms team. This led to the degradation of tactical airpower doctrine, equipment, training, and technology, severely limiting the effectiveness of cross-domain, air-to-ground fires as the US Army entered WWII. While modern technology and new TTPs have improved the overall effectiveness of CAS in counterinsurgency and stability operations over the past 17 years, the combined arms principle of close multi-domain cooperation remains a matter of debate.[57]

To avoid poor cross-domain coordination in future conflicts, the services must prioritize combined-arms effectiveness higher than the pursuit of service-specific theories or dogma. During the interwar period, the Army Air Force's dogged determination to achieve independence from Army Ground Forces led not only to development of an incompatible theory of air operations, but also to minimal participation in pre-war maneuvers, depriving air and ground personnel of the opportunity to develop effective CAS TTPs in training.

As Clausewitz argued, critical thinking about military theory requires objective analysis of relevant historical case studies. Only this sort of unbiased critical analysis, combined with realistic and arduous training, can enable the conversion of theory into sound, well-tested doctrine. Without this critical thinking and effective combined arms training, the US military remains at risk of relearning the same difficult lessons about the use of airpower in the next large-scale combat operation.

Additionally, friction among coalition partners can further degrade the combat readiness of an allied force. This challenge, caused by many factors including differing cultural perspectives and operational concepts, plagued the Anglo-American Allies throughout WWII, leading to disagreements over the proper use of airpower and difficulty reaching a common understanding, much less consensus, when planning air support for major operations.

Finally, senior leaders must look for and enable change agents, much like Marshall and Arnold did for Pete Quesada. While he could do little to effect bombardment theory's stranglehold over interwar airpower concepts, Quesada acted as an agent of change in the employment of tactical air support of ground troops. His close cooperation with ground commanders, careful observation and development of cross-domain TTPs, and passionate leadership of the IX Tactical Air Force kept tactical air-to-ground support alive despite the hostile climate created by the embrace of bombardment theory and the cultural and theoretical differences that created friction among the Anglo-American Allies. Quesada's efforts as an agent of change emerged as one of WWII's most significant contingent events. Today's senior military leaders must empower such change agents to overcome the deleterious effects of decades of air-ground animosity and doctrinal inconsistency—a challenge that remains operative to this day.

Although today's US Air Force has supported ground troops with CAS during 16 years of combat in Afghanistan and Iraq, its pilots have not flown CAS in contested airspace or against a near-peer threat. As the US Army shifts its focus to large-scale combat operations, Army-Air Force relationships must form and doctrine must develop in an objective, collaborative manner to avoid another instance of learning in combat what the services could have practiced in pre-war training.

Notes

1. Rick Maze, "Radical Change Is Coming: Gen. Mark A. Milley Not Talking About Just Tinkering around the Edges," 13 December 2016, accessed 18 May 2018, https://www.ausa.org/articles/ radical-change-coming-gen-mark-milley-not-talking-about-just-tinkering-around-edges; Lieutenant General Michael D. Lundy, Commander, US Army Combined Arms Center reinforced these concerns in his foreword to the Army's most recent operational doctrine. See Department of the Army, Field Manual (FM) 3-0, *Operations* (Washington, DC: 2017).

2. US Army Capabilities Integration Center, "Multi-Domain Battle: Evolution of Combined Arms for the 21st Century, 2025–2040," December 2017.

3. Carl von Clausewitz, *On War*, ed. Michael Howard and Peter Paret, trans. Michael Howard and Peter Paret (Princeton, NJ: Princeton University Press, 1984), 122.

4. von Clausewitz, 156.

5. Russell B. Fette, "Ebb and Flow: Maintaining the Close Air Support Relationship through History" (master's thesis, US Army School of Advanced Military Studies, 2016). The term "close air support" was not yet in use during World War II; both air and ground personnel typically referred to "direct support to ground forces" or simply "air support." For consistency, CAS is used throughout.

6. Fette, 82–84.

7. Giulio Douhet, "The Command of the Air," in *Roots of Strategy: Book 4*, ed. David Jablonsky (Mechanicsburg, PA: Stackpole Books, 1999), 260–407; William Mitchell, "Winged Defense," in *Roots of Strategy: Book 4*, 408–515; for more detail on the historical context in which strategic bombing theory developed, see Azar Gat, "Futurism, Proto-Fascist Italian Culture, and the Sources of Douhetism," in *A History of Military Thought: From the Enlightenment to the Cold War* (New York: Oxford University Press, 2001), 561–597.

8. Thomas A. Hughes, *Overlord: General Pete Quesada and the Triumph of Tactical Airpower in World War II* (New York: The Free Press, 1995), 54.

9. Hughes, 52–55.

10. David M. Kennedy, *Freedom from Fear: The American People in Depression and War, 1929–1945* (New York: Oxford University Press, 2001), 615–19; Hughes, *Overlord: General Pete Quesada*, 53–54, 79.

11. Quoted in Hughes, *Overlord: General Pete Quesada*, 55.

12. For more on agents of change, see Kirk C. Dorr, "Developing Agents of Change" (master's thesis, School of Advanced Military Studies, 2003), accessed 3 June 2018, http://cgsc.cdmhost.com /u?/p4013coll3,17; Hughes, *Overlord*, 59–63.

13. Hughes, *Overlord*, 47–49.

14. Hughes, 47–49, 75.

15. Hughes, 82.

16. Hughes, 82.

17. Hughes, 79–81.

18. Hughes, *Overlord*, 84–86; For a description of the Americans' first tank battle with German forces, see Freeland A. Daubin, "The Battle of Happy Valley" (Monograph, The Armored School, 1948).

19. Eisenhower to Churchill, "The Papers of Dwight David Eisenhower," Johns Hopkins University Press, accessed 17 April 2018, https://eisenhower.press.jhu.edu, 741; Hughes, *Overlord*, 86–87.

20. Eisenhower to Arnold, "Eisenhower Papers," 654; Eisenhower to Combined Chiefs of Staff and British Chiefs of Staff, "Eisenhower Papers," 747.

21. Eisenhower to Arnold,19 January 1943 "Eisenhower Papers," 778; Eisenhower to Marshall, 8 February 1943, "Eisenhower Papers," 810n1.

22. Daniel R. Mortensen, *A Pattern for Joint Operations: World War II Close Air Support, North Africa* (Washington, DC: Office of Air Force History and US Army Center of Military History, 1987), 84–88.

23. Quoted in Hughes, *Overlord*, 109; for more on the War Department reorganization in March, 1942, see Forrest C. Pogue, *George C. Marshall: Ordeal and Hope, 1939–1942* (New York: Viking Press, 1966), 289–297; Mortensen, *A Pattern for Joint Operations*, 86.

24. "Foreign Relations of the United States" (Washington, DC: Government Printing Office, 2010), accessed 3 June 2018, https://history.state.gov/historicaldocuments/frus1943Cairo Tehran; Eisenhower Memorandum for Diary, 6 December 1943, "Eisenhower Papers," 1408; Eisenhower to Marshall, 17 December 1943, "Eisenhower Papers," 1423.

25. Eisenhower to Marshall, 17 December 1943, 1423.

26. Eisenhower to Marshall, 23 December 1943, 1426; Eisenhower to Marshall, 26 December 1943, 1439.

27. Eisenhower to Marshall, 25 December 1943, 1428; Hughes, *Overlord*, 111–114.

28. Eisenhower Memorandum (for the record), 22 March 1944, "Eisenhower Papers," 1601.

29. Hughes, *Overlord*, 121.

30. Dorr, "Developing Agents of Change," accessed 3 June 2018, http://cgsc.cdmhost.com/u?/p4013coll3, 17; Hughes, *Overlord*, 126.

31. Martin Blumenson, *Breakout and Pursuit*, US Army in World War II: European Theater of Operations (Washington, DC: US Army Center of Military History, 1961; repr., 2005), 207–208; Steven L. Ossad, *Omar Nelson Bradley: America's GI General, 1893–1981* (Columbia: University of Missouri Press, 2017), 210–211; Hughes, *Overlord*, 129, 159–169; Michael D. Doubler, *Closing with the Enemy: How the GIs Fought the War in Europe, 1944–1945*, Modern War Studies (Lawrence, KS: University Press of Kansas, 1994), 63–86.

32. Army Air Forces Historical Studies No. 36, "Ninth Air Force, April to Nov 1944, 140–170.

33. Dwight D. Eisenhower, "Report by the Supreme Commander to the Combined Chiefs of Staff on the Operations in Europe of the Allied Expeditionary Force, 6 June 1944 to 8 May 1945" (Washington, DC: Center of Military History, 1994), 28.

34. Blumenson, *Breakout and Pursuit*, 13–15.

35. Eisenhower to Marshall, "The Eisenhower Papers," 1796.

36. Blumenson, *Breakout and Pursuit*, 10–13; William C. Sylvan and Francis G. Smith Jr., *Normandy to Victory: The War Diary of General Courney H. Hodges & the First US Army*, ed. John T. Greenwood (Lexington, KY: University Press of Kentucky, 2008), 30, 55; Steven L. Ossad, *America's GI General,* 197; Doubler, *Closing with the Enemy*, 31–62.

37. Blumenson, *Breakout and Pursuit*, 209–10.

38. Eisenhower to Bradley, 8 July 1944, 1810.

39. Eisenhower to Bradley, 1 July 1944, 1794 (emphasis in the original).

40. Eisenhower to Bradley, 1 July 1944, 1794.

41. Quoted in Blumenson, *Breakout and Pursuit*, 190; Eisenhower to Bradley, 1 July 1944, 1794.

42. Blumenson, *Breakout and Pursuit*, 188–196

43. Blumenson, 172–82.

44. Blumenson, 220–21.

45. Ossad, *America's GI General*, 205.

46. Ossad, 212–20.

47. Ossad, 220–23.

48. "9th Air Force Operations, 1–30 June, 1944, With Special Study of Close Support in the Assault on Cherbourg."

49. Ossad, *America's GI General*, 217–21; "9th Air Force Operations, 1–30 June 1944, With Special Study of Close Support in the Assault on Cherbourg."

50. Blumenson, *Breakout and Pursuit*, 228–29.

51. Blumenson, 231–36.

52. Mark T. Calhoun, *General Lesley J. McNair: Unsung Architect of the US Army* (Lawrence, KS: University Press of Kansas, 2015), 320–26; Smith to Marshall, "Eisenhower Papers," 1803.

53. Quoted in Ossad, *America's GI General*, 225.

54. Blumenson, *Breakout and Pursuit*, 273.

55. Mark J. Reardon, *Victory at Mortain: Stopping Hitler's Panzer Counteroffensive* (Lawrence, KS: University Press of Kansas, 2002), 12, 294–95; Doubler, *Closing with the Enemy*, 63–86; Hughes, *Overlord*, 163–91; 228.

56. Fette, "Ebb and Flow," 80.

57. Fette, 82–84.

Chapter 10

Fires and Combined Arms Maneuver: The Battle of Vimy Ridge, 9 April 1917

David Thuell and Thomas G. Bradbeer

Throughout the period of trench warfare, the objective of all the combatants on the Western front was the restoration of mobility to the battle. While a visualisation of the battlefield would suggest that its static nature was due to the rows of trenches and belts of barbed wire, it was essentially, the superiority of defensive firepower of that of the offensive which led to both the struggle's indecisiveness and its appalling levels of bloodshed. The principal source of this firepower was the artillery; manoeuvre in the face of unsuppressed modern ordnance proved an extremely hazardous and costly operation.[1]

—Albert Palazzo

The Industrial Revolution of the 19th Century, brought about a technical revolution in the development of weapons. This revolution increased the efficiencies of the weapons to the point where, by 1914, they completely dominated the battlefield. The battlefield being comprised of three key elements—firepower, mobility, and protection. At the start of the First World War, firepower was the dominant element, and the main source of firepower during the war was artillery. It is estimated that 60 percent of all casualties during the war were inflicted by artillery fire.[2] This dominance is the reason why all large-scale offensive operations failed to achieve their objectives on the Western Front until April 1917.

On 9 April 1917, the Canadian Corps as part of the British First Army, launched a well-coordinated and synchronized attack against three German divisions of the German Sixth Army defending Vimy Ridge just north of Arras, France. At the same time the British Third Army, under the command of Sir Edmund Allenby, attacked along the Scarpe River toward Arras. The Canadian Corps attack was significant in that it was the first time the four Canadian divisions, totaling 97,184 men, operated in combat together.[3] The British 5th Infantry Division was attached to the Canadian Corps for this operation. Attacking on a four mile front, the Canadians pushed the entrenched German divisions off of Vimy Ridge in a four day battle. Vimy Ridge would prove to be one of the greatest tactical successes for the British Expeditionary Force (BEF) during the entire war.[4] More importantly "For Canadians, Vimy Ridge was a nation-building experience.

For some, then and later, it symbolized the fact that the Great War was also Canada's war of independence."[5]

The Canadians were able to overcome the superiority of firepower over the offensive and achieve all of their objectives assigned to the Corps by capturing the ridge that rose 480 feet above the Douai plain. Since October 1914 the Germans had defended the ridge against the French Army and fought off two major attacks, in May and September 1915 respectively, and inflicting more than 150,000 French casualties.[6] The ridge was significant in that it enabled the German defenders to possess a commanding view of the allied lines for many miles in three directions.

The Canadians were able to capture Vimy Ridge for a number of reasons. First and foremost, the soldiers were well led, well trained, and adequately equipped.[7] They were also, for the most part, combat veterans, having fought on the Western Front since their introduction to combat during the Battle of Second Ypres in April 1915. They gained even more experience during the Battle of the Somme in 1916. By early 1917 the Canadian soldier had earned a reputation of being among the best soldiers in the BEF.[8]

Significant to the performance of the Canadian Corps during the battle of Vimy Ridge was the fact that the Canadians applied three significant changes to their doctrine in the months before the operation. The first two changes involved the use of artillery; the third change had to do with the employment of infantry during offensive operations.

During the winter of 1916–1917, the British and Canadian artillery changed its tactical doctrine from conducting artillery barrages aimed at destroying enemy targets and instead implemented barrages that would neutralize the target. The second change in artillery doctrine involved the creation of the Counter-Battery Staff Office (CBSO). This was done to increase the effectiveness of the British artillery against its German counterpart. The third doctrinal change took place in the area of small unit tactics, empowering platoon commanders to use their initiative and to make decisions that would normally be done by their company or battalion commanders. "Regardless of how much planning preceded an attack, lone soldiers or small parties were often the only means of overcoming stubborn resistance on the Great War battlefields."[9]

Artillery in the Great War

The application of British Artillery in First World War went through four distinct phases between 1914 and 1918. The first phase was "Inadequacy," where the artillery was ill-prepared for the many challenges they would experience, most especially in the areas of fire-planning, massing guns, and concentrating fires where it would influence the battle. In 1915 the second phase evolved into "Experimentation and Build up," with more advanced guns and howitzers being developed, along with better and larger supplies of ammunition, to include the use of gas. Tactically, the artillery formations learned that if an infantry assault was to be successful they had to produce a barrage that would better protect the attacking infantry. The result was the "lifting" barrage.[10]

By 1916 the third phase, "Destruction," became the focus, most especially on the Western Front. The "lifting barrage" was still used but evolved into the "rolling barrage," and British leaders decided that the only way to defeat an entrenched enemy was to conduct a massive days or weeks long bombardment that would "crush" all resistance. Within the British Army, the Royal Artillery was "tasked to restore infantry mobility by winning the firefight at the cost of surprise."[11] Massing and concentrating fires was evolving, and the inclusion of an artillery commander in every British corps headquarter, greatly improved both command and control of resources but also improved combined arms coordination. The close battle remained the focus. During the BEF's major offensive operation on the Western Front in 1916, the Battle of the Somme, the Royal Artillery divided its fire support plan into three phases: the preliminary bombardment (which was planned to last seven days), the protective barrage (as the infantry walked across no-man's land), and the exploitation and consolidation phase (if and when the German lines were breached).[12] A major consideration for the use of "destruction" fires was the vast amount of logistics support required, primarily the amount of artillery ammunition. It took weeks to transport and stockpile the enormous amounts of ammunition required for a two or three day barrage prior to the star of an offensive operation. No matter how many guns were available to support an attack, if there was not enough ammunition to sustain a high rate of fire, both before and during the attack, British and French commanders would reduce the scale of the operations and narrow the sector of attack based on the density of fire available.[13]

By early 1917 the Royal Artillery began to focus on "Neutralization," the fourth and final phase.[14] The artillery's primary purpose was no longer to aid the infantry by destroying machine guns and obstacles, such as dense belts of barbed wire but instead shifted to neutralizing enemy artillery.

The Canadian Corps attack on Vimy Ridge represented a half way point between destruction and neutralization, as the preparatory artillery barrage was to be destructive, but the creeping barrage that was to be fired during the actual attack was to neutralize the enemy artillery. "The British First Army's Artillery Plan for the attack on Vimy Ridge in February 1917 identified that . . . at the opening of the Infantry attack the policy of destruction must give way to neutralization."[15]

The creeping barrage, the use of heavy machine guns, the firing of smoke, and gas barrages all represented fundamental changes in the use of artillery. While three of these types of artillery barrages could be lethal to exposed infantry, they were not intended to be destructive. They were all intended to neutralize the Germans entrenched in their defensive positions.

The creeping barrage that was fired by the artillery in support of the Canadian Corps attack on Vimy Ridge was in fact a neutralizing barrage. "The concentrated drumfire from artillery and machine guns keeps the enemy in his deep dugouts. When the barrage lifts he hasn't time to come out of his subterranean galleries to work his machine guns before our infantry are on top of him."[16] By forcing the Germans to remain under cover, the creeping barrage provided the attacking infantry with the protection they needed to close with the enemy.

As Lieutenant Colonel Chalmers Johnston, Commander of the 2nd Canadian Mounted Rifle Battalion, noted about his battalions advance on the day of the attack. "Owing to the rapid advance behind our curtain fire, enemy machine guns had no time to get into action."[17] There was no advantage to be gained by spending additional time and ammunition in trying to destroy the enemy's dugouts, when the creeping barrage would prevent the Germans from firing on the advancing Canadians.

The Use of Smoke and Gas Barrages

Before launching their attack on Vimy Ridge, the infantry brigade commanders from the 4th Canadian Division requested that their artillery support include a smoke barrage to conceal the infantry's advance from the German defenders on Hill 145 (the highest point of the ridge) and the knoll even further north of the ridge known as "The Pimple."[18] The 4th Canadian Division's senior artillery commander agreed that "the most efficient plan was to neutralize [The Pimple] with smoke."[19]

At 0530 on Easter Monday, 9 April, the Canadian artillery began to fire a creeping barrage as the infantry left their trenches. Though the artillery fired a smoke barrage throughout the morning on Hill 145 and The Pimple, the wintry weather conditions gradually opened major gaps in the smoke screen and the greatest fears of Major General David Watson, the commanding general of the 4th Division, came true. The Germans entrenched on the Pimple poured a murderous fire into the attacking Canadian infantry as they crossed no-man's land toward Hill 145. The Canadians also included a heavy machine gun barrage to help minimize the enfilade fire coming from the Pimple, but regardless of the smoke screen and machine gun fire, the 4th Division suffered heavy casualties with several battalions sustaining more than 50 percent casualties.[20] By the end of the first day of the battle, Hill 145 and the Pimple remained under German control. It would be another 24 hours before the Canadians captured these two key terrain features. The untested 85th Infantry Battalion from Nova Scotia captured Hill 145 after a dusk attack on 10 April, amazingly without an artillery barrage to support them.[21]

Gas artillery shells began to arrive in the Canadian Corps sector in March 1917. Lieutenant Colonel Andrew McNaughton, as Canadian Counter-Battery Officer (CCBO,) took a page from a French Army officer, Lieutenant Colonel Pascal Lucas who wrote, "the neutralization of personnel [by gas] could supplement the always incomplete destruction of defensive organizations."[22] As a result the Canadian Corps artillery began using gas shells primarily against German artillery positions. At this point in the war, both sides had effective anti-gas drills in place and suffered relatively few casualties from gas. The British and Canadians used gas primarily as a harassing agent at this point of the war. By firing it at the German artillery positions, it would force the gun crews to wear their gas masks while they tried to fire their guns, effectively reducing their rate of fire by nearly half.[23]

Figure 10.1. "The Taking of Vimy Ridge, Easter Monday 1917." Courtesy of the Canadian War Museum.

Firing a neutralizing gas barrage did not require the same level of accuracy as attempting to fire a destructive, high explosive barrage. The gas shells could actually miss the German batteries but still be close enough that the crews would be forced to wear their protective masks, decreasing their efficiency. On the actual day of the attack gas barrages were fired on most of the German artillery batteries. Hauptmann Behrmann, Reserve Infantry Regiment 261, noted the results. "Many of the guns were swiftly overrun. Hundreds of horses were killed in the initial gas attack, so there was no means of dragging them to the rear when they were threatened."[24] By killing the horses in the initial gas barrage, the artillery actually immobilized the German artillery batteries, allowing the attacking Canadian infantry to capture 63 German artillery pieces during the battle of Vimy Ridge.[25]

The Use of Machine Guns for Neutralizing Fires

In February of 1917, the Canadian Corps began using heavy machine guns to assist the Field and Heavy artillery with their barrages. From 4 February 1917, the War Diaries of the 2nd Canadian Infantry Brigade, provide a list of some of the targets assigned to the heavy machine guns: "Brigade machine guns carried out programme of indirect fire against German trench railways, Roads, X Roads, Hqrs & Field Kitchens."[26] The 4th Canadian Division noted that in the nights leading up to the attack, its machine guns fired "on average 15,000 rounds a night, spread out over the whole German rear area, communications and overland tracks."[27]

The effect of these nightly machine gun barrages on the Germans ability to resupply their front lines was noted in a 4th Canadian Division after battle report. "Prisoners stated definitely that the only way they got their rations was by each relief bringing up sufficient rations for its stay in the trenches."[28] Heavy machine guns were an appropriate weapon to engage all of these targets as neutralizing them was just as effective as destroying them, and significantly more efficient.

The heavy machine guns also fired creeping barrages in support of the infantry's advance during the attack on the ridge. On 9 April, the opening day of the attack, 2nd Canadian Infantry Brigade noted that upon advancing into the former German rear area "that many of the German dead were killed by Machine gun fire, indicating that Machine Gun barrage . . . was [very] effective."[29]

The Counter Battery Staff Officer

During the planning for the attack on Vimy Ridge, Lieutenant General Sir Julian Byng, General Officer Commanding (GOC), Canadian Corps, identified four priorities for his artillery commanders: counter-battery fire, destruction of the German fighting positions, destruction of the German barbed-wire obstacles, and interdiction of enemy re-supply efforts.[30] During this same period, the British Royal Artillery identified the requirement for a counter-battery expert to serve on division and corps staffs who was "free to devote their whole time, energy and brains to the one end of defeating enemy guns."[31] Thus, the Counter Battery Staff Officer (CBSO) was created to deal specifically with the task of locating, destroying or neutralizing the German artillery within their respective corps and division areas of operations:

> The British recognition of the necessity for an artillery intelligence organisation enhanced their capabilities in target identification and selection, ordnance utilisation, and munition allocation.

Figure 10.2. Lieutenant General Sir Julian Byng, General Officer Commanding (GOC) Canadian Corps. Photo courtesy of the Imperial War Museum CO 1370.

The overall product of these intellectual improvements was an enormous increase in effective firepower and a higher degree of success in counter-battery fire.[32]

The primary objective for the CBSO "was to have such effective knowledge of the enemy's artillery dispositions that his batteries could be swamped, harassed and hampered by a deluge of accurately aimed H.E. [high explosives] and gas shells just before the critical moment of the assault and while it continued."[33]

The CBSO would consist of a senior artillery field-grade officer (Lieutenant Colonel or Colonel) as well as a small "centralized staff of artillery personnel dedicated to the suppression of the enemy's batteries through the analysis and tactical application of intelligence."[34] They would be attached to all army corps and divisions within the BEF operating in France and Belgium. The CBSO continually sought to gain and maintain an advantage in artillery firepower over the Germans, by any means possible.

In turn, the Canadian Corps established the Canadian Counter-Battery Officer (CCBO) on 27 January 1917 when General Byng appointed 31-year-old Lieutenant Colonel Andrew G. L. McNaughton to be the first CCBO in the Canadian Corps.[35] McNaughton had joined the Canadian Militia in 1909 and was commanding an artillery battery when the war began. He had been wounded twice and done much to advance gunnery techniques as the war progressed. During the Battle of the Somme he commanded the 11th (Howitzer) Brigade.[36] Prior to the war McNaughton was a professor of engineering at McGill University in Montreal and brought a scientist's enquiring mind to every problem he faced.[37] He had an excellent reputation within the artillery community and was instrumental in convincing infantry commanders of the necessity for the synchronization of the artillery fire-plan with the maneuver plan prior to any offensive operation. He was well liked by the soldiers who served in his units and highly respected by his senior leaders for both his expertise as well as his critical thinking abilities.[38]

One of McNaughton's specified tasks was "to gather enemy intelligence so as to harass enemy operations and destroy opposing artillery forces."[39] Under McNaughton's leadership, the CCBO staff would gather intelligence from any and all sources to include aerial observation, aerial photographs, sound-ranging, flash spotting, forward artillery observers, prisoners, signalers intercepting German transmissions, night patrols, trench raids, and even snipers who, "passed along information seen through their telescopes." [40] These sources were to be exploited by the CCBO to assist in developing detailed target analysis against the German artillery. Without the CCBO there would have been no possible way to combine and interpret all of the different sources of information, from all of the different branches of the army. Since ever division and corps in the BEF had a counter-battery officer, they were able to share tactics, techniques and procedures and eventually develop doctrine for the use of counter-battery fires which in turn greatly improved the overall effectiveness of the British Army's counter-battery fire in the last year and a half of the war.[41]

Prior to the attack on Vimy Ridge, McNaughton visited with his French and British counterparts to discuss the lessons they had learned on the application of artillery during the Battles of Verdun and the Somme, respectively.[42] From the British he learned much about a variety of techniques used with flash-spotting and sound ranging and would incorporate these techniques into his planning for the counter-battery fight against the German artillery behind Vimy Ridge.[43] Under McNaughton's leadership, Canadian artillerymen using sound-ranging techniques were able to calculate the position of the enemy gun within an accuracy of 25 yards. They were also able to identify its type, caliber, and the target it was registered on, all in less than three minutes under good weather conditions.[44]

The Artillery Plan for Vimy Ridge

The preliminary bombardment in support of the attack on Vimy Ridge began on 20 March and consisted of five phases. Phase One began in early March and consisted of the pre-positioning of artillery batteries and the stockpiling of artillery ammunition. This proved to be a logistics miracle in itself. In all, more than 1,000 guns and howitzers had to be moved into their firing positions to support the attack with one howitzer to every 20 yards of front and one field gun for every ten yards.[45] 1,005,000 rounds of 18-pdr gun ammunition would be issued to the 480 18-pounder guns that would take part in the preliminary bombardment.[46] Phase Two was the start of the preliminary barrage that was planned to last from 20 March through 2 April. Phase Three was the final week of the preliminary barrage from 3–9 April. Phase Four was the bombardment to support the initial attack and phase five identified contingencies for the consolidation and exploitation of the ground captured.[47]

During Phase One the command relationships and coordination between the Major General Royal Artillery (MAGRA), First Army, Major General H. F. Mercer and the Brigadier General Royal Artillery (BGRA) E.W.B. Morrison, commander of the Canadian Corps artillery, was finalized. Fourteen heavy artillery brigades, consisting of 114 60-pounder guns, 144 6-inch howitzers, 56 9.2-inch howitzers, 40 8-inch howitzers, and numerous other smaller caliber guns and howitzers would support the three week preparatory barrage. Added to this list of artillery firepower were the guns and howitzers of the divisional artillery units belonging to the 1st, 2nd, and 3rd Canadian Divisions as well as the division artillery's of the 5th, 31st, and 63rd (RN) British divisions. The British 5th and 11th Brigades, Royal Field Artillery (RFA) served as the divisional artillery for the 4th Canadian Division with a further eight brigades of artillery providing reinforcing fires to the Canadian Corps once the attack began. In total, these units provided an additional 480 18-pounders and 138 4.5-inch howitzers to support the assault on Vimy Ridge. Finally, six brigades of Heavy Artillery were assigned the specific task of conducting counter-battery fire prior to and during the assault.[48] During phase one nearly all of the field guns were moved forward during the hours of darkness to occupy firing positions only 500 yards behind the Canadian forward trenches. These guns conducted registration on German targets at the start of the preparatory barrage and then fell silent for the next two and a half weeks so as to not be located by German observers.[49]

In addition to the artillery, 150 of the 358 Vickers heavy machine guns in the Canadian Corps were allocated to support the preliminary bombardment. The Canadians would use the Vickers as an indirect fire system very effectively in the assault on Vimy Ridge.[50]

When Phase Two began on 20 March, General Byng directed that only half of the artillery would participate, primarily to conserve ammunition and to preserve the barrel life of the guns.[51] Counter-battery fires during this phase concentrated on located German artillery batteries via aerial observers or by flash-spotting and sound ranging. When the location of the enemy batteries were confirmed, they were added to the fireplan list and would not be fired upon until the last few days of phase three, just before the attack started.

"The Symphony of Hell"

When all of the available British and Canadian artillery opened fire at the start of Phase Three on 2 April, the effects of the barrage could be felt 12 miles away, breaking windows in the French city of Douai.[52] The bombardment went on non-stop for 23 hours a day for six days allowing little respite to the three German divisions dug-in and along Vimy Ridge. The guns fell silent for one hour each day to allow the aircraft of Number 16 Squadron, Royal Flying Corps (RFC) the chance to conduct battle damage assessment. The aircrews of 16 Squadron made a major contribution to

Lieutenant Colonel McNaughton's counter battery operations by providing aerial photographs as well as directing artillery fire both before and during the attack on Vimy Ridge.[53]

In what the Germans would later state was "The Symphony of Hell" or "the Week of Suffering," the German positions were pounded with high explosives and gas for six days preventing reinforcements and supplies from reaching the forward units on Vimy Ridge.[54] With each passing day, the British and Canadian artillery increased their rates of fire incrementally with 90,000 rounds being fired on 5 April alone.[55] The bombardment destroyed several German trench systems and obliterated huge segments of the barbed-wire obstacles in front of the German trenches. To make matters worse the German artillery experienced a shortage of ammunition as their logistics system began to break down due to the effects of the British and Canadian long range fires.

At 0530 on Easter Monday, 9 April 1917, the attack on Vimy Ridge began when 21 infantry battalions from the four Canadian divisions left their trenches and began the trek across no-man's land. With a thunderous roar that deafened friend and foe alike "the most concentrated and powerful bombardment of the war thundered into the German Lines on Vimy Ridge."[56] A freak snowstorm with pounding snow and sleet fell on the advancing infantry in the pre-dawn light. Even in the poor visibility German opposition began to stiffen the closer the Canadians came to the enemy trenches.

As the Canadian infantry moved forward, they hugged the creeping barrage in front of them which advanced 100 yards every three minutes. Simul-

Figure 10.3. Canadian MK V 8-inch howitzers in action, April 1917. Photo courtesy of the Canadian War Museum.

taneously, the standing barrage moved forward 150 yards of the creeping barrage, bombarding the objectives along the "Black Line" while 300 yards further on the heavy artillery pounded the rear slopes of the ridge and McNaughton's counter-battery brigades silenced nearly 85 percent of the German guns still in action.[57] Of the more than 400 7.7.cm field guns available to the German Army Group commander defending Vimy Ridge, the majority were destroyed and those that were not were effectively neutralized.[58]

By the end of the first day, three of the four Canadian divisions had captured all of their objectives. Only the 4th Division was unable to capture Hill 145 and The Pimple; these critical positions were captured the following day. By 12 April the Canadians had achieved a success unparalleled in the war to that time. The success achieved by the Canadian Corps was due to many reasons. First and foremost it started with General Byng and his infantry and artillery commanders. Their focus on synchronization and planning, as well as the development and execution of an intense training plan prior to the battle, proved to be combat multipliers that enabled the successful assault on Vimy Ridge. Just as important, platoon commanders and section leaders were given the authority to use their judgment as they saw fit to maintain the initiative during the attack. In doing so this also enabled small units to accomplish their assigned missions. It was this combination of "mission command" with a well-planned and executed artillery fire-plan that led to the defeat of the Germans on Vimy Ridge.

As for the success of the CCBO, it can be summarized in this brief report sent by Brigadier General E.W.B. Morrison 60 minutes after the start of the attack. "C.B.S.O.—Everything going splendidly. All our troops on the RIDGE. . . . Practically no hostile barrage."[59] Another measure of the success of the CCBO was that, "By all available means the Canadian counter-battery staff discovered 176 of the estimated 212 guns the Germans had available to defend themselves."[60] This severely diminished the firepower the attacking infantry faced when they assaulted the ridge.

The change from destructive artillery barrages to neutralizing barrages, which began in April 1917, would become doctrine within both the British and Canadian artillery until the end of the war. Creeping barrages which included smoke and gas shells, and heavy machine gun fire, would all continue to play significant roles in offensive operations conducted by the BEF. Given the importance of artillery in support of offensive operations on the Western Front, the creation of the CBSO by the British Army in the winter of 1917, may be one of the most important doctrinal changes of the war. Interestingly enough, the Germans were never able to duplicate the CBSO within their armies.[61]

Changes in Infantry Doctrine prior to Vimy Ridge

Shortly after the conclusion of the Battle of the Somme, BEF General Headquarters issued several directives that would incorporate numerous lessons learned from that five month campaign. The two that impacted the infantry most directly were *SS143—Instructions for the Training of Platoons for Offensive Action* and *SS144—The Normal Formation for the Attack.*

These new tactics represented a major change in infantry doctrine within the British Army, placing greater responsibility at the lowest echelon—the platoon commander. This pushed the actual command of offensive operations down to the platoon level. There were two primary reasons for this change: the lack of communications between battalion headquarters and the advancing platoons once the companies and platoons left their trenches and began crossing no-man's land, and additional firepower being allocated to the infantry platoons to make them more lethal. The addition of grenade launchers attached to the infantryman's Lee-Enfield rifles as well as providing more of the very effective Lewis light machine guns increased the lethality of the infantry platoon.[62]

The battalion commander of the 22nd Battalion noted, "Once the attack is launched the Battalion Commander is practically impotent . . . company and platoons were cut off from higher headquarters."[63] When the company or platoon ran into a German strong-point, such as a machine gun post, they would stop and call for support from the artillery. They would remain stationary until support arrived. Communications between advancing infantry and the headquarters was almost impossible, and when possible could take hours. This would effectively stop the advance of the infantry, thereby losing initiative and thus jeopardizing the whole offensive operation.

In the months prior to the attack on Vimy Ridge, General Byng had directed his staff to conduct a detailed analysis of small unit tactics and training. When the British General Staff issued *SS143* and *SS144* in February 1917, it directed that one of the infantry platoons in each company transition into three sections consisting of bombers (hand grenades), rifle-bombers (rifle grenades) and Lewis machine gun teams to assist the infantry company with suppressing or neutralizing enemy strongpoints. The increase in firepower at the platoon level was a major lesson learned from the Battle of the Somme. It was believed that this change to the infantry structure would combine to provide the companies and platoons with enough firepower to deal with almost any defensive obstacle missed by the artillery. General

Byng directed that *SS143* and *SS144* be incorporated immediately into the revised training plan for every soldier in the Canadian Corps.[64]

In order for the new tactics and weapons to be successful at overcoming the superiority of defensive firepower, the infantry needed extensive training on how to operate these weapons, and then on how to carry out the new tactics. Light machine gunners, bombers, and rifle grenadiers had to learn how to operate their individual weapons but more importantly, they needed to learn how to operate together as a team. A 4th Division weekly report published just five days before the attack on Vimy Ridge, stated that 146 men completed courses of instruction on use of the Lewis Gun, the Mills Bomb (grenade) and Rifle Grenade.[65]

As part of the revised training program, General Byng directed that in the coming battle every platoon would be given a specific objective. More importantly, he provided the time for every company and platoon to conduct rehearsals in the rear area so that they could develop battle drills. A scale model of Vimy Ridge was built near First Army headquarters and every soldier was to understand his role as well as the man alongside him. Byng also provided 45,000 maps so that every platoon commander, platoon sergeant and section commanders had a map and knew how to use it to assist them in achieving their objectives.[66]

Once the individual soldiers had completed training on their new weapons, they would return to their platoons and begin, "training under the Brigade and Battalion arrangements in the new organization of Platoons etc."[67] For the four Canadian divisions, this training continued right up until the day before the attack on Vimy Ridge. This intense training regime provided the attacking infantrymen the knowledge they needed to successfully deal with and overcome the German strongpoints they would encounter.

Now with the new tactics, weapons, and training, when the artillery barrages failed to neutralize a German strong point, the platoon would be able to effectively deal with these positions and continue advancing toward their objectives.

After the Canadian Corps's successful assault and capture of Vimy Ridge, Major General Henry E. Burstall, commander of the 2nd Canadian Division, reflected on the two directives and their impact on his platoons:

> The platoon organization has fully justified its introduction. Whenever preparations for an attack have been complete, i.e. wire properly cut and trench destruction thoroughly carried out, the Infantry have been able to advance with comparatively small

casualties as the new organization has enabled them to overcome opposition with the weapons at their own disposal.[68]

The Canadian Corps was able to apply these changes to infantry doctrine because of an intense training program which contributed greatly to capturing Vimy Ridge from an entrenched, well-led, disciplined and motivated enemy, proving the soundness and effectiveness of the new doctrine. Major General Sir Arthur Currie, commander of the 1st Canadian Division at Vimy Ridge and future commander of the Canadian Corps, stated "There is no use in waiting until the end of the war to make necessary changes."[69]

Conclusion

On 12 April 1917, German resistance ended and with it the Battle of Vimy Ridge. The four Canadian divisions were positioned on the high ground along a six mile front. The German Sixth Army, having sustained more than 20,000 casualties, including 4,000 soldiers who became prisoners of war, retreated more than four miles eastwards across the Plains of Douai and took up defensive positions where they prepared for the next Allied attack.[70] The Canadian Corps suffered 10,602 over the four day battle with 3,598 soldiers killed and 7,004 were wounded. It would prove to be the highest casualty rate every suffered by the Canadians in their history. Despite the casualties, the British and Canadians considered Vimy Ridge an overwhelming success. General Byng would be promoted to command Third Army and Major General Currie received a knighthood from King George V on the battlefield and then assumed command of the Canadian Corps where he would prove to be one of the most capable corps commanders on either side during the entire war.[71] Shortly after the battle, the Canadians received perhaps the greatest tribute when the French Army General Staff sent a group of senior officers to meet with the leaders of the Canadian Corps to analyze how and why the Canadians had been so successful at Vimy Ridge. "One of the greatest armies in the world was not too proud to learn from an army of citizen soldiers."[72]

By implementing neutralizing and destructive artillery barrages across BEF, creating the position of counter-battery staff officer at the corps and division level, and incorporating new tactics at the infantry platoon level, the Canadian Corps was able to overcome the superiority of defensive firepower, and achieve a major tactical victory during the Battle of Vimy Ridge. This successful large-scale combat operation demonstrated that by conducting detailed planning at all levels—from Army to platoon—and by synchronizing fires with maneuver, well-trained and well-led soldiers could defeat a near-peer enemy defending key terrain under extreme environmental conditions.

One of the greatest strengths of the Canadian Corps prior to the Battle of Vimy Ridge (and for the remainder of the war), was its highly integrated and flexible organization. The Canadian Corps staff, under the exceptional leadership of General Byng, effectively planned and coordinated the employment of all multi-domain capabilities across the operational framework. This is just one of the many lessons that the Battle of Vimy Ridge offers present day military professionals. As the US Army reorients its doctrine toward the conduct of large-scale combat operations to prevent peer and near-peer adversaries from gaining positions of strategic advantage, it is highly recommended that military professionals of all ranks study and analyze how the Canadian Corps, operating as a small national army, prepared for and successfully accomplished its assigned mission of capturing Vimy Ridge in 1917.

Notes

1. Albert Palazzo, "The British Army's Counter-Battery Staff Office and Control of the Enemy in World War I," *Journal of Military History* 63, Issue 1, 1999, 55–74.

2. Tim Cook, "The Gunners at Vimy," in *Vimy Ridge: A Canadian Reassessment*, eds. Geoffrey Hayes, Andrew Iarocci, and Mike Bechthold, (Waterloo, Canada: Laurier Centre for Military Strategic and Disarmament Studies and Wilfrid Laurier University Press, 2007), 110.

3. David T. Zabecki, "Vimy Ridge, France," *Military History Magazine* 27, no. 2, July 2010, 76.

4. Tim Cook, *Vimy: The Battle and the Legend*, (Toronto: Penguin Random House Canada Limited, 2018), 147–149. See also Mike Chappell, *The Canadian Army at War* (Oxford, UK: Osprey Publishing Ltd., 1985), 14–15; Brenda Ralph Lewis, "Vimy Ridge 1917," *War Monthly* 19, September 1975, 26–33.

5. Desmond Morton, as quoted in Edward Humphreys *Great Canadian Battles: Heroism and Courage through the Years,* (London: Arcturus Publishing Limited, 2008), 304.

6. Zabecki, "Vimy Ridge, France," 76.

7. Alexander Turner, *Vimy Ridge 1917: Byng's Canadians Triumph at Arras* (Oxford: Osprey Publishing Ltd., 2005), 24–25.

8. Alexander Turner, *Vimy Ridge 1917: Byng's Canadians,* 24–25.

9. Andrew Iarocci, in *Vimy Ridge: A Canadian Reassessment*, 159.

10. Paddy Griffith, ed. *British Fighting Methods in the Great War* (London: Frank Cass & Co. Ltd., 1996), 29.

11. Griffith, 31–35.

12. Griffith, 31–35.

13. Griffith, 34.

14. David T. Zabecki, *Steel Wind: Colonel Georg Bruchmuller and the Birth of Modern Artillery* (Westport, CT: Praeger Publishers, 1994), 6.

15. Zabecki, 115.

16. Cook, "The Gunners at Vimy," 109.

17. Geoffrey Hayes, "3rd Canadian Division," in *Vimy Ridge: A Canadian Reassessment*, 201.

18. Bill Rawlings, *Surviving Trench Warfare: Technology and the Canadian Corps, 1914–1918* (Toronto: University of Toronto Press, 1992), 120.

19. Library and Archives Canada, War Diaries, RG9-III-D-3, volume 4862, file number 168, "War Diaries—4th Canadian Division, General Staff," 144, accessed 9 March 2018.

20. Tim Cook, *No Place to Run: The Canadian Corps and Gas Warfare in the First World War* (Vancouver: UBC Press, 1999), 109. See also Alexander McKee, *The Battle of Vimy Ridge*, (Toronto: The Ryerson Press, 1966), 137.

21. Alexander Turner, *Vimy Ridge 1917: Byng's Canadians*, 79–80.

22. Cook, *No Place to Run: The Canadian Corps and Gas Warfare in the First World War,* 112.

23. Cook, 112.

24. Jack Sheldon, *The German Army on Vimy Ridge 1914–1917* (London: Pen & Sword Books Ltd., 2008), 299.

25. Michael Krawchuk, *Wall of Fire: The Battle of Vimy Ridge* (Calgary: Detselig Enterprises Ltd.), 330.

26. Library and Archives Canada, War Diaries, RG9-III-D-3, volume 4871, file number 206, "War Diaries, 2nd Canadian Infantry Brigade," 5, accessed 9 March 2018.

27. Library and Archives Canada, War Diaries, RG9-III-D-3, volume 4862, file number 168, "War Diaries - 4th Canadian Division, General Staff," 143, accessed 10 March 2018.

28. Library and Archives Canada, War Diaries, RG9-III-D-3, volume 4862, file number 168, "War Diaries - 4th Canadian Division, General Staff," 143, accessed 10 March 2018.

29. Library and Archives Canada, War Diaries, RG9-III-D-3, volume 4871, file number 206, "War Diaries, 2nd Canadian Infantry Brigade," pg155, accessed 10 March 2018.

30. Turner, *Vimy Ridge 1917: Byng's Canadians*, 36.

31. General Sir Martin Farndale, *History of the Royal Regiment of Artillery: Western Front 1914-18*, (Dorchester, UK: The Dorset Press, 1986), 186.

32. Palazzo, "The British Army's Counter-Battery Staff," 55–74.

33.. McKee, *The Battle of Vimy Ridge,* 79.

34. Palazzo, "The British Army's Counter-Battery Staff," 55–74.

35. Pierre Berton, *Vimy* (Toronto: McClelland and Stewart Limited, 1986), 109–11.

36. Michael Krawchuk, *Wall of Fire: The Battle of Vimy Ridge* (Calgary: Detselig Enterprises Ltd., 2009), 220.

37. Cook, *Vimy: The Battle and the Legend*, 45.

38. Lieutenant Colonel Andrew G.L. McNaughton was an advocate for the development of advanced gunnery techniques within the Canadian Field Artillery (CFA) throughout the war. He analyzed the wear on gun barrels, muzzle velocity, the effects of weather on artillery rounds once they left the tube and was a major advocate for sound-ranging and flash spotting of enemy artillery. According to Pierre Berton, one of Canada's most renowned historians, McNaughton was considered by the British, French and German's as the best artillery officer in the BEF. In the Second World War he commanded the 1st Canadian Division, 1939-1940; the Canadian Corps, 1940–1942 and the First Canadian Army, 1942–1943.

39. Cook, "The Gunners at Vimy," 111.

40. Bill Rawlings, *Surviving Trench Warfare*, 111.

41. Palazzo, "The British Army's Counter-Battery Staff," 55–74.

42. Berton, *Vimy*, 110–11.

43. Berton, 110–11.

44. Berton, 165–66.

45. McKee, *The Battle of Vimy Ridge,* 53.

46. Farndale, *History of the Royal Regiment of Artillery*, 175.

47. Turner, *Vimy Ridge 1917: Byng's Canadians,* 44–45.

48. Farndale, *History of the Royal Regiment of Artillery*, 175.

49. Farndale, 175.

50. Turner, *Vimy Ridge 1917: Byng's Canadians,* 46.

51. Turner, 47.

52. Turner, 48.

53. Turner, 42–43.

54. Berton, *Vimy,* 183.

55. Lewis, "Vimy Ridge 1917," 28.

56. Farndale, *History of the Royal Regiment of Artillery*, 175.

57. Farndale, 175–76. See also Stephen Bull, *Canadian Corps Soldier versus Royal Bavarian Soldier: Vimy Ridge to Passchendaele, 1917* (Oxford: Osprey Publishing, 2017), 33.

58. Turner, *Vimy Ridge 1917: Byng's Canadians,* 47.

59. Library and Archives Canada, War Diaries, RG9-III-D-3, volume 4957, file number 503, "War Diaries, General Officer Commanding, Royal Artillery, Canadian Corps," 169, accessed 11 March 2018.

60. Rawlings, *Surviving Trench Warfare,* 111.

61. Palazzo, "The British Army's Counter-Battery Staff," 55–74.

62. Bull, *Canadian Corps Soldier versus Royal Bavarian Soldier*, 13–18. By 1916 each infantry battalion had 16 Lewis guns, with one Lewis in each platoon. By 1918 each battalion would have 36, two per platoon plus four held at battalion headquarters to serve in the anti-aircraft role.

63. Rawlings, *Surviving Trench Warfare,* 81.

64. Turner, *Vimy Ridge 1917: Byng's Canadians,* 37–38.

65.Library and Archives Canada, War Diaries, RG9-III-D-3, volume 4862, file number 168, "War Diaries—4th Canadian Division, General Staff," 140, accessed 12 March 2018.

66. Turner, *Vimy Ridge 1917: Byng's Canadians,* 39.

67. Library and Archives Canada, War Diaries, RG9-III-D-3, volume 5070, "War Diaries, 5th Division-Miscellaneous," 23, accessed 12 March 2018.

68. David Campbell, "The 2nd Canadian Division," in *Vimy Ridge: A Canadian Reassessment*, 184.

69. Rene Chartrand, *The Canadian Corps in World War I* (Oxford: Osprey Publishing Ltd., 2007), 20.

70. Humphreys, *Great Canadian Battles*, 310–11.

71. Humphreys, 311. See also Cook, *Vimy: The Battle and the Legend*, 123.

72. Mike Chappell, *The Canadian Army at War* (Oxford, UK: Osprey Publishing Ltd., 1985), 15.

Chapter 11

The Future of Fires: Dominating in Large-Scale Combat Operations

Major General Wilson A. Shoffner and
Colonel Christopher D. Compton

Success in large-scale combat operations (LSCO) is dependent on the Army's ability to fight with fires. The Army's long and storied past provides rich examples—several of which are highlighted in this volume—of the successful application of fires in LSCO. As the Army prepares to defeat technologically advanced peer and near-peer threats capable of challenging US forces in all domains, the ability to fight with fires will be just as critical to success in the future as it was in previous conflicts. Army fires must be organized and equipped in a way that maximizes the timely, accurate integration and employment of cross-domain fires throughout the depth of an increasingly lethal, expanded battlespace.

As history has shown, fighting with fires is inextricably linked to maneuver. The ability to integrate fires *and* maneuver is essential to success in future large-scale combat; we will not dominate our adversaries if we only do one and not the other. The Army's recently published "Functional Concept for Fires 2020-2040" (TRADOC Pamphlet 525-3-4) is a foundational document for developing future fires capabilities. The concept addresses this relationship in the opening lines of the document: "The principle role of fires is to enable freedom of maneuver, while maneuver forces compel the enemy to concentrate when they place something of value at risk."[1] Over the past two decades, potential adversaries have invested heavily in long-range fires and integrated air defense systems (IADS)—making it even more critical that the US Army possess the ability to maneuver and deliver fires in depth. Solving this dilemma requires building a fires force capable of penetrating the enemy's Integrated Air Defenses and destroying the fires-strike complex from standoff ranges. To that end, land-based fires must be capable of power projection across all domains, achieve overmatch for Army forces in close combat, and ensure joint force freedom of maneuver.[2]

Required Capabilities for the Future

Creating a fires force with the capacity, range, and lethality to achieve overmatch in multi-domain operations (formerly multi-domain battle) requires a shift in current fires force organization, capability, and employment. Peer adversaries already employ a fires-strike complex with long-range fires as well as integrated sensor networks along with counter-rocket, artillery, mortar and air defense systems designed to offset the maneuver and technological advantages of US forces. To face the increasingly lethal threats of today and tomorrow, the Army requires a formidable fires complex capable of delivering precise, responsive, effective, and multifunctional fires against targets in all domains (land, air, maritime, space, cyberspace) and at all echelons (tactical, operational, strategic). This requires both reinvesting in and developing new ground-based fires capabilities as well as reorganizing Army fires forces, especially in echelons above brigade (EAB).

The newly formed Cross-Functional Teams (CFTs) for long-range precision fires (LRPF) and air missile defense (AMD) will increase both range and lethality in fires platforms and munitions. The main role of the CFTs is to accelerate the development of the most critical capabilities needed for the future and get those capabilities into the hands of the warfighter as soon as possible. But material solutions only solve part of the problem. Equally important is the force structure required to integrate and employ those capabilities on the battlefield. Analysis to determine the optimal fires force structure is occurring through the development of Operational and Organizational (O&O) concepts that merge future material solutions with robust mission command for integrating and employing cross-domain fires at echelon.

How We Got Here: AirLand Battle to Modularity

The starting point for this modernization effort involves at least a cursory review of the past. Historically, the great strength of Army fires was the ability to deliver timely and accurate massed fires with Field Artillery (FA) and provide protection of critical assets with Air Defense Artillery (ADA) throughout the depth of the battlefield to enable maneuver and set conditions for victory. Army fires units assigned to formations at all echelons—supported by joint enablers—formed the necessary structure to fight with fires and win. Success depended upon the right capability and the right organizations.

The fires force from World War II through Operation Desert Storm was organized to fight and win against peer and near-peer adversaries. The Army invested heavily in FA and ADA in the 1970s through 1990s to optimize for large-scale combat. The Army had tactical, operational, and strategic fires capability that ranged the depth of the battlefield to counter peer adversary air and ground capabilities. The Army organized effectively at echelon to deliver accurate massed fires as well as create integrated layers and redundancies of air defense to maximize capability and lethality against a threat with superior numbers.

The post-Cold War operational environment drove the Army to its current structure, characterized by the term modularity. Today's army maximizes the readiness and lethality of the brigade combat team (BCT) along with interoperable, rapidly deployable division and corps headquarters capable of providing mission command of multiple BCTs and supporting units or serving as a joint task force for a range of military operations. While this transition meant an overall reduction in fires capacity—especially at echelons above BCT—advancements in target acquisition and precision munitions coupled with significant improvements in joint integration have made today's fires force a lethal and highly effective arm of the US Army.

Fires in MDO: Optimizing for the Future Fight

While the past provides a useful reference point for determining the right capability and organizations, re-optimizing for LSCO today requires adapting to an operational environment (OE) where the US military will be contested in all domains as well as in the information environment. This emerging OE is the driving force behind the Army's Multi-Domain Operations (MDO) concept and is redefining how the Army will employ fires on the future battlefield.

Threat anti-access/area denial strategies (A2AD) capabilities may challenge our ability to maintain air and maritime dominance throughout all phases of conflict, creating the need to establish temporary windows of advantage across multiple domains in time and space to enable joint force operations. To that end, Army fires forces must be structured to employ effective cross-domain fires, that is, capable of employing lethal and non-lethal effects across all domains to create multiple dilemmas for an adversary and enable joint Force operations.

The seamless integration and synchronization of cross-domain fires throughout the depth of an expanded and contested battlefield will require tailored fires capacity at each echelon with the right mix of capability and leadership to provide precise and responsive fires. While echelon requirements are different, each requires certain organic lethal and non-lethal delivery capability, enhanced sensor-to-shooter linkages, and the ability to conduct cross-domain targeting and fire control using an integrated fire control network. The following analysis examines how the Army that is optimized for LSCO could employ cross-domain fires capability at the tactical, operational, and strategic levels.

Tactical Cross-Domain Fires: Supporting the Close Fight

The BCT continues to be the primary ground maneuver force designed to close with and destroy enemy forces, largely enabled by cross-domain fires. Lethal fires delivered by an assigned FA battalion equipped with the soon-to-be-fielded extended-range cannon artillery (ERCA) and Short-Range Air Defense (SHORAD) will provide the BCT the ability to shape the close fight and protect maneuver forces while maneuvering in the close area. The brigade fires cell must have the ability to provide the BCT commander with timely access to both see and strike in all domains, including space and cyberspace. While the BCT must be able to internally integrate cross-domain fires, success in LSCO will depend heavily on effective shaping operations from EAB formations.

In order to shape for BCTs, divisions must be capable of integrating and employing cross-domain fires beyond the range of the BCT's cannon artillery. To optimize for LSCO, the division requires a fires organization that can plan for and employ deep shaping fires as well as protect the division's maneuver forces and critical command and control (C2) nodes. In addition to integrating fires, this organization should have the ability to provide mission command of assigned long-range rockets, SHORAD, and other fires capability that provide the division with increased flexibility and lethality to support BCT operations in the close area and provide the division commander options for weighting the main effort.

The division must retain the advantages of the current Joint Air-Ground Integration Center (JAGIC), but must expand this proven capability to be fully cross-domain by incorporating cyber electro-magnetic activities (CEMA), air defense and air management (ADAM), and information operations (IO). Additionally, given the division's increased long-range fires capability coupled with a growing demand for engaging targets at greater ranges, a division will require improved ISR that is capable of both accurately locating and rapidly engaging targets in the division's deep area.

Operational Fires: Shaping the Deep Area

The employment of ground-based operational fires is perhaps the most critical requirement for the Army to optimize for LSCO because it directly counters the enemy's strength—the long-range fires and IADS complex. At the corps level, effective multi-domain convergence includes employing the lethal fires capability of FA rockets and missiles and protective air missile defense capability along with non-lethal fires capability from intelligence, cyberspace, electronic-warfare, and space (ICEWS). These capabilities allow a Corps to be fully capable of executing core operational fires requirements such as Joint Suppression of Enemy Air Defense (J-SEAD), operational strike, and shore-to-ship fires through enhance sensor-to-shooter linkages over an integrated fires network.

Like the division, fires at this level must be well-integrated and synchronized through operational targeting and fire planning. To support the Corps as a joint task force (JTF), fires formations must be organized to maximize interoperability with Joint, Interagency, and Multi-National (JIM) partners. Conceptually, these capabilities give a corps headquarters what it does not have today—a force fires headquarters with the ability to engage the enemy beyond the fire support coordination line (FSCL) at ranges well beyond current rocket and missile capabilities. The robust cross-domain fires capability, including the integrating functions residing within the headquarters, will provide a corps or JTF commander with true operational reach to strike peer adversaries attempting to engage US forces from standoff ranges.

Strategic Land-Based Fires: Enabling the Theater Army

The Army requires a strategic ground-based fires capability as well as a Theater Fires Command capable of integrating cross-domain fires at the theater or regional combatant command level. Expanding the Army Air Missile Defense Command (AAMDC) and the Battlefield Coordination Detachment (BCD) force structure into a single theater enabling command with strategic attack capability would help optimize the Army for LSCO and provide significant shaping capability for the joint force commander.

The most notable addition to this concept is the inclusion of strategic surface-to-surface fires capable of striking targets beyond operational distances. Conceptually, this unit could be equipped with munitions capable of providing additional support to corps/JTF operations or striking targets in support of the joint force with long-range precision strike capability. This deep strike capability—coupled with air and missile defense units equipped with THAAD and Patriot launchers to provide protection for strategic nodes in the theater—the Theater Army would have fully integrated surface-to-surface and surface-to-air capability.

Another unique capability that has both strategic and operational implications is the development of the multi-domain task force (MDTF). This formation is designed specifically to counter threat A2AD strategies by opening windows of advantage for joint force exploitation. The MDTF's ability to position forward in theater during the competition period and protect critical nodes early in operational phases of conflict provides increased decision space for the joint force commander, flexibility to address emerging threats with massed cross-domain fires, and the capability required to prevent sequential threat escalation activities. The MDTF's ability to employ cross-domain fires to disrupt and destroy threat formations prior to their interdiction of the joint force sets the conditions for follow-on operations and campaigns. In addition, the MDTF provides the Army with the ability to experiment with different concepts in the employment of ICEWS capabilities.

Conclusion

Optimizing for LSCO against emerging peer and near-peer threats requires a force capable of employing precise, responsive, and multi-functional cross-domain fires throughout the depth of the battlefield. The Army is no stranger to LSCO and has—throughout its history—risen to meet the challenges posed by peer and near-peer threats of the past. As the Army adapts to the current and future operational environment, developing a capable fires force that meets the challenging demands of our most capable adversaries is a critical component to the solution. By building on our knowledge of the past, expanding on the advancements in the current fires force, and adapting to the changing demands of the emerging operational environment, the Army can once again regain the technological and organizational advantage required to fight and win in LSCO.

Fighting with fires on the future battlefield is not an option. As such, the Army must not only continue its pursuit of material solutions in long-range fires and air defense to improve range and lethality but must also build the right force structure at each echelon to integrate and employ cross-domain fires throughout the depth of the battlefield. Future large-scale combat requires the return of the Fires to a position of dominance on the battlefield, but it must be coupled with the integration of multi-domain capability that creates multiple dilemmas for the enemy and enable friendly freedom of maneuver.

Notes

1. Department of the Army, TRADOC Pamphlet 525-3-4, "The US Army Functional Concept for Fires 2020-2040," February 2017, iii.
2. Department of the Army, TRADOC Pamphlet 525-3-4, iii.

About the Authors

G. Kirk Alexander

Lieutenant Colonel G. Kirk Alexander is an active-duty field artillery officer and serves as the Battalion Commander for 1st Battalion, 31st Field Artillery, Basic Combat Training at Fort Sill, Oklahoma. He earned an MA from Webster University and a Master's in Military Art and Science from the US Army Command and General Staff College's School of Advanced Military Studies. His assignments include three combat deployments to the Middle East while supporting Operation Enduring Freedom and Operation Iraqi Freedom.

Joe R. Bailey

Joe R. Bailey is the Assistant Command Historian for the US Army Combined Arms Center and Fort Leavenworth, Kansas. He earned a BS in History, an MA in Military History from Austin Peay State University, and a PhD in American History from Kansas State University. He is the co-general editor of *Essential to Success: Historical Case Studies in the Art of Command at Echelons Above Brigade* (Fort Leavenworth, KS: Army University Press, 2017). His research areas include American Military History and History and Memory.

Thomas G. Bradbeer

Lieutenant Colonel (Retired) Thomas G. Bradbeer is the Major General Fox Conner Chair of Leadership Studies for the US Army Command and General Staff College at Fort Leavenworth, Kansas. He earned a BA in History from the University of Akron, Master's in Adult Education from the University of Saint Mary and in Military Art and Science from the US Army Command and General Staff College, and a PhD in History from the University of Kansas. His chapter on General Matthew B. Ridgway appeared in *The Art of Command: Military Leadership from George Washington to Colin Powell,* 2nd ed. (Lexington, KY: University of Kentucky Press, 2017) and his Spring 2010 *Army History* article "General Cota and the Battle of the Hurtgen Forest: A Failure of Battle Command?" received the Army Historical Foundation Distinguished Writing Award in 2010. His research areas include Air Warfare—specifically the First and Second World Wars, the British Army in the 20th Century, and the Korean War.

Mark T. Calhoun

Lieutenant Colonel (Retired) Mark T. Calhoun is an Associate Professor at the US Army School of Advanced Military Studies at Fort Leavenworth, Kansas. He earned a BS in Chemistry from the University of Louisiana at Lafayette; a Master's in Military Art and Science from the US Army Command and General Staff College's School of Advanced Military Studies and a PhD in History from the University of Kansas in 2012. His published works include *Lesley J. McNair: Unsung Architect of the U.S. Army* (Lawrence, KS: University Press of Kansas, 2015), the first comprehensive biography of General Lesley J. McNair. He also wrote a chapter in *Unifying Themes in Complex Systems, Volume V* (New York City: Springer Press, 2011), "Clausewitz and Jomini: Contrasting Intellectual Traditions in Military Theory" in the Summer 2011 *Army History*, and various encyclopedia entries and book reviews. His research centers on the US Army during the interwar period and World War II.

Christopher D. Compton

Colonel Christopher D. Compton is the Chief of Concepts Development Division, Fires Center of Excellence at Fort Sill, Oklahoma. He has Master's degrees in Public Administration from the University of Oklahoma, in Strategic Studies from the Army War College, and in National Security and Strategic Studies from the Naval War College. He had two combat deployments in support of Operation Iraqi Freedom. His recent assignments include Deputy Chief of Staff, US Army Central; Chief of Fires, 25th Infantry Division; and Commander of 2nd Battalion, 2nd Field Artillery. He is co-author of "The Fires Complex: Organizing to Win in Large-Scale Combat Operations," *Fires Journal*, May 2018; "Confronting Conflict in the Gray Zone," *Breaking Defense*, June 2016; "Gray Zone: Why We're Losing the New Era of National Security," *Defense One*, June 2016, and "Outplayed: Regaining Strategic Initiative in the Gray Zone," *Strategic Studies Institute*, June 2016.

Boyd L. Dastrup

Boyd L. Dastrup received his PhD from Kansas State University in 1980 and is currently the US Army Field Artillery School Historian. He is the author of numerous books, including *The U.S. Army Command and General Staff College: A Centennial History* (1982), *Crusade in Nuremberg: Military Occupation, 1945–1949* (1985), *King of Battle: A Branch History of the U.S. Army's Field Artillery* (1992, 1993), *Modernizing the King of Battle: 1973–1991* (1994, 2003), *The Field Artillery: History and Sourcebook* (1994), *Cedat Fortuna Peritis: A History of the Field Artillery School* (2011), and *Artillery Strong: Modernizing the Field Artillery for the 21st Century* (2018). He has also served as a subject matter expert for the History Channel on "Dangerous Missions: Forward Observation" (2001) and for the Discovery Channel on "Artillery Strikes" (2005).

Mark E. Grotelueschen

A 1991 graduate of the US Air Force Academy (USAFA), Lieutenant Colonel (USAF-Retired) Mark E. Grotelueschen teaches in the Academy's Department of Military and Strategic Studies. He previously served as Professor of History at USAFA. He received an MA from the University of Calgary and a PhD from Texas A&M University. He is the author of *Doctrine Under Trial: American Artillery Employment in World War I* (2000); *The AEF Way of War: The American Army and Combat in World War I* (2007), which has been named repeatedly to the US Army Chief of Staff's Professional Reading List; and *Into the Fight: April–June 1918* (2018), a volume in the US Army Center of Military History's *World War I* commemoration series.

David M. Rodriguez

General (Retired) David M. "Rod" Rodriguez is a 1976 graduate of the United States Military Academy at West Point. In his last assignment, he was Commander, Joint Task Force-82 in Afghanistan. His most recent commands included Commander of the US Africa Command (2013–2016); Commanding General of the US Army Forces Command (2011–2013); Commander, International Security Assistance Force Joint Command (IJC), and Deputy Commander, US Forces–Afghanistan (US-FOR-A) from 2009–2011. He also commanded the 82nd Airborne Division; the 2nd Brigade, 82nd Airborne Division; and the 2d Battalion, 502nd Infantry Regiment, 101st Airborne Division. Rodriguez's extensive combat experience included G-3 Planner, XVIII Airborne Corps, Operation Just Cause, 1989–1990; Operations Officer, 1st Battalion, 505th Parachute Infantry Regiment, 82nd Airborne Division, Desert Shield/Desert Storm, 1990–1991; Assistant Division Commander, 4th Infantry Division (Mechanized), 2002– 2003; Commander, Multi-National Division–Northwest, 2005; Special Assistant to the Commander, Multi-National Corps–Iraq, 2006. He received a Master of Arts in National Security and Strategic Studies from the US Naval War College and a Master's of Military Art and Science from the US Army Command and General Staff College's School of Advanced Military Studies in 1989.

Wilson A. "Al" Shoffner

Major General Wilson A. Shoffner is a 1988 graduate of the US Military Academy at West Point, where he earned a Bachelor of Science degree in International Relations. Major General Shoffner's command experience includes B Battery, 3rd Battalion, 319th Field Artillery Regiment, 2d Battalion, 319th Airborne Field Artillery Regiment, and the 18th Fires Brigade. Operational deployments include Saudi Arabia and Iraq during Operation Desert Shield and Desert Storm, and Afghanistan in 2003 as the Chief of Plans, 82nd Airborne Division during Operation Enduring Freedom. From 2003–05, Major General Shoffner served as the Deputy Chief of Plans for the NATO Allied Rapid Reaction Corps. Prior to assuming command of Fort Sill and the Fires Center of Excellence in November 2017, he served on the Army Staff in the Pentagon as Director, Army Talent Management Task Force, and Director of Operations, Army Rapid Capabilities Office. He earned a Master of Military Art and Science from the US Army Command and General Staff College's School of Advanced Military Studies and a Master of Arts in National Security and Strategic Studies from the Naval War College.

David Thuell

David Thuell earned a BA in Economics from Carleton University in 1996. He has worked in the telecommunications industry and is pursuing a Master's degree in History at Norwich University. His primary area of research is the Western Front, First World War.

Lincoln R. Ward

Major Lincoln R. Ward recently completed a tour of duty as a Joint Plans Officer, Combined Joint Task Force–Horn of Africa, in Djibouti. He earned a BA in History from Washington State University, a Master's of Education from Western Kentucky University, and a Master's in Military Art and Science from the US Army Command and General Staff College's School of Advanced Military Studies. He is a field artillery officer and has served with infantry, heavy, and Stryker brigade combat teams in Korea, Iraq, and Afghanistan.

Jeffrey S. Wright

Major Jeffrey S. Wright is assigned to the Department of Military Instruction, US Military Academy. Previously he was Operations Officer for 3-16th Field Artillery, 2d Armored Brigade Combat Team, 1st Cavalry Division. He earned a BS in European History from the US Military Academy, an MA in International Relations from Webster University, and a Master's in Military Art and Science from the US Army Command and General Staff College's School of Advanced Military Studies.

Printed in Great Britain
by Amazon